INTERIOR LIGHTING FOR DESIGNERS

INTERIOR LIGHTING FOR DESIGNERS

THIRD EDITION

Gary Gordon, IALD, IES
the late James L. Nuckolls, IALD

Illustrations by Gregory F. Day

John Wiley & Sons, Inc.

New York   Chichester   Brisbane   Toronto   Singapore

Cover photo description:

Glowing bubbles are etched into the mirror of a mahogany bars salvaged from the ocean liner SS Caronia at the Manhattan restaurant One Fifth Avenue. To illuminate the bubbles, the original mirror was moved 5½ inches forward, creating a narrow cavity, painted matte white, that forms a light box. Optical fibers supply light to snack bowls. "Porthole" fixtures from the Caronia are fitted with opal glass luminaires to diffuse light evenly. A miniature striplight causes flecks of gold leaf on the ceiling to glitter. These four luminous elements combine to recall the tranquil yet brilliant and inviting atmosphere created by an exotic aquarium or the moonlit sea.

Gary Gordon received a 1993 International Association of Lighting Designers (IALD) Citation for this project. The Award reads, "to recognize lighting installations which illustrate the synergy of architectural and lighting design by displaying high aesthetic achievement backed by technical expertise."

Library of Congress Cataloging-in-Publication Data:

Gordon, Gary, 1957–
    Interior lighting for designers / Gary Gordon, James
L. Nuckolls. — 3rd ed.
      p.   cm.
    Rev. ed. of: Interior lighting for environmental designers / James
L. Nuckolls. 2nd ed. c1983.
    Includes index.
    ISBN 0-471-50970-1 (cloth : alk. paper)
    1. Electric lighting. 2. Lighting, Architectural and decorative.
I. Nuckolls, James L. II. Nuckolls, James L. Interior lighting for
designers.   III. Title
TK4175.G67 1995
729' .28 — dc20   94-17915

Printed in the United States of America

10 9

For
Eve Becker
who was my biggest fan

PREFACE

This new edition of Interior Lighting for Designers goes beyond the scope of Jim Nuckoll's earlier work, which focused primarily on the mechanics of producing light. This 3rd Edition emphasizes the design of light in interiors; tools and techniques are presented as a means by which to achieve the design.

This is an architectural approach to lighting design; it is based on an inspiring apprenticeship with the enormously talented architect and lighting designer Carroll Cline and on 12 years of professional experience designing light for interiors around the world.

I have been influenced by the writings of the late architect and lighting professor John Flynn, by the work of the late architect and lighting designer Richard Kelly, and by my warm friendship and professional collaboration with the lighting-fixture-design genius Edison Price.

The 3rd Edition has been written to serve both as a textbook for architecture and interior design students and as a manual for students and practicing professionals. It provides a simple framework for understanding the lighting design process. More than 200 line drawings, photographs, and color plates accompany the text to illustrate its principles.

The book's basic tenet is that lighting design is not a mysterious art form. It is a process, and, like any process, it can be learned. Regardless of the space to be lighted—a gallery, an office, a restaurant, a school—and regardless of the light sources available for use, the process is always the same.

This book presents the steps of the lighting design process in roughly the same order as a professional would apply them. Design, of course, is not always a linear process. At times, some of these steps are used simultaneously. But, on the whole, the order of the material corresponds to professional practice.

I developed this approach while teaching undergraduate and graduate courses at the Parsons School of Design Lighting Institute. Its success is proved by the great number of former students who practice lighting design professionally today. It is my hope that the reader will benefit in a similar way.

Gary Gordon
New York City
December 1994

ACKNOWLEDGMENTS

This book is the happy result of the combined effort of many talented people. It owes a great debt to the thorough copy and technical edit provided by Edison Price. It is also the product of a thorough technical edit by William Blitzer and an equally thorough copy edit by Linda Segretto.

Invaluable copy-editing assistance was provided by Val Clarke, Matthew Michaels, and Alan Rackham. Research assistance was provided by Andrew Brody, Chad Rains, and David Weiner of Gary Gordon Architectural Lighting, Inc.

Encouragement in the writing process was provided by Therese Eiben, Mary Hebert, Rachel Herr, and the Ragdale Foundation. I am grateful for the support of Karen Goldstick at Flack + Kurtz, Alan Rackham, and the late Tim Alger.

The concepts and techniques presented in this book were cultivated while working on actual projects at Gary Gordon Architectural Lighting, Inc. That firm prospered because of the support and encouragement of its competitors Howard Brandston, Helen Diemer, Karen Goldstick, Barbara Horton, Jules Horton, and Hayden McKay; of its clients James Biber, Cynthia Filkoff, Richard Dattner, Rendell Fernandez and Simone Corno, Arlene and Arnold Goldstein, Steven Haas, Evelyn and Leonard Lauder, Nancy Olnick and Giorgio Spanu, Adam Rose and Peter McQuillan, Coty Sidnam, Marc and Martha Spector, Wayne Turett, and Don Zivkovic and Brian Connolly; and to the patience and inspiration of Carroll Cline and the spark that was first ignited by James Nuckolls.

The book appears in its current form only through the efforts of Val Clarke, Andrew Lewis, and Judith Aisen, Linda Bathgate, Peggy Burns, Amanda Miller, and Millie Torres at Wiley. Stephen Kliment provided the impetus for this new work when he was at Wiley.

This work was supported by a grant from the National Endowment for the Arts.

CONTENTS

INTRODUCTION

Perception of the world around us is based on the quantity of contrast: the differences between light and dark. Contrast is a stimulus that influences mood and affects productivity. The degree of contrast in a space induces the level of stimulation felt by its occupants. Rather than asking how much light is required for a room or an activity, lighting designers should be asking how much contrast is required.

The first step in the lighting design process is to identify how a space is going to be used. The designer then determines the degree of contrast required to achieve the necessary level of stimulation.

Patterns of light and shade provide degrees of contrast. Yet, patterns of light and shade are evident only after they are received by a surface. Therefore, the selection of surface materials and surface finishes is as important as the light sources and lighting fixtures that produce light.

The designer chooses a light source that has the ability to provide the required degree of contrast, and then uses a variety of techniques to modify the direction and distribution of that light source. This modification is provided by lighting fixtures and architectural details. Selecting the fixture or detail is easy at this point in the process because the specific objectives of the space have ruled many of the options. Last, the designer creates a lighting plan that locates the lighting equipment.

A common mistake when providing light is to select the lighting equipment first. What's important is not what produces light, but rather where it lands.

Selecting lighting fixtures is the last part of the lighting design process. The key to successful lighting design is to decide what you want to light first, then work backward toward a solution.

To be successful, lighting design must be integrated into the fabric of the architecture. The objective is to use modern lighting techniques in a manner sympathetic to, and expressive of, the spirit of the architectural concept.

In the completed space, one should not be aware of the mechanics of light production—only of a comfortable environment that enhances one's sense of well-being. Thus, it is not only the quality of light that we are concerned with, but the quality of life.

CHAPTER 1

PERCEPTION

What is perceived as light is a narrow band of electromagnetic energy, ranging from approximately 380 nanometers (nm) to 760 nanometers. Only wavelengths in this range stimulate receptors in the eye that permit vision (figure 1.1). These wavelengths are called *visible energy,* even though we cannot directly see them.

In a perfect vacuum, light travels at approximately 186,000 miles per second. When light travels through glass or water or another transparent substance it is slowed down to a velocity that depends on the density of the medium through which it is transmitted. This slowing down of light is what causes prisms to bend light and lenses to form images (figure 1.2).

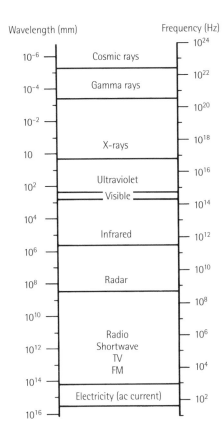

Figure 1.1 Visible light is a narrow region of the total electromagnetic spectrum, which includes radio waves, infrared, ultraviolet and x-rays. The physical difference is purely the wavelength of the radiation, but the effects are very different. Within the narrow band to which the eye is sensitive, different wavelengths give different colors. See also color plate 5.

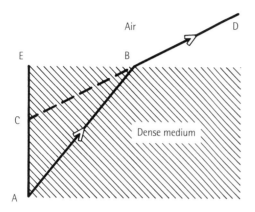

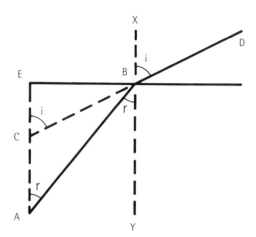

Figure 1.2 The Law of Refraction (the "sine law") states when light passes from a medium A into a medium B the sine of the angle of incidence bears a constant ratio to the sine of the angle of refraction.

When light is bent by a prism, each wavelength is refracted at a different angle so that the emergent beam emanates from the prism as a fan of light, yielding all the spectral colors. (See color plate 1.)

All electromagnetic radiation is similar. The physical difference between radio waves, infrared, visible light, ultraviolet, and X-rays is their wavelength. Spectral color, or hue, is light of a specific wavelength.

THE EYE AND THE BRAIN

A parallel is often drawn between the human eye and a camera. Yet visual perception involves much more than an optical image projected on the retina of the eye and "photographically" interpreted by the brain.

The eyes supply the brain with information coded into chains of electrical impulses. But the "seeing" of objects is determined only partially by these neural signals. The brain searches for the best interpretation of available data. The perception of an object is a hypothesis, suggested and tested by sensory signals and knowledge derived from previous experience.

Usually the hypothesis is correct, and we perceive a world of separate solid objects in a surrounding space. Sometimes the evaluation is incorrect; we call this an *illusion*. The "ambiguous shapes" seen in figures 1.3 and 1.4 illustrate

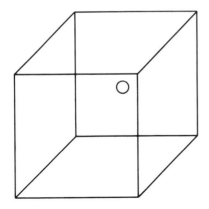

Figure 1.3 Necker cube

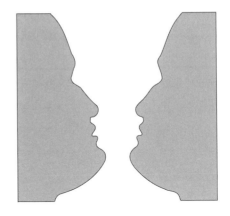

Figure 1.4 Ambiguous figures

how the same pattern of stimulation at the eye gives rise to different perceptions.

The human eye is primarily a device which gathers information about the outside world. Its focusing lens throws a minute inverted image onto a dense mosaic of light-sensitive receptors, which convert the patterns of light energy into chains of electrical impulses that the brain will interpret (figure 1.5).

The simplest way to form an image is not with a lens, however, but with a pinhole. In figure 1.6, a ray from each point of the object reaches only a single point on the screen, the two parts being connected by a straight line passing through the pinhole. Each part of the object illuminates a corresponding part of the screen, so an upside-down image of the object is formed. The pinhole image is dim because the hole must be small if the image is to be sharp.

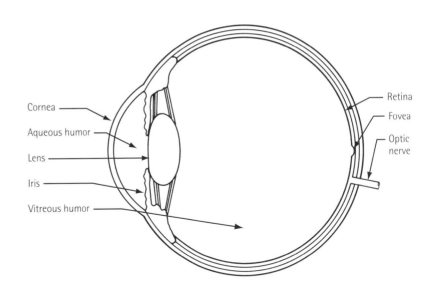

Cornea
Aqueous humor
Lens
Iris
Vitreous humor

Retina
Fovea
Optic nerve

Figure 1.5 The human eye

A lens is able to form a much brighter image. It collects a bundle of light rays from each point of the object and directs it to a corresponding point on the screen, thus giving a bright image (figure 1.7).

Figure 1.6 Forming an image with a pinhole

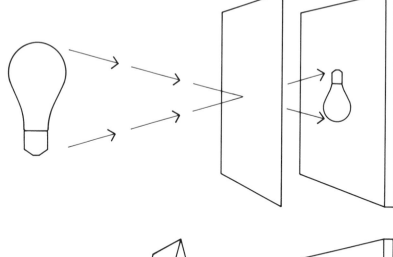

Figure 1.7 Forming an image with a lens. A lens is actually a pair of prisms, but image-forming lenses have curved surfaces.

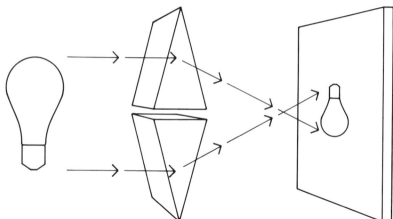

The lens of the human eye is built up from its center, with cells being added all through life, although growth gradually slows down. The center is thus the oldest part, and as the cells age they become more compact and they harden. As a result, the lens stiffens and is no longer able to change its shape to accommodate varying distances (figure 1.8).

Lenses only work well when they fit properly and are adjusted correctly. Sometimes the lens of an eye is unsuitable to the eye in which it finds itself, and it is adjusted wrongly: (1) the lens focuses the image in front of or behind the retina instead of on it, giving "short" *(myopic)* or "long" *(presbyopic)* sight; (2) the lens is not truly spherical, giving distortion and, in some directions, blurring of the image; or (3) the cornea is irregular or pitted.

Fortunately, almost all optical defects can be corrected by adding artificial lenses called *glasses*. Eyeglasses correct for errors of focus (called *accommodation*) by changing the power of the lens of the eye; they correct for distortion (called *astigmatism*) by adding a non-spherical component. Ordinary glasses do not correct damage to the surface of the cornea, but *corneal lenses*, fitted to the eye itself, serve to give a fresh surface to the cornea.

The *iris* is the pigmented part of the eye. It is found in a wide range of colors, but the color has no impact on vision as long as it is opaque. The iris is a muscle that forms the *pupil*. Light passes through the pupil to the lens which lies immediately behind it. This muscle contracts to reduce the aperture of the lens in bright light and also when the eyes converge to view near objects.

The *retina* is a thin sheet of interconnected nerve cells, which include the light-sensitive cells that convert light into electrical impulses. The two kinds of light-receptor cells—the *rods* and the *cones*—are named after their appearance as viewed with a microscope (figure 1.9).

The cones function in high illuminance and provide color vision. The rods function under low illuminance and yield only shades of gray. Color vision, using the cones of the retina, is called *photopic;* the gray world given by the rods in dim light is called *scotopic.*

BRIGHTNESS PERCEPTION

We speak of *intensity* of light entering the eye, called *luminance*, which gives rise to *brightness*. Intensity is the physical energy of the light, which is measured by various kinds of photometers, including the familiar photographer's exposure meter.

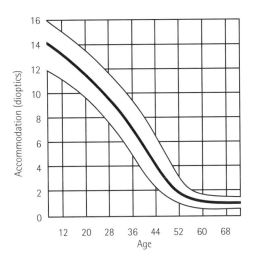

Figure 1.8 Loss of accommodation of the lens of the eye with aging.

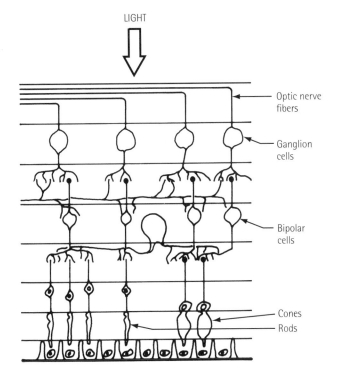

Figure 1.9 The retina

Brightness is an experience. We hear someone say, "What a bright day!" and we know what is meant by that. This sensation is only roughly related to the intensity of light entering the eyes. Brightness is a function of the intensity of light falling on a given region of the retina at a certain time, the intensity of light that the retina has been subject to in the recent past (called *adaptation*) and the intensities of light falling on other regions of the retina (called *contrast*).

Figure 1.10 demonstrates how the intensity of surrounding areas affects the perception of brightness. A given region looks brighter if its surroundings are dark, and a given color looks more intense if it is surrounded by its complementary color.

If the eyes are kept in low light for some time they grow more sensitive, and a given quantity of light will seem brighter. This "dark adaptation" is rapid for the first few seconds, then slows down. The cone and rod receptor cells adapt at different rates: cone adaptation is completed in about seven minutes; rod adaptation continues for an hour or more.

Figure 1.10 Simultaneous contrast

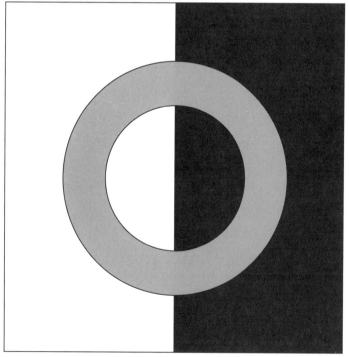

As the eye becomes dark adapted, it loses acuity while it gains sensitivity. With a decrease of intensity and the compensating dark adaptation, the ability to make out fine detail is lost.

COLOR PERCEPTION

Brightness is also a function of color. For a given intensity, the colors at the middle of the spectrum look brighter than those at the ends. The sensitivity curves for rods and cones are different. Their shape is similar, but the cones are most sensitive to yellow, while the rods are most sensitive to green. This change with increasing intensity is known as the *Purkinje Shift* (figure 1.11).

The visible spectrum is comprised of five colors of light (not of pigment): red, yellow, green, blue, and violet. These colors can be mixed: Yellow is obtained by combining red with green light.

Mixing colors of light is achieved by using filters, prisms, or diffraction gratings. By mixing two colors of light, a third color is formed in which the two mixed colors cannot be identified.

By mixing three colors of light and adjusting their intensities, any spectral hue can be produced. White can be made, but not black or nonspectral colors such as brown. (See color plate 2.)

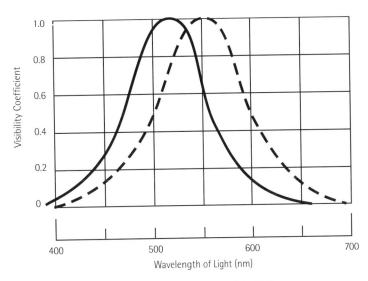

Figure 1.11 The Purkinje Shift

When speaking technically about color vision, we do not refer to "colors" but rather to "hues." This is to avoid difficulty with the term "colors," which is descriptive of the physiological sensations to which we give specific names, such as "red" or "blue." We therefore speak technically of "spectral hues," rather than "spectral colors."

Another important distinction is to be found between *color as a sensation* and *color as a wavelength* (or a set of wavelengths) of light entering the eye. Technically, light itself is not colored: It gives rise to sensations of brightness and color, but only in conjunction with a suitable eye and nervous system. When we speak of "yellow light" it means light that gives rise to a sensation described by the majority of people as "yellow."

All the colors of the spectrum are interpreted to the eye by only three kinds of receptors: red, green, and violet. The three color-sensitive kinds of receptors (cones) respond to orange–red, pure green, and blue–violet; all colors are seen by a mixture of signals from the three systems.

The eye accepts as white not a particular mixture of colors, but rather the general illumination, whatever this is. A candle or lamplight that looks white by itself appears yellow when "white" lights are present for comparison.

The reference for what is taken as white shifts. Knowledge of the normal color of objects is called *color constancy;* it leads us to expect that a tomato will be red. The brain's stored knowledge and expectations exert a strong influence on color perception: Objects such as oranges and lemons, for example, take on a richer color because they are recognized as orange and yellow.

Grass is a plant found on lawns and we call the sensation of color it gives "green," but we identify grass by characteristics other than its color—its presence as a lawn, the form and density of the blades, and so forth. If we do confuse the color, sufficient additional evidence is available to identify it as grass. We know it is supposed to be green and we call it green, even when this is doubtful as in the dim light of dusk.

Neurophysiologists discovered in 1992 that an alignment of brain cells forms the basis of visual memory. The cells are stacked in columns; depending on which columns are excited by an object, the brain is able to instantly recognize complex images such as faces even at odd angles or when only part of the face is visible. Yet it remains a mystery how the contributions from separate channels for brightness, color, shape, and movement—with their own locations in different regions of the brain—come together to form consistent perceptions.

CHAPTER 2

PSYCHOLOGY

The psychology of light includes an understanding of perception, luminance contrast, and subjective impressions of space. It is possible, of course, to simply introduce general illumination into a room to permit vision, but it is the emotional impact of an appropriate lighting system that provides the substantial challenge to the creative designer.

Perception is independent of the quantity of light entering the eye; it is based on the degree of contrast. A certain quantity of light is necessary for a person to see, yet the eye responds not to the total but to the average intensity in the field of view.

The sense of sight, therefore, is contrast sensitive. It is a mechanism for the detection of differences: of figures on a ground, of objects in a surround. Subjective impressions of space are a function of luminance contrast: the relationship of surfaces that are lighted (the focus or foreground) to those that are left in comparative darkness (the surround or background).

LUMINANCE CONTRAST

Reliance on published standards for illuminance on the workplane leads unintentionally to environments that are sterile and unstimulating. Proper attention to the manipulation of luminance contrast as a principal technique for the design of lighting systems results in environments that are inviting and inspiring.

If all objects and surfaces in a room receive equal emphasis from light, contrast is lost. Over time, the lack of contrast causes people to feel listless and depressed. Without contrast, the environment produced has the quality of a cloudy, overcast day.

People feel more alert, energetic, and positive on a sunny day, a day marked by bright highlights and crisp shadows. By providing patterns of luminance contrast, an environment may be created that has the attributes of a sunny day. The significant difference between a "dull, dreary day" and a "bright, cheerful" one is the quality of light.

To establish patterns of luminance contrast, the lighting designer must first evaluate the activities or tasks that will occur in the space. Some activities and tasks benefit from a high degree of contrast to encourage participation and stimulate enjoyment. Other activities and tasks benefit from a minimum of contrast to help a person feel contented, comfortable, and relaxed. And, although individuals react differently to the same environment, there is a high degree of similarity in people's reactions to light.

Environmental psychologists use the terms high load and low load to describe degrees of stimulation or arousal. The more stimuli that must be processed by a person, the higher the load. Environments that are complex, crowded, asymmetrical, novel, unfamiliar, surprising, or random are high load. Environments that are simple, uncrowded, symmetrical, conventional, familiar, unsurprising, or organized are low load.

If the task to be performed is complex or unusual—reading an exciting suspense story, summarizing an important report, or writing an essay—the load is great enough that one's degree of arousal is fairly high; additional load from the environment will increase stimulation to such a point that the task is avoided. One becomes distracted, annoyed, or frustrated, and performance falls off sharply.

Tasks that are simple or routine—writing checks, making a shopping list, or other familiar chores benefit from a mildly stimulating environment. Daydreaming or dozing may result without increased stimulation. This is why such work often fails to be performed in studies or offices designed for paperwork; instead it is done in kitchens, dining rooms, or living rooms, which have a higher degree of stimulation.

The lower the load of the task, the more it requires a high load setting for optimum performance. Boring tasks are boring because they are nonstimulating (simple or overly familiar) and often unpleasant. Within reason, the more stimulation provided, the more pleasant the task becomes. For many, basic housework is monotonous; playing background music increases stimulation, enabling one to complete boring domestic chores.

Patterns of luminance contrast evoke positive emotions in the same way as background music. They have impact on the performance of tasks, on the behavior of people in work or play settings, and on the degree of contentment and pleasure.

After the activity or task has been identified, luminance contrast is established by developing patterns of light and shade. The relationship between foreground and background is determined by selecting specific surfaces and objects to receive lighting emphasis while leaving others in comparative darkness (figure 2.1).

Figure 2.1 Patterns of light and shade establish luminance contrast.

Architectural lighting design involves the skillful balance of three elements of light: (1) general or ambient light, (2) focal or task light, and (3) sparkle or glitter. The proportions of these three elements establish the desired emotional setting.

The late lighting designer Richard Kelly poetically defines the three kinds of light: To Kelly, general light is

> ambient luminescence; it is a snowy morning in open country . . . twilight haze on a mountain top or a cloudy day on the ocean . . . the light in a white tent at noon . . . moonlight coming through the fog.

> Ambient luminescence is shadowless illumination. It minimizes form and bulk. It dematerializes. It reduces the importance of things and people. It fills people with a sense of freedom of space and suggests infinity. It is usually reassuring and restful.

> The best example is a foggy day on a mountain top. There is an even glow without incidence all around; there are no shadows, nothing to tell you what to look at. In that sense it's confusing, but it is also relaxing and restful, as there is no excitement, no interest. It minimizes man—think about a figure moving through that fog—and destroys form (figure 2.2).

Task light, for Kelly, is

> focal glow . . . the campfire of all time, the glowing embers around which stories are told, or the football rally bonfire. Focal glow is the limelight, the follow spot on the stage, and an aircraft beacon. . . . It is the light burning at the window or the welcoming gleam of the open door.

> Focal glow is the sunburst through the clouds and the shaft of sunshine that warms the far end of the valley. It is the pool of light at your favorite reading chair, your airplane-seat light, or matchlight on a face. Focal glow is the end of the rainbow; it commands attention, creates interest, fixes the gaze, and tells people what to look at. Focal glow is the focus. It separates the important from the unimportant, establishes precedence, can induce movement, and can control traffic.

> Focal light is directive, creates a bright center; it tells us what to look at, organizes, marks the most important element. It creates a sense of space; you can organize depth through a sequence of focal centers (figure 2.3).

Figure 2.2 Ambient luminescence

Figure 2.3 Focal glow

To Kelly, sparkle is

> a play of brilliants . . . the sensation of a cache of diamonds in an opened cave or the Versailles Hall of Mirrors with its thousands of candle flames . . . a ballroom of crystal chandeliers. Play of brilliants is Times Square at night . . . sunlight on a tumbling brook . . . the heaven full of stars . . . birch trees interlaced by a motor car's headlights.

> Play of brilliants excites the optic nerves . . . stimulates the body and spirit and charms the senses. It creates a feeling of aliveness, alerts the mind, awakens curiosity, and sharpens the wits. It quickens the appetite and heightens all sensations. It can be distracting or it can be entertaining.

Figure 2.4 Sparkle

Sparkle is scintillation. It is a tiny microscopic bombardment of points of light—the most exciting kind of light there is. It stimulates and arouses appetites of all kinds; chandeliers in dining rooms, sequins on dresses, and lights on theatre marquees all take advantage of the fact (figure 2.4).

Balance of Luminance

Outdoors, during daytime, the sky provides the ambient light. Objects and surfaces that are illuminated by the sun, such as a meadow, trees, or the side of a building, are the focal glow. The reflection of the sun from specular surfaces such as moving water, dew on leaves, or polished metal on a building supplies the sparkle.

At the beach, the ambient light provided by the sky is balanced by the diffuse reflected light from the sand. Objects that are lighted by the sun (sandcastles, people, bright beach blankets, and bathing suits) become the focus. The glistening of the sun on the agitated water or on wet stones at the water's edge is the sparkle.

Indoors, the proportions of these same elements— ambient light, focal light, and sparkle—always and everywhere determine the emotional setting.

Figure 2.5 Low-contrast lighting

Figure 2.6 Low-contrast lighting

A space lighted with a large proportion of ambient light and a small amount of focal light and sparkle is a low-contrast environment. General lighting systems that flood a space with diffused light from overhead reduce contrast, yielding a low-contrast setting. Low-contrast spaces are low in stimulation. They are behaviorally neutral: there are few stimuli to respond to (figure 2.5).

Low-contrast lighting systems are intended to provide easy seeing for visual tasks, to allow random circulation, and to permit flexible relocation of work surfaces. This diffuse lighting technique provides a uniformly-illuminated working environment—an area suitable for difficult and sustained visual tasks (figure 2.6).

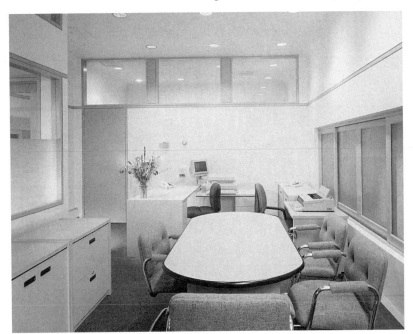

Highly diffuse light produces a shadowless environment; forms are ill-defined and textural perception is poor. Although this is adequate for task vision, it ignores the problem of the bland psychological reaction that is characteristic of a cloudy day.

A space lighted with a small amount of ambient light and a large proportion of focal light is a high-contrast environment. High-contrast lighting systems render patterns of light and shade. High-contrast spaces increase stimulation; they are intended to evoke specific moods or emotions (figure 2.7).

Attention is involuntarily drawn toward areas of luminance that contrast with the visual background. When a person approaches an unfamiliar space or activity, luminance contrast and color contrast help to establish an initial response. High-contrast environments are useful for guiding the circulation of people entering an unfamiliar room (figure 2.8).

Figure 2.7 High-contrast lighting

Figure 2.8 High-contrast lighting

A single spotlight on a stage is an extreme example of the influence of luminance contrast in creating focal points. A room lighted in this way dominates the people in it; the luminance contrast directs their attention and holds their interest, producing visual direction and focus.

Some luminance patterns influence one's impressions of activity, setting, or mood. The balance of light and shade establishes an emotional setting that reinforces the intended activity.

Other luminance patterns affect one's personal orientation and understanding of a room's surfaces and objects. For example, object and display lighting affect attention and awareness; wall lighting and uplighting affect impressions of room size and shape. These lighting techniques shape our understanding of space.

SUBJECTIVE IMPRESSIONS

The late professor John Flynn documents that, as the patterns of luminance contrast change, the strength of visual stimuli also changes, altering our impressions of space.

While looking for evidence that the light changes alone elicit significantly different reactions, Flynn tested six lighting schemes without making other changes in the room (figures 2.9 to 2.14). These light changes induce consistent responses in three areas: spaciousness, perceptual clarity, and pleasantness.

Figure 2.9 Overhead downlighting, low intensity

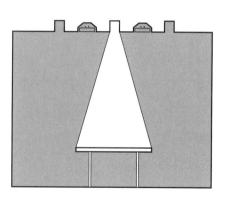

Figure 2.10 Peripheral wall lighting, all walls

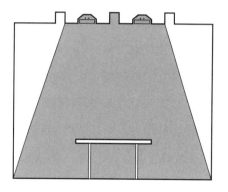

Figure 2.11 Overhead diffuse, low setting

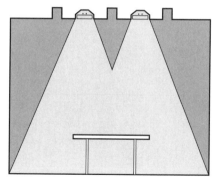

Figure 2.12 Combination: Overhead downlighting + end walls

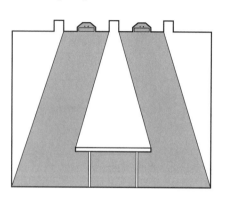

Figure 2.13 Overhead diffuse, high intensity

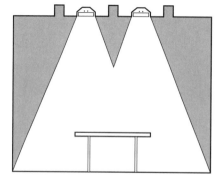

Figure 2.14 Combination: Overhead downlighting + overhead diffuse

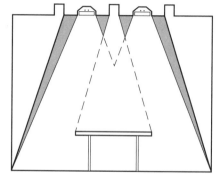

Impressions of Spaciousness An impression of largeness or smallness is affected by the intensity and uniformity of the room perimeter. Differences in the quantity of horizontal illuminance from overhead systems have negligible influence on impressions of pleasantness. Differences in quantity of illuminance significantly alter impressions of perceptual clarity and spaciousness. The higher illuminance values are described as "clear," "bright," "distinct," "large," and "more spacious" (figure 2.15).

Impressions of Perceptual Clarity Nothing is more important than how people's faces appear. Lighting schemes that are rated high in facial clarity are considered more public; schemes that are rated low in facial clarity are considered more private.

Figure 2.15 Impressions of spaciousness (large-small). Improvement in visual contact continues to approximately 25 fc of ambient horizontal illuminance, beyond which it stabilizes.

Public space implies intermingling and bringing people together. The potential for visual contact improves as the intensity of general illuminance is increased. Increasing intensities reduce anonymity and bring people together because facial expressions and gestures are more clearly perceptible (figure 2.16).

Private space suggests separating people and keeping them apart. Shadow and silhouette strengthen feelings of detachment and privacy because these lighting techniques inhibit the ability to perceive precise facial detail; even nearby individuals become more anonymous (figure 2.17).

In a crowded space, when it is impossible to separate people physically by distance, it is possible to separate them visually by lighting. This technique is used in cocktail lounges, fine restaurants, and reception rooms.

Figure 2.16 Impressions of public space

Figure 2.17 Impressions of private space

Figure 2.18 Impressions of pleasantness

Impressions of Pleasantness   The nonuniform luminance produced by the downward concentrating system rates more favorably than the uniform luminance produced by the diffuse system. The nonuniform luminance is rated as more "friendly," "pleasant," "sociable," and "interesting." (figure 2.18)

When wall lighting is added, ratings shift to the positive for all three categories of impression. Lighted vertical surfaces strengthen feelings of spaciousness, clarity, and pleasantness.

VARIATION

Lack of variation in the built environment is an obstacle that lighting helps to overcome. Monotony results in boredom and depression: Even a string of consecutive, bright, sunny days will become boring through over-familiarity. Variation increases stimulation and impressions of pleasantness.

To increase the load of office or factory environments, introduce stimuli that vary over time; otherwise, workers quickly become accustomed to the setting. For example, coffee and lunch breaks in areas with greater contrast and sparkle than in the workplace introduce variety by change of the lighting atmosphere and at the same time encourage sociability and conversation.

Performing low-load tasks in dull settings benefit enormously from pleasant and mildly stimulating diversions. If one must wade through low-load paperwork that calls for a fairly high-load environment (reading reports, reviewing dull proposals, or composing an answer to a customer complaint), productivity is increased when offices are provided with a means of altering the lighting condition. If workers are performing complex and dangerous tasks, however, a pleasant low-load lounge brings the degree of stimulation down to an optimal point.

A fixed, ideal lighting solution that will increase performance while a person is doing a monotonous task is unattainable: a controllable variability of the lighting environment is needed and is beneficial. Changing all the lamps in a factory to an improved-color light source is insufficient, for example; in time, such a static modification loses much of its stimulating value.

People using a library, as those in the office and factory, benefit from more stimulating lighting systems in areas used for taking breaks, socializing, having a cup of coffee, or simply daydreaming for relief from the fatigue caused by concentrated work. The typical library has quiet stacks and cubicles conducive to study and other areas for relaxed reading and scanning periodicals. People prefer less loaded settings for difficult, complex materials, and more loaded spaces for casual, pleasant reading.

In addition to the lighting system, surface finishes, textures, and colors also contribute to the environmental load. In practice, they all must be considered at the same time.

CHAPTER 3

LUMINANCE

DIRECTION AND DISTRIBUTION OF LIGHT

Patterns of luminance are determined by the direction and distribution of light. A luminaire emits light in one of three directions—downward, upward, or multidirectional—and in one of two distributions—concentrated or diffuse.

Downward light from properly designed luminaires has a restricted angular spread; glare is prevented by this spread and the human eyebrow shielding upward view. Upward light usually covers a large area of the ceiling; the light reflected from the ceiling is of low luminance and is unlikely to cause distracting glare. Multidirectional light cannot emit much of its output sideways without causing objectionable glare.

Upward and downward light is emitted in patterns that vary from narrow to wide. *Concentrated* distribution focuses light in a narrow pattern; *diffuse* distribution disperses light in a wide pattern.

Luminaires with narrow beamspreads that lack an upward component of light produce *concentrated downward*, or *direct*, distribution (figure 3.1). From low ceilings, concentrated downward beams—with *spreads* of 30° or less—create areas of high luminance on the floor with dark areas in between. To avoid this unevenness, luminaires must be placed inordinately close to

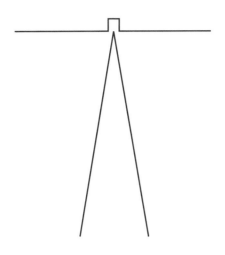

Figure 3.1 Concentrated downward distribution

Figure 3.2 An example of concentrated downward distribution

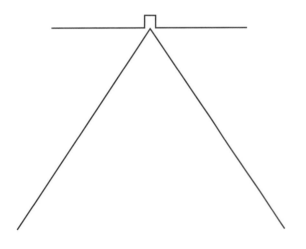

Figure 3.3 Diffuse downward distribution

Figure 3.4 An example of diffuse downward distribution

each other. From high ceilings, concentrated downward beams overlap and avoid such light and dark areas, but only horizontal surfaces and the tops of objects are lighted; faces and walls receive little light and appear in shadow. This yields a high contrast space, one of low ambient luminance with high luminance accents (figure 3.2).

Luminaires with diffuse beamspreads and a downward distribution produce *diffuse downward* light (figure 3.3). Diffuse downward beams—with spreads from 80° to 120°—offer a more practical light distribution for many purposes. A luminaire with a 100° beamspread, emitting most of its light below a *cutoff* angle of 40° from horizontal, is offered by most well-designed downlights today. A greater percentage of light at higher angles increases incident light on vertical surfaces, "models" faces, and reduces the concentration of luminance within the space. This yields a low–contrast setting (figure 3.4).

A *concentrated upward*, or *indirect*, distribution directs light toward the ceiling (figure 3.5). With light directed upward and the downward component removed, the ceiling becomes visually prominent. It also becomes a secondary light source because of its reflective properties.

When mounted in close proximity to the surface being lighted, concentrated upward beams create isolated areas of high luminance. The nonuniformity of *concentrated upward* distribution reduces the strong contrast that results from a concentrated downward system by adding visual interest through luminance variation (figure 3.6).

If this is the main source of room illumination, as in areas with low ceiling heights, the "spots" of

Figure 3.5 Concentrated upward distribution

Figure 3.6 An example of concentrated upward distribution

high luminance on the ceiling become uncomfortable and cause direct glare. When placed farther from the surface to be lighted, however, concentrated upward beams produce uniform luminance: Each beam covers a wider area and multiple beam patterns overlap. In areas with higher ceiling heights, the concentrated beam has sufficient distance to spread; the ceiling is lighted uniformly, reducing luminance and glare (figure 3.7).

A *diffuse upward* distribution directs light toward the ceiling and the upper side walls (figure 3.8). This technique is used to create uniform ceiling luminance for the prevention of glare in areas with visual display terminal (VDT) screens and to emphasize structural form or decorative detail in or near the ceiling plane. Because each point on the ceiling reflects light in every direction, diffuse upward distribution produces a "flat," low–contrast environment: The reflected light reduces contrast and shadow; objects and faces have the washed-out appearance caused by an overcast day (figure 3.9).

Figure 3.7 An example of concentrated upward distribution with the light source placed farther from the illuminated surface

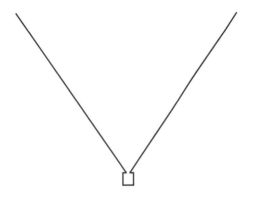

Figure 3.8 Diffuse upward distribution

Figure 3.9 An example of diffuse upward distribution

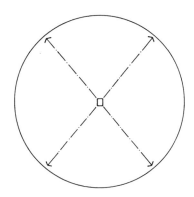

Figure 3.10 Multidirectional distribution

Figure 3.11 An example of multidirectional distribution

Wall lighting is sometimes a substitute for the indirect ceiling lighting: It lightens shadow and reduces excessive contrast. It works especially well when the walls are high in relation to the size of the room. Another solution is direct downlights in combination with a light floor: The floor reflects light back to the ceiling as though indirect lighting were being used. The floor must be kept clean for this technique to be successful.

The ideal lighting arrangement is often a combination of direct and indirect light, where the direct light takes the place of the sun, casting shadows and modeling shapes, and the indirect light softens the shadows, acting as a blue sky or the photographer's "fill" light. *Direct/indirect* schemes are produced either with separate systems for downward and upward light or with one system that provides both downward and upward distribution.

Multidirectional distribution is produced by luminaires that deliver both upward and downward components of light (figure 3.10). These luminaires emit light in several directions at the same time—toward the ceiling and walls as well as toward the floor. The reflected light from the ceiling and the interreflection of light in the space diffuse the downward distribution, reducing shadow and contrast and creating a high luminance, uniform interior (figure 3.11).

Luminaires that deliver both direct and indirect components of diffuse light, but no side lighting, are called *multidirectional diffuse* (figure 3.12). They provide efficient use of light on work surfaces while relieving contrast by reflection from the ceiling plane.

Multidirectional distribution created with concentrated beamspreads is called *multidirectional concentrated* (figure 3.13). A higher contrast, nonuniform luminance condition is produced with concentrated distributions present in both the upward and downward components. The upward component reduces excessive contrast in a space; however, the nonuniform light reflected from wall or ceiling surfaces is insufficient to "wash out" all shadow and contrast. This lack of diffusion yields moderate contrast (figure 3.14).

Figure 3.12 An example of multidirectional diffuse distribution

Figure 3.14 An example of multidirectional concentrated distribution

Figure 3.13 Multidirectional concentrated distribution

SURFACE FINISHES AND REFLECTANCES

What is perceived as "brightness" is not the incident light on a surface, but the light that is *reflected* from that surface toward the eyes. Brightness results from the intensity of light that initially strikes a surface *and* the reflecting or transmitting properties of that surface.

Whether it is of high or low intensity, some amount of incident light from luminaires or from interreflection falls on all room surfaces. The relative size of these surfaces and the intensity of light reflected from them determine their visual prominence in an interior composition.

Reflected light is usually diffuse and multidirectional, causing interreflection between all surfaces and objects. This interreflection fills in shadows, reduces contrast, and yields more uniform luminance.

Dark–colored, low–reflectance finishes absorb much of the light that strikes them, reflecting only a small amount toward the eye. This gives an impression of a dark, high–contrast space regardless of the amount of illuminance (figures 3.15 and 3.16).

Figures 3.15 and 3.16 The overall brightness results from the distribution of reflected light, which, in turn, depends on the reflectance properties of the surfaces in the space. If all the room surfaces are dark, there is little interreflection; contrast is high.

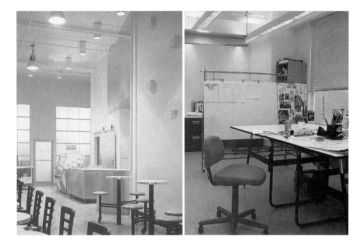

Figures 3.17 and 3.18 If all of the room surfaces are light colored, interreflections will fill in shadows and reduce contrast.

Light-colored and high-reflectance finishes reflect much more of the incident light, contributing to a higher luminance and a greater diffusion of light (figures 3.17 and 3.18). This interreflection is independent of the distribution of light, whether it is concentrated or diffuse.

The choice of surface finishes augments or negates the initial distribution of light from luminaires. This influence of reflected light must be accounted for: Understanding the relationship between lighting equipment and room surfaces is critical to successful lighting design.

SECONDARY LIGHT SOURCES

Any object or surface that reflects or transmits light becomes a secondary light source. The moon is an example: It is incapable of producing light. The "moonlight" we see is produced by a primary source—the sun—which is reflected by the moon's surface.

Figure 3.19 An architectural surface as a secondary light source

Similarly, a lighted wall or ceiling becomes a secondary light source that illuminates a room through reflection. The result is then dependent on the reflected light from the lighted surface, rather than on the initial distribution of light from the luminaire (figure 3.19).

SURFACES AND OBJECTS

In addition to altering our perception of space, the direction and distribution of light affect the perception of surfaces and objects in a room.

All three-dimensional form is seen as a pattern of luminance contrasts, often consisting of highlights and shadows. A change in this pattern, caused by a change in the direction and distribution of light, alters visual impressions of form and surface.

Lighting alters perception of texture. *Grazing light*, from luminaires located close to a surface being lighted, strengthens highlights and shadows. It enhances the perception of depth by emphasizing the natural textures and sculptural relief of the surface. It is also used for inspection to detect surface blemishes and errors in workmanship (figures 3.20 and 3.21).

Grazing light is appropriate for lighting heavily textured surfaces such as rough plaster, masonry, or concrete. It is disastrous for "flat" walls of smooth plaster or gypsum board, however, because such walls are not truly flat and because minor surface imperfections such as trowel marks, tape, and nail-head depressions are magnified by the shadows that result from grazing light.

Conversely, diffuse *wash light* reduces the likelihood that surface flaws will be noticed and strengthens an impression of surface smoothness. This is more suitable for a gypsum board wall or an acoustical tile ceiling. Diffuse wash light from the front is particularly successful at reducing or removing shadows and small luminance variations (figures 3.22 and 3.23).

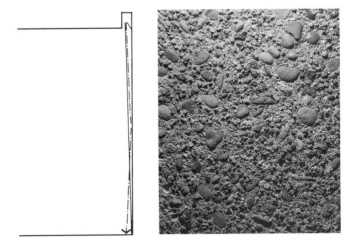

Figures 3.20 and 3.21 Grazing illumination

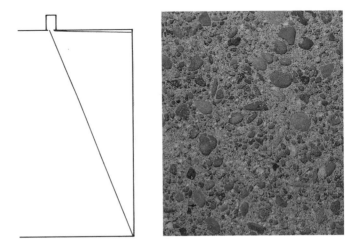

Figures 3.22 and 3.23 Diffuse wash light

Concentrated direct lighting on objects produces drama and emotional excitement. Yet the same sharp shadows that contribute to the dramatic impact also reduce visibility of detail. This diminishes the ability to study and appreciate all aspects of the object accurately (figure 3.24).

A diffuse lighting distribution, on the other hand, illuminates the entire object, reducing shadows and facilitating study of workmanship and detail. Although it is often desirable, this kind of lighting sacrifices the dramatic impact and visual excitement (figure 3.25).

In practice, objects being exhibited or photographed are often lighted from two sides to reduce excessive shadows. One side has a concentrated beam-spread to enhance drama and function as the sun's directional rays; the other side receives diffuse illumination to soften shadows and replicate the sky's diffusing quality. The background may be lighted separately to distinguish the object from its surround and to add visual depth.

Sharp highlights and dark shadows create a dramatic setting and strengthen impressions of texture and form; however, they are distracting in a working environment. Some shadows on a work surface are mildly irritating, such as those cast by a hand or pencil while one is writing under a concentrated light source.

Other shadows are extremely distracting and even hazardous, such as those on an assembly line. During a period of sustained visual activity, the extreme concentration and constant readaptation required by workers in high contrast settings result in visual fatigue, errors, and accidents.

Sometimes highlight and shadow are desirable in a work environment. Just as the highlights and shadows of a sunny day are emotionally stimulating, carefully placed highlights and shadows in an interior provide visual relief and interest. Office and factory workers benefit from the stimulation and variation provided by greater luminance contrast in corridors, washrooms, lunchrooms, lounges, and other meeting places. On most *work* surfaces, however, diffuse light distribution is desirable to minimize highlights and shadows.

Experience and memory also influence our perception of objects. Through the course of time, people have come to expect midday sunlight to emanate from

Figure 3.24
Sculpture lighted with concentrated direct lighting from below

Figure 3.25
Sculpture lighted with diffuse lighting from above

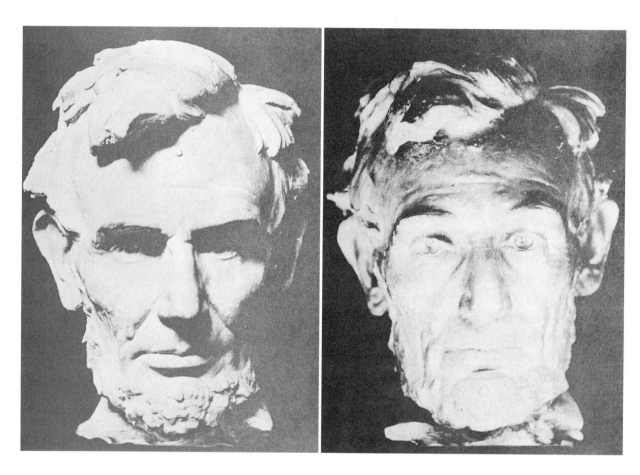

Figure 3.26 Bust of Lincoln lighted from above   **Figure 3.27** Bust of Lincoln lighted from below

a concentrated source overhead, at an angle less than 45° from *nadir* (straight down) and skylight to be a diffuse, multidirectional source.

When a lighting system alters the expected direction of light, it changes the normal relationship between highlights and shadows. An unnatural impression results, inducing mystery or anxiety (figures 3.26 and 3.27).

GLARE AND SPARKLE

Excessive contrast or luminance is distracting and annoying. This negative side of luminance is called *glare*. In the extreme, glare cripples vision by reducing or destroying the ability to see accurately.

Glare is often misunderstood as "too much light." It is light coming from the wrong direction, the result of an extreme luminance within the normal field of view. The difference between high and low beams of car headlights at night demonstrates that glare for the approaching driver is a function of direction as well as intensity. It also demonstrates that glare is present in a space with little light.

Glare is also a function of luminance area. Although a small area of luminance is tolerable, a larger area of the same intensity becomes uncomfortable. It is desirable to reduce luminance intensities as the area of luminance becomes more dominant in the field of view.

In addition, glare is a function of location. Within limits the human eyebrow shields glare from overhead luminaires, but not from poorly-shielded, wall-mounted luminaires or high-luminance wall surfaces, as these elements are directly in the field of view (figure 3.28).

Direct Glare

The late afternoon sun or an unshielded electric light source are examples of the distracting influence of direct glare in the environment. *Direct glare* is caused by the lighting system; it is defined as excessive light misdirected toward the eye.

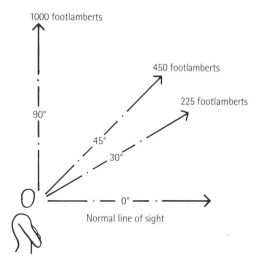

Figure 3.28 Acceptable luminance values decrease as the source approaches the center of the visual field.

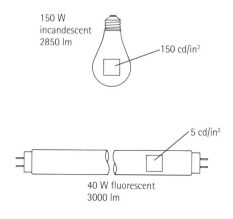

Figure 3.29 Unshielded lamp luminance for equivalent light output

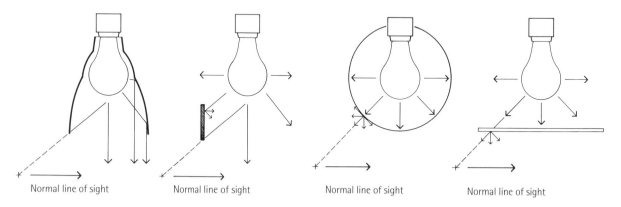

Figure 3.30a Limiting the amount of light emitted toward the eye

Figure 3.30b Increasing the area from which light is emitted

Figure 3.30 Control of direct glare

Usually, the uncontrolled luminance of an exposed light source produces glare. For this reason, bare lamps are rarely used in architectural applications (figure 3.29).

When direct glare occurs in the normal field of view, two main control techniques are available: (1) Limit the amount of light emitted in the direction of the eye, or (2) increase the area from which light is emitted (figure 3.30).

Shielding devices such as the hand, used instinctively, and sun visors improve visibility and restore visual comfort. Another solution to the problem of direct glare is directional control: the car headlights redirected below the line of sight demonstrate that changing the direction of the beam aids visual comfort.

This second method is more efficient; it uses accurate control devices to redirect light in the desired direction. Typical devices are reflectors and refracting lenses that limit the distribution of stray light emitted toward the eye.

Visual comfort results from the reduction of glare and distracting luminance in the field of view. Excessive luminance is physiologically disconcerting and reduces the ability to see detail accurately. The quality and comfort of vision depend upon the avoidance of distracting or disabling luminances.

VISUAL COMFORT PROBABILITY (VCP)

A *visual comfort probability* (VCP) rating is defined as the percentage of people who, if seated in the least desirable location in an office work space, will find a lighting installation comfortable. VCP depends on the size and shape of the room, the reflectances of room surfaces, and the location and light distribution of the luminaires.

A VCP of 70 or more is recommended for office use, and of 80 or more for office areas using visual display terminals (VDTs). VCP is only applicable for direct lighting systems.

Reflected Glare

Visual comfort also includes reflected luminance and surface properties as well as the luminance of the lighting system. *Reflected glare* is excessive uncontrolled luminance reflected from objects or surfaces in the field of view.

Figure 3.31

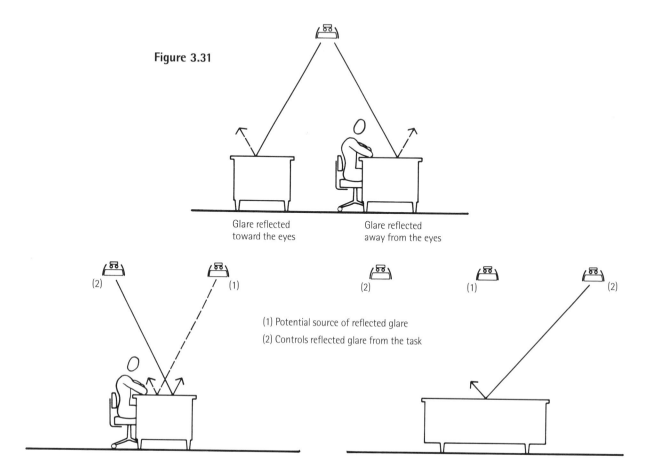

Glare reflected toward the eyes

Glare reflected away from the eyes

(1) Potential source of reflected glare

(2) Controls reflected glare from the task

Figure 3.32

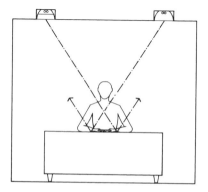

Figure 3.33 Proper desk lighting

Specular surfaces have reflecting properties similar to those of a mirror. The luminance reflected is the mirrored image of the light source or of another lighted surface within the reflected field of view.

These properties make specular surfaces useful as reflectors for light control in luminaires, but polished or specular interior surfaces such as desks, floors, walls, and ceilings introduce problems of reflected glare. Diffuse surfaces prevent highlights and are uniformly bright from all angles of view.

Reflected images on glass and other transparent materials form a visual barrier. At night, large areas of glass may become black mirrors. If surfaces viewed through the transparent material are higher in luminance than the reflected images, a sense of transparency is achieved.

Most work surfaces reflect light both diffusely and specularly. Diffuse reflectance is dependent on the quantity of illuminance on the surface. Specular reflectance is dependent on the luminance of the source: the reflected image of the lamp or luminaire. This reflected image causes a veiling image on the work surface that obscures surface detail.

In the visual task area, remove glossy surfaces wherever possible. A glass–covered or highly polished desk top is quite specular; reflected images become distracting. Matte (low–gloss) finishes should always be used for work surfaces.

It is helpful to think of the work surface as a mirror when orienting task luminaires (figure 3.31). Proper lighting fixture location controls reflected glare from the task (figure 3.32). When luminaires are located on either side of the desk, shadows cast by the luminaires are filled in and light is reflected away from the worker's eyes (figure 3.33).

VISUAL DISPLAY TERMINALS (VDTS)

VDTs are glossy *vertical* work surfaces. Screen reflections are caused by variations in luminance being "seen" by the screen surface and reflected into the worker's eyes. Screens that are convex and inclined upward, in particular, reflect into the eyes large areas of ceilings, walls, windows, and the surrounding space.

Screen positioning and angling, low-reflectance screens, blinds on windows, and dark smocks for workers are techniques that will relieve many reflection problems. Reflections caused by the lighting system can be controlled with properly designed deep–cell parabolic louvers to prevent lamp images from appearing on the VDT screen.

In addition to reflections on the screen surface, which make viewing the screen images difficult, two lighting problems that cause concern for VDT users are: (1) proper lighting for the non-VDT tasks the worker must also perform, and (2) lighting of the area in the worker's field of view.

Sometimes the ambient room illuminance in VDT areas is set low in the belief that this improves screen visibility. The opposite is true. While low quantities of ambient light reduce screen reflections, the room visually appears gloomy; there also will be areas of high contrast between the screen and the dark surround. Low ambient illuminance is unstimulating, especially when contact with the outdoors via windows is missing.

It is the *variation* in room luminance that is extremely critical, however. All surfaces and objects reflected by the VDT screen into the worker's normal line of sight—especially room surface finishes such as system divider panels, vertical surfaces of filing cabinets, and the ceiling plane—must be of more or less equal luminance if distracting images are to be prevented.

Indirect lighting systems are sometimes used to avoid luminaire reflections in the screen. The ceiling must be high enough to all pendant- or floor-mounted luminaires to distribute light evenly or excessive contrast is created in a different way (see figure 13.18). Even when uniform ceiling luminance is achieved, the diffuse reflected light may have a "washing out" effect that reduces the visibility of the screen. Moreover, because all of the light in the space is diffuse, indirect systems also create a bland interior. Many high-quality VDTs are now furnished with integral low-reflectance screens; in time, VDTs may cease to be a lighting problem.

Sparkle

The main difference between glare and sparkle is the relationship between luminance intensity and luminance area in the field of view. Large areas of

Figure 3.34 Direct sparkle

Figure 3.35 Reflected sparkle

Figure 3.36 Transmitted sparkle

luminance are distracting and disconcerting; relatively small areas of similar or higher intensity are points of sparkle and highlight that contribute to emotional excitement and visual interest.

- *Direct sparkle.* Examples include Christmas tree lights; small, exposed, clear filament lamps, and perforated shielding materials (figure 3.34).

- *Reflected sparkle.* Examples include textured metal and pebbled surface finishes (figure 3.35).

- *Transmitted sparkle.* An example is a crystal chandelier. Clear filament lamps combined with crystal glass, particularly when that glass has been faceted, introduce subtle color highlights via the prisms that disperse "white" light into the rainbow of colors that comprise it (figure 3.36).

The presence or absence of sparkle, highlight, and shadows constitute the main visual attribute that makes a sunny day interesting and stimulating and a cloudy, overcast day flat and dull. The emotional stimulation provided by carefully controlled sparkle is equally significant in the interior.

CHAPTER 4

COLOR

The color of an object or surface is determined by its reflected or transmitted light. Color is not a physical property of the things we see—it is the consequence of light waves bouncing off or passing through various objects. What is perceived as color is the result of materials reflecting or transmitting energy in particular regions of the visible spectrum.

Green glass transmits the green portion of the spectrum, absorbing almost all of the other regions; yellow paint reflects the yellow portion, absorbing almost all other wavelengths. White or neutral gray materials reflect all wavelengths in approximately equal amounts.

Pure spectral colors are specified by their wavelength, which is usually expressed in nanometers. A nanometer (nm) is one billionth of a meter or about 39 billionths of an inch.

The reflectance chart (see color plate 4) shows that butter absorbs blue light and reflects a high percentage of all other colors; these other colors combine to produce what we call yellow. Green lettuce reflects light with wavelengths primarily in the 500 nm to 600 nm region and absorbs all of the energy at other wavelengths. A tomato is red only because it reflects visible energy at 610 nm while absorbing almost all of the other wavelengths.

A light source that emits radiant energy comparatively balanced in all visible wavelengths appears "white" in color. Passing a narrow beam of this white light through a prism spreads and separates the individual wavelengths, allowing the eye to distinguish among them. The resulting visual phenomenon is called a color spectrum. (See color plate 5.)

"White" light sources emit energy at all or almost all visible wavelengths, but not always in an ideal proportion. Almost all sources are deficient at some wavelengths yet still appear to be white. This deficiency influences the perception of colors; the effect is known as color rendition. It causes the graying of some colors while enhancing the vividness of others.

To provide accurate color perception, a light source must emit those wavelengths that a material reflects. Lighting a tomato's surface with a white light source makes the surface appear red, because only red wavelengths of light are reflected toward the eye. All other wavelengths are absorbed.

If the tomato is lighted with a green source, however, it will appear dark gray because no red energy is available to be reflected. The eye can see only the colors of a surface that are present in the source of illumination.

Because the proportion of colors in "white" light varies, what we call "white" light is a broad category. Within this category, the most common variations are described as warm or cool. A warm "white" light emphasizes the long (high nm) end of the spectrum, with hues of yellow through orange to red. Warm light sources that emphasize these hues include the sun and incandescent, tungsten-halogen, and high-pressure sodium lamps. Conversely, a cool "white" light source emphasizes the short (low nm) end of the spectrum, with hues of blue through green to yellow. Cool light sources that emphasize these hues include north skylight and some fluorescent and metal halide lamps.

Spectral distribution charts, available from lamp manufacturers, express the relative color composition of light sources. Because these charts are of limited practical value in predicting how colors will appear, simplified systems of color notation and color rendition have been developed.

COLOR TEMPERATURE

Color temperature describes how a lamp appears when lighted. Color temperature is measured by kelvins (K), a scale that starts at absolute zero (−273°C).

At room temperature an object such as a bar of steel does not emit light, but if it is heated to a certain point it glows dull red. Instead of a bar of steel, physicists use an imaginary object called a blackbody radiator. As the steel bar, the blackbody radiator emits red light when heated to 800 K; a warm, yellowish "white" at 2800 K; a daylight-like "white" at 5000 K; a bluish, daylight "white" at 8000 K; and a brilliant blue at 60,000 K. The theoretical blackbody is necessary because the bar of steel would melt at these higher temperatures.

Incandescent lamps closely resemble blackbody radiators in that they emit a continuous spectrum of all of the visible colors of light. Consequently, the incandescent spectrum is accurately specified by color temperature in kelvins. Fluorescent and high-intensity discharge lamps produce a discontinuous spectrum with blank areas punctuated by bands at specific frequencies. These bands combine to give the impression of "white" light, which is specified by its apparent or correlated color temperature.

Because color temperature describes chromaticity and not actual temperature, it is expressed in kelvins only (not in degrees). Incandescent lamps used in architectural lighting have color temperatures in the 2600 K to 3100 K range; fluorescent lamps are available with apparent color temperatures from 2700 K to 7500 K; north skylight is arbitrarily called 10,400 K.

Unfortunately, the apparent color temperature of discontinuous spectrum light sources fails to provide information about its spectral energy distribution. For example, cool white and cool white deluxe fluorescent lamps have the same apparent color temperature, yet their spectral distribution curves and their effects on colored objects and materials are quite different. This same limitation applies when using color temperature notations for high-intensity discharge sources, including mercury, metal halide, and high-pressure sodium lamps.

COLOR RENDERING

Color rendering expresses how colors appear under a given light source. For example, a shade of red will be rendered lighter or darker, more crimson or more orange, depending on the spectral distribution properties of the light falling on it.

The most accepted method to determine the color-rendering ability of a light source is a rating system called the Color Rendering Index (CRI).

The CRI first establishes the real or apparent color temperature of a given light source. Second, it establishes a comparison between the color rendition of the given light source and of a reference light source. If the color temperature of a given source is 5000 K or less, then the reference source is the blackbody radiator at the nearest color temperature. If the given color temperature is above 5000 K, then the reference source is the nearest simulated daylight source.

The comparison is expressed as an R factor, on a scale of 100, which is a percentage indicating how closely the given light source matches the color-rendering ability of the reference light source. Comparisons are valid only for a specific color temperature reference. Therefore, it is inappropriate to compare two light sources unless their color temperature is similar—within 100 K to 300 K.

R is an average of the color rendering ability of eight test colors; better performance at some wavelengths is concealed when averaged with poorer performance at other wavelengths. As a consequence, two lamps that have the same color temperature and CRI may have different spectral distributions and may render colored materials differently.

Some typical CRIs appear in Table 1 in the Appendix.

The color properties of the light source significantly affect the appearance of people. Because incandescent sources are rich in red wavelengths, they complement and flatter complexions—imparting a healthy, ruddy, or tanned quality to the skin. HID and cool fluorescent sources that emphasize the yellow or blue range produce a sallow or pale appearance.

SUBJECTIVE IMPRESSIONS

The color of light has a profound effect on subjective impressions of the environment. The Amenity Curve indicates that warmer light is desirable for low luminance values (figure 4.1). It also shows that a room uniformly lighted to

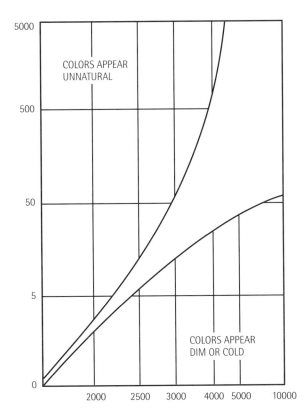

Figure 4.1 Amenity curve

20 footcandles (fc) will be unpleasant with either kerosene lamps (about 2000 K) or lamps that simulate daylight (about 5000 K).

With the warm-toned kerosene source, the quantity will seem too high and the space too greatly lighted. With simulated daylight the same quantity of light will seem dark and dingy. Both warm fluorescent (3000 K) and standard incandescent lamps (2600 K to 3100 K) fall within the acceptable range on the chart.

In addition, a warm atmosphere suggests friendliness or coziness. A cool atmosphere implies efficiency and neatness. Flynn evaluates subjective responses to colors of "white" light that are produced by electric light sources in interior spaces at intermediate illuminance values.

Flynn's subjects categorized their impressions of visually warm versus visually cool space as follows: Cool colors (4100 K) strengthen impressions of "visual clarity." Warm colors (3000 K) reinforce impressions of pleasantness, particularly when a feeling of relaxation is desirable.

Patterns of sparkle plus saturated warm (orange-red) hues strengthen impressions of playfulness and merriment; this is particularly strong with random patterns of light and color. Patterns of sparkle plus saturated cool (violet-blue) hues reinforce impressions of enchantment; this is particularly strong with rhythmic or regimented patterns of light and color.

Diffuse light plus warm (orange-red) hues strengthen impressions of tension and anxiety. Diffuse light plus cool (violet-blue) hues reinforce impressions of somberness; at low luminance values, they create an impression of gloom.

SURFACE FINISHES AND COLOR OF LIGHT

The relationship between the spectral distribution of light and the colors of fabrics, walls, and other elements in the interior is pivotal. Some objects appear to be the same color under a certain light source although they are different in spectral composition. If the light source is changed, however, the object color differences become apparent.

It is advisable to appraise, match, and specify colored materials using light sources identical in color to those that will be used in the completed installation. When this is unknown, two light sources of different spectral character may be used to examine the samples. One of the sources ought to be predominantly blue in spectral distribution, such as a daylight fluorescent lamp; the other ought to be predominantly red, such as an incandescent lamp.

INCANDESCENT SOURCES

Incandescent lamps emit energy in a smooth curve beginning with a small amount of deep blue radiation in the near ultraviolet range and increasing into the deep red portion of the spectrum. The color of incandescent light is warm in tone, with most of the energy concentrated in the red and yellow range. Although this "white" light is deficient in blue and green, and tends to gray these colors, it complements the appearance of warm colors and human faces.

Incandescent lamps enjoy one slight advantage over other lamps in color rendering—not because they render colors more naturally, but because decades of use have established them as a norm. Incandescent lamps produce light as a by-product of heat, similar to other sources of light that have been familiar for thousands of years: the sun, open fire, candles, oil lamps, and gas lamps. All of these give warm-colored light and all are point sources.

Good color rendition is usually interpreted to mean the familiar appearance of familiar objects: Things assume familiar colors by frequently being seen under certain kinds of light sources, such as daylight or incandescent. (See color plate 6.)

Tungsten-halogen lamps (3000 K) have more blue and less red energy than standard incandescent lamps; they appear whiter than the slightly yellowish standard incandescent lamps (2700 K).

FLUORESCENT SOURCES

Fuorescent lamps produce a discontinuous spectrum: peaks of energy at specific wavelengths. Variations in the composition of the phosphors that coat the inside of the lamp produce differences in the color of emitted light. Three principal color temperatures are available with fluorescent lamps: (1) warm (3000 K) lamps are compatible with incandescent lamps; (2) cool (4100 K) lamps are compatible with daylight; and (3) 3500 K are compatible with both.

Fluorescent lamps also fall into three groups with regard to efficiency and color rendition: (1) standard, (2) deluxe, and (3) rare earth. Standard white— both cool and warm kinds—produce high efficiency and poor color rendition. (See color plates 13 and 14.)

Deluxe white lamps produce improved color rendering with an approximately 25 percent sacrifice in lighting efficiency. The reduction in light quantity is often imperceptible, however, because of the vivid and accurate colors that improve contrast and portray tones that are grayed with standard lamps. (See color plates 15 and 16.)

For both high color rendering and high luminous *efficacy*, rare earth lamps are used. Three kinds of rare-earth lamps are available: (1) triphosphor RE-70, (2) triphosphor RE-80, and (3) quad-phosphor RE-90.

Triphosphor rare-earth lamps produce light in accordance with the theory that the human eye reacts to three *prime* colors—blue–violet, pure green, and orange–red. (See color plate 17.) When these three prime (not primary) colors are combined in a triphosphor lamp, only those wavelengths are emitted; the brain fills in the remainder of the spectrum. This yields more colorful interiors because the three narrow-emission prime-color phosphors compress all hues into the eye's color response system, increasing color contrast. (See color plates 18, 19, and 20.)

RE-70 lamps use a coat of conventional phosphors and a thin coat of narrow-emission, rare-earth phosphors, producing CRIs of 70 to 79. *RE-80* lamps use a thick coat of the narrow-emission, rare-earth phosphors, producing CRIs of 80 to 89.

Quad-phosphor RE-90 lamps do not use the narrow-emission phosphors; they contain four wider-emission phosphors that produce CRIs of 95 at 3000 K and 98 at 4100 K. Rare-earth lamps with CRIs of 95 to 98 are the highest color-rendering fluorescent lamps available.

HIGH–INTENSITY-DISCHARGE (HID) SOURCES

As with fluorescent lamps, high-intensity-discharge *(HID)* lamps produce a discontinuous spectrum. The different metals in the arc of the various HID sources yield different color-rendering abilities.

If you were to throw salt on a barbecue, the sodium chloride would make the flames appear yellow. Similarly, the sodium in high-pressure-sodium lamps makes their color appear yellow. If you were to throw mercury on a barbecue, although this is not recommended because it would cause mercury poisoning, the mercury would make the flames appear blue. Similarly, the mercury in mercury-vapor lamps makes their color appear blue.

The clear mercury lamp produces a cool, white light of predominantly blue and green energy. The lack of energy at the warm (red) end of the spectrum results in poor color rendering; people appear ghastly. Clear mercury-vapor lamps exhibit particularly poor rendering of red. Rendering of other colors is fair, but blues appear purplish. (See color plate 7.)

Applying a phosphor coating to the inside surface of the outer bulb of a mercury lamp slightly improves the color-rendering properties, but also reduces efficiency. The phosphor converts invisible ultraviolet energy into visible light. (See color plate 8.)

Metal-halide lamps are similar in construction to mercury lamps, except that various metal halides have been added. These halides add missing wavelengths that improve the mercury lamp's spectral distribution, yielding a more uniform spectrum and better color rendering, but reds are slightly muted. (See color plate 9.) A broad range of color-rendering quality exists in the different metal-halide lamps; many experience lamp–to–lamp color inconsistency and color shift over the lamp life.

High-pressure-sodium lamps produce predominantly yellow light at 2100 K, which creates a shift in almost all observed colors. Reds, greens, blues, and violets are muted. (See color plate 10.)

By further increasing the gas pressure inside the lamp, white high-pressure-sodium lamps produce incandescent–like color at 2700 K with good color-rendering properties and a CRI of 80. (See color plate 11.)

Low-pressure-sodium lamps emit all visible energy at 589 nm, which means that they will render only materials that reflect light at that wavelength. All other colors appear gray. (See color plate 12.)

A "best" lamp color is nonexistent, as is "true" color. Each spectral distribution results in different object colors, whether it comes from natural sources such as sunlight or skylight or from electric sources such as incandescent, fluorescent, or HID lamps. The "right" color source for a given application depends upon an evaluation of trade-offs including directional control, familiarity, color rendition, efficiency, absence of glare, maintenance, and cost.

CHAPTER 5

DAYLIGHT

A principal characteristic of daylight is its variability. The color of daylight changes with the time of day, the cleanliness of the atmosphere, and the interreflection of surrounding objects. The intensity of the sun changes with the time of day, the time of year, and the latitude of the site. The luminance of the sky depends on whether the light is coming from an overcast sky, from a clear sky only, or from a clear sky and direct sunlight.

Daylight has two components: (1) sunlight and (2) skylight. Sunlight is the directional beam emitted by the sun; skylight is the diffuse reflection of light from particles in the atmosphere.

Direct sunlight is usually an impractical source for interiors unless it is shielded. Just as electric luminaires are designed to reduce glare, direct sunlight entering interior spaces requires careful control. For critical seeing tasks, sunlight often causes excessive luminance differences that result in discomfort and poor visibility. This high contrast in the field of view inhibits the eye's ability to adjust, leading to visual fatigue and disturbing the accommodation needed for clear vision.

Skylight, on the other hand, is a useful source without shielding. Although special building configurations or controls are necessary to make skylight acceptable for horizontal tasks at the workplane or for displaying art, it is used with less control to light noncritical seeing areas such as corridors, stairwells, cafeterias, and seating areas.

People require changing stimuli to remain sensitive and alert. Gazing out the window at distant objects provides relief for the muscles of the eye; a cloud passing in front of the sun supplies stimulation or respite through variation in luminance. The constantly changing nature of daylight satisfies the biological need of the mind and body for change.

The proper introduction of daylight into the interior is the simplest way to provide this change. A view of the sky provides information about the time of day and weather conditions which helps to maintain our biological cycles. The varying light intensity helps to reduce monotony. The goal of daylight design is to provide visual variety with controlled luminance contrasts.

Comfort requires moderate changes. Monotony will cause fatigue, but so will overstimulation. Excessive contrast provides emotional appeal but also impairs visual performance. The sudden appearance of a beam of sunlight on a task will provide momentary change and relief; if it remains it will soon cause visual fatigue and stress.

Daylight and view do not necessarily go together and often are achieved through different building openings. The criteria for producing a view to the exterior are different from the criteria for producing good interior daylight.

The more complex the view and the more frequent the changes, the greater will be our satisfaction. Although large windows are sometimes desirable, people's basic need for a view of the outside can be satisfied with comparatively small openings.

DAYLIGHT DESIGN

Window size and height above the work surface are factors in daylighting design. Of course, as the window becomes larger in size the amount of daylight increases. But the height of the window is the more significant factor.

The higher the window opening, the deeper the daylight can penetrate into the room, and if it is high enough it may prevent exterior luminance from causing glare. This high-entry light is softened and spread by proper design of the room surfaces. Interreflections between these surfaces cause the luminance patterns to become more uniform; visibility and seeing comfort are increased.

Windows and other daylight openings that are set flush in a wall or ceiling produce excessive contrasts between exterior luminance and the immediately adjacent interior surfaces. This contrast is often harsh and uncomfortable.

A softer transition is achieved with the use of splayed jambs, rounded jambs, and deep window wells. Instead of the sharp contrast between adjacent surfaces, these designs provide a zone of intermediate luminance which softens the change (figure 5.1). The jambs of the window become light-reflecting shelves that reflect the light indirectly into the interior. Using white paint around the windows or hanging draperies or blinds are other solutions.

Figure 5.1 Splayed and rounded window jambs soften contrasts.

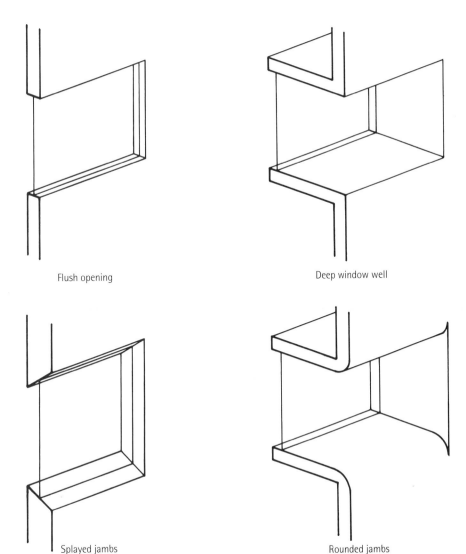

Flush opening

Deep window well

Splayed jambs

Rounded jambs

For comfortable seeing, the ratio between fenestration and adjacent surfaces ought to be less than 20:1. This ratio is also desirable for the surface luminance of luminaires and adjacent surfaces. It is advisable to limit luminance ratios anywhere in the field of view to less than 40:1.

Fenestration Sections

Windows placed on a single side of the room (figure 5.2) are the usual method of fenestration. To achieve useful work surface illuminance throughout the room, limit the depth of the room to twice the height from the floor to a full room–width window head. For example, if the window head height is 10'-0", the optimum room will be no more than 20 ft deep. Somewhat narrower windows provide slightly lower illuminance values, but the difference is minor.

Figure 5.2 Unilateral section

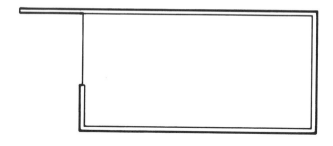

This ratio of 1:2 may be increased to 2:5 as long as the reflectances of interior surfaces are high and carefully controlled. If these ratios are exceeded, people seated in the deepest part of the room will feel cheated, even if they are provided with adequate electric lighting.

Windows placed on opposite sides double the feasible room depth for daylighting. The opposite windows need only occupy the upper part of the wall; the quantity of interior light will be almost the same as if the windows were full height, with the added benefit of reducing the possibility of glare (figure 5.3).

Figure 5.3 Bilateral section

Skylights are tools for delivering daylight deep into interior areas of one-story buildings or into the top floors of multistory buildings. They also bring daylight into the lower floors of multistory buildings through light wells and reflective devices.

Skylights come in a variety of shapes and sizes. They are made of clear, patterned, or translucent glass or various kinds of plastic. Clear, gray-tinted, or milk-white acrylics are best for this purpose; their optical properties are similar to glass and they are easier to maintain.

Flat skylights have both drainage and dirt-accumulation problems. Domed or slanted skylights mitigate these drawbacks (figure 5.4). Although the domed skylight is "self-cleaning" on the outside, dirt still collects on the inside, making a program of periodic cleaning as important with skylights as it is with electric luminaires.

Depending on the shape of the room and the location and size of the skylight, luminance control will be necessary in areas with demanding visual requirements. If directly exposed to view from below, at angles in the *glare zone,* skylights often produce excessive luminance and cause disabling veiling reflections on tasks. Light from skylights is controlled with the use of deep wells, splayed wells, and louvers, preventing any view of the skylight at unsuitable angles and minimizing veiling reflections.

Diffuse (milk–white) plastic or glass skylights diminish the biological benefits of daylight by obscuring the view of the weather. Clear glass or plastic skylights, however, produce more heat gain for a given unit of illuminance at the work surface below and may admit direct sunlight in undesirable ways.

An exterior shield that shades the skylight from direct sun but allows daylight to penetrate reduces the heat load. For colder climates, *double glazing* made of two thicknesses of glass or plastic with an air space between reduces conductive heat loss in winter.

Clerestories have all the attributes of skylights; because they occur in the vertical rather than the horizontal plane, they can be oriented to prevent the penetration of direct sun (figure 5.5). When built in combination with a

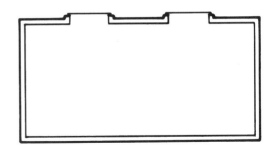

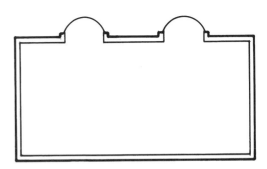

Figure 5.4 Skylight sections

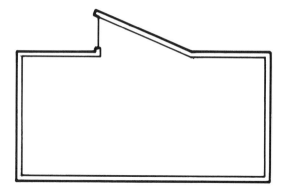

Figure 5.5 Clerestory section

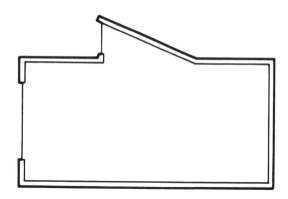

Figure 5.6 Clerestory and main window

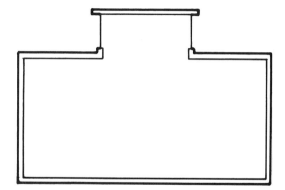

Figure 5.7 Roof monitor section

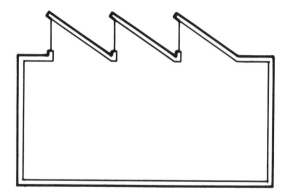

Figure 5.8 Sawtooth section

lightshelf, a clerestory reflects great quantities of daylight against the upper ceiling yet blocks the view of the glaring sky from below.

When facing the same (or opposite) direction as the main windows, the clerestory extends the room–depth limitations (figure 5.6). When clerestories are located on walls opposite each other, as was often the case in early church buildings, these vertical glazing sections are called roof monitors (figure 5.7). A series of parallel clerestories is suited for large, low–roofed structures such as factories and warehouses, and is called a sawtooth section (figure 5.8).

To maximize the light delivered by the clerestory, it is recommended that the roof directly below the clerestory and the adjacent interior ceiling area be diffuse and highly reflective.

Heat Gain

When buildings use glazing to admit daylight, a single layer of ordinary glass exposed to the sun also admits warming radiant energy—heat. This helps in cold winters, but poses a problem in hot summers.

If buildings are properly designed to use daylight, they reject most of the direct light from the sun yet still admit an ample supply of skylight. Just as the sun's light can be controlled, there are many ways to control the sun's radiant heat; it may be admitted or excluded as seasonally required without passing up the benefits of daylighting.

Orientation is a primary method for managing solar heat radiation because the sun strikes differently-oriented surfaces with widely varying intensity. The size and placement of glazed areas are also factors in capturing the sun's energy for cold-weather heat gain.

For example, a house benefits if its walls and roof are oriented to receive heat from the sun in the winter and shed it in the summer. If the principal facade of a house faces due south or within 30° of due south, the south-facing walls may be designed to absorb radiation from the low winter sun; the roof may be designed to reject the sun's heat by reflecting the high summer sun.

It is possible with any building orientation to achieve good quality daylighting indoors. North light is inherently softer, cooler, and more uniform; because of the sun, south light is more intense and variable. But the same high quality of illumination that comes naturally from the north sky can be achieved with any other orientation by the proper use of daylight controls.

SHADING DEVICES

Shading devices used on the inside of the building reflect some of the radiant heat energy back outdoors, reducing the energy gain from the sun by as much as 60 to 70 percent. Exterior shading devices can reduce that energy penetration even more—by 90 to 95 percent. Exterior shading devices are more expensive to build and maintain, but with hot climates and/or high energy costs, air-conditioning savings often give prompt paybacks.

A variety of shading devices are employed to deliver daylight to where it is needed and to reduce glare by limiting excessive luminance in the field of view. Shading devices are divided into two categories: (1) moveable and (2) stationary.

Moveable controls adjusted in response to varying sky conditions are the most efficient, but they require a human operator or an automatic device. Stationary (static) controls are less expensive, but are also less efficient, because they are unresponsive to daily and seasonal changes.

Moveable Controls

Draperies and screens are available with a wide range of materials that vary in their openness of weave and surface reflectivity. They provide almost any desired degree of light transmission or a complete blackout. Greater flexibility is achieved with two separately tracked draperies over a window area—one used to reduce light and the second to block it completely.

Light–colored venetian blinds (interior horizontal louvers) can be adjusted to exclude direct sunshine but reflect light to the ceiling, increasing its penetration into the space while still allowing a view of the outdoors (figure 5.9). Or they can be closed completely, blocking both light and view.

But for venetian blinds to function appropriately under changing sky conditions they must be operated with an understanding of their potential by someone who has the opportunity and the incentive to perform the task. Venetian blinds collect dirt easily and are tedious to clean; they are subject to mechanical failure of support straps and control strings.

Double–glazed windows are available with a narrow venetian blind positioned between the inner and outer glass, which eliminates the dirt-collection problem. These blinds are fully operable and reject heat more efficiently than interior blinds or other shading devices such as roller shades or draperies.

Moveable shading devices on building exteriors are difficult to maintain and they deteriorate rapidly unless made of stainless steel or a copper alloy. Awnings are highly reliable, but their aesthetic appeal is limited.

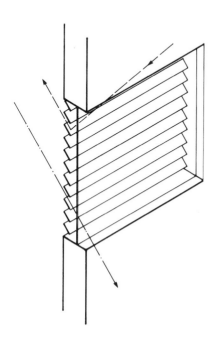

Figure 5.9 Properly adjusted venetian blinds reflect daylight to the ceiling and do not prevent a view outside.

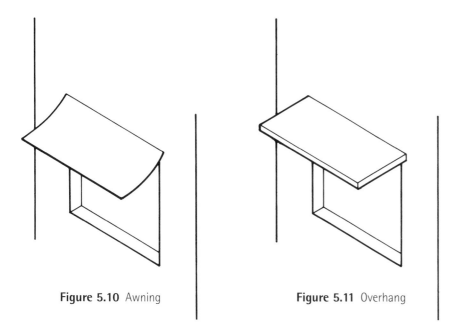

Figure 5.10 Awning

Figure 5.11 Overhang

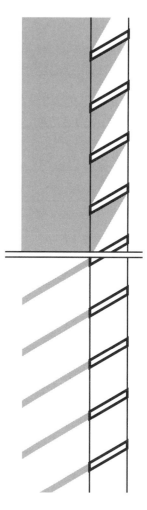

Figure 5.12 High sun and low sun angles at exterior louvers

Stationary Controls

Building overhangs and fixed awnings serve to shade direct sunlight and reduce glare through the upper area of windows (figure 5.10). They also reduce the daylight entering the room, decreasing the illumination close to the window and the penetration into the room. The maximum depth of useful light penetration is calculated from the outer edge of the overhang, instead of the vertical plane of the window.

Although they reduce the quantity of skylight entering the building, overhangs can collect light from a light-colored exterior surround and reflect it into the interior. This results in a more even distribution of light.

An overhang located on the southern side of a building is especially efficient at controlling both light and heat from the sun (figure 5.11). In the summer, the overhang shields the glass from the sun's direct rays yet allows daylight to enter from the lower sky and by reflection from the ground. In the winter, the overhang allows the low-angle sun to penetrate for warmth, but seating must be oriented to avoid direct sun glare.

Exterior horizontal louvers may pick up direct sun, causing excessive luminance and discomforting or disabling glare (figure 5.12). Exterior or interior vertical louvers are useful for low sun angles that occur in the early morning

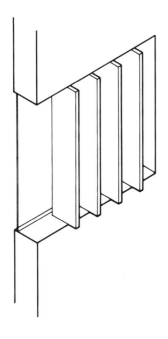

Figure 5.13 Vertical louvers

or late afternoon, particularly on building walls oriented toward the east or west (figure 5.13). When it is necessary to control both high sun and low sun, "egg-crate" louvers are used because they combine horizontal and vertical shielding.

Direct sunshine from flat skylights, or from pitched skylights facing east, south, or west, must also be controlled. Interior louvers or translucent shades will reduce glare and heat, but exterior controls provide superior shading.

Exterior sun shades can be oriented to shade light and heat from the sun during warm weather yet allow penetration during the cold seasons, or be designed to eliminate direct sun from the interior all year long (figure 5.14).

A difficulty with fixed overhangs and awnings is that the amount of shading follows the solar seasons rather than the climatic seasons. The middle of the summer for the sun is June 21, but the hottest days occur from the end of July to the middle of August. The overhang designed for optimal shading on September 21, when the weather is still warm and solar heat gain is unwelcome, causes the same shading on March 21—when temperatures are lower and solar heat gain is welcome (figure 5.15).

Figure 5.14 Skylight shades

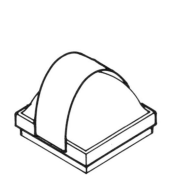
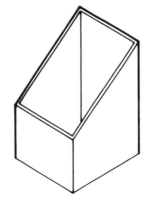
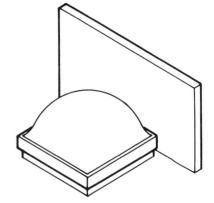

Vegetation, which follows the climatic seasons, provides excellent shading year-round. On March 21 many plants are without leaves and do not obstruct the passage of sunlight. On September 21, however, the leaves are still full and provide good shading. Deciduous trees or an overhanging trellis with a climbing vine that sheds its leaves in winter provide a natural climatic control when placed in front of south-facing windows.

Glazing Materials

Glazing materials are available with a wide range of heat and light transmittance, color, and prismatic control. Because of its resistance to abrasion, glass is the preferred medium; where breakage is a concern, acrylic or polycarbonate is substituted. Both glass and plastic can be tinted in warm, neutral, or cool gray tones to reduce the transmission of light and heat yet remain transparent to vision. Saturated colors are to be avoided except in carefully-designed art ("stained") glass windows.

Translucent glazing materials that transmit diffused light but obscure vision include etched, sandblasted, opal, and patterned glass and plastic. Many translucent materials become excessively glary with exposure to the sun and will be distracting when seen from task areas. Because they prevent a view of the outside, their psychological value is minimal. As diffusion increases so does the area of luminance and the possibility that the window or skylight will become a source of glare.

Selectively-transmitting materials pass the desirable wavelengths of the visible spectrum but reflect or absorb the radiant heat energy. Directionally-selective glass blocks and prismatic glass or plastics refract light for directional control.

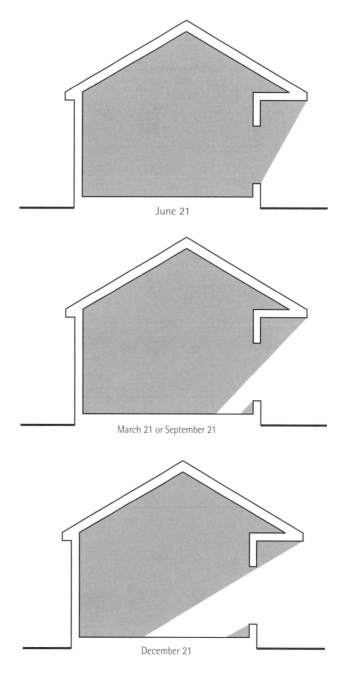

June 21

March 21 or September 21

December 21

Figure 5.15 Shading a south window with a fixed overhang (at solar noon)

When installed vertically, prismatic glass-block walls are used to reflect day-light onto the ceiling of a room, increasing illuminance values deep in the interior and removing the glaring sky from view (figure 5.16). When installed horizontally, as with glass-block pavers, they transmit light yet maintain a low surface luminance even when exposed to direct sun.

Quantity

Because of the great variety of changing sun and sky conditions, it is imprac-tical to predict precisely the interior illuminance patterns derived from day-lighting. By knowing the size and position of windows, however, and using tables of average daylighting conditions for various locations and orienta-tions, the average amount of available daylight that will enter a space can be determined, but not the precise amount at any moment.

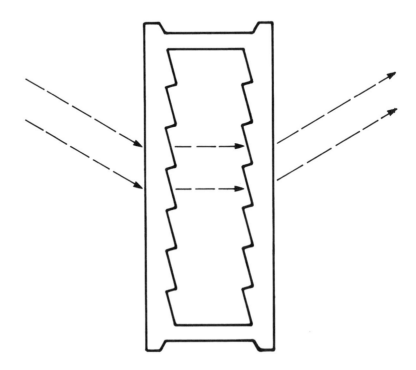

Figure 5.16 Prismatic glass block directs daylight toward the ceiling.

Interior daylight illuminance values are often expressed as a daylight factor. The daylight factor accounts for light received directly from the sky, light reflected from external surfaces, and interreflections within the room. It is a measure of the proportion of the outdoor illumination to the daylight illumination received indoors.

Average interior daylight illuminance is also calculated by graphic methods, such as the Libbey-Owens-Ford™ "Sun Angle Calculator," and by computer programs that consider geographic location, time of day, time of year, fenestration, room shape, and interior finishes. The most sophisticated programs produce a rendering of the interior showing the relative luminances of room surfaces.

The simplest, most versatile, and most reliable technique for studying the aesthetics of daylighting is simulation by constructing a scale model. Daylight behaves in the same way in a scale model as in an actual building. If studied under similar sky conditions, the interior of the scale model appears exactly as the interior of the building. Miniature photoelectric cells are placed inside the model to read illuminance values. But identical sky conditions are difficult to achieve by placing the model outdoors; this has led to the development of sky simulators that reproduce almost any sky condition.

Energy Control

Photocells (light-sensing devices) automatically switch luminaires off when the daylight contribution at selected interior locations reaches prescribed levels. The luminaires are automatically switched on as the available daylight decreases. This kind of switching has the disadvantage of calling undue attention to the change; it may be abrupt and jarring.

Dimming systems that allow a gradual increase and decrease in light quantity are more satisfactory. This is more pleasant and may even go unnoticed. Sophisticated systems are designed with a built-in delay so that a cloud passing rapidly across the sun triggers no response.

CHAPTER 6

INCANDESCENT LAMPS

The incandescent lamp is a simple device—a hot wire (the filament) sealed in a glass jar (the bulb). An electric current passing through the wire heats it to incandescence and the wire emits light. The filament wire diameter and length determine the amount of electrical current consumed by the lamp, regulating its light output (figure 6.1).

Figure 6.1 Incandescent lamp components

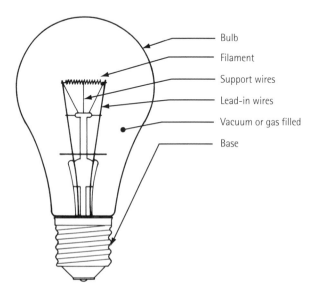

Bulb

Filament

Support wires

Lead-in wires

Vacuum or gas filled

Base

The incandescent lamps discussed in this chapter are commonly referred to as "large" lamps. This designation does not refer to large physical size, but has traditionally described lamps that are operated on standard-voltage circuits. The "large lamp" category now includes lamps of many voltages commonly found in residential, commercial, and industrial use.

"Miniature" lamps, conversely, are not necessarily small, although many of them are. They are lamps that operate at less common voltages, powered by storage batteries or by transformers that reduce or increase the standard voltage to the voltage required by the lamp. Their predominant use is in transportation vehicles and instruments.

The large lamp family contains about 100 combinations of glass and quartz bulb shapes and sizes. These variations are designated by a two–part abbreviation: the first part, one or more letters, indicates the shape of the bulb; the second part, a number, indicates the diameter of the bulb in eighths of an inch. For example, an A19 lamp is an **a**rbitrary-shaped lamp that is $^{19}/_8$ or $2^3/_8$ inches in diameter (figure 6.2).

A	**a**rbitrary (with familiar teardrop shape)
AR	**a**luminum **r**eflector
B	flame (smooth)
C	**c**one shape
CA	**ca**ndle
F	**f**lame (irregular)
G	**g**lobe shape
GT	**g**lobe-**t**ubular
MR	multifaceted **m**irror **r**eflector
P	**p**ear shape
PAR	**p**arabolic **a**luminized **r**eflector
PS	**p**ear–**s**traight neck
R	**r**eflector
S	**s**traight side
T	**t**ubular

Figure 6.2 Incandescent bulb shapes at ¼ actual size

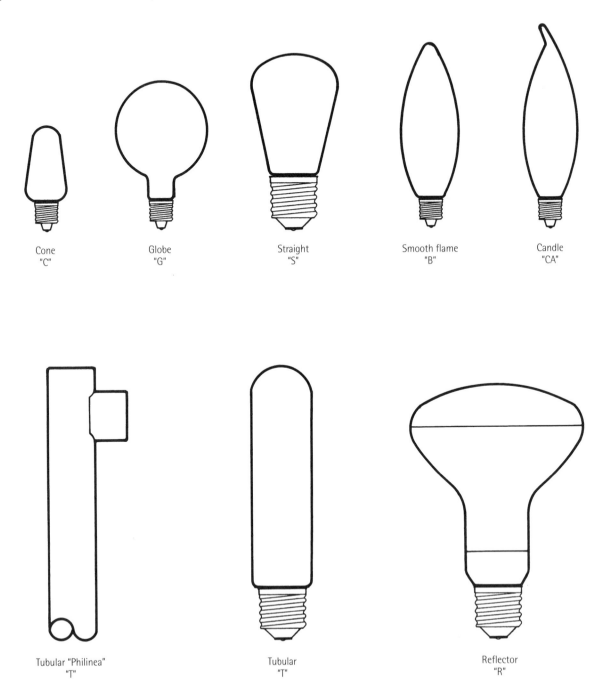

Cone
"C"

Globe
"G"

Straight
"S"

Smooth flame
"B"

Candle
"CA"

Tubular "Philinea"
"T"

Tubular
"T"

Reflector
"R"

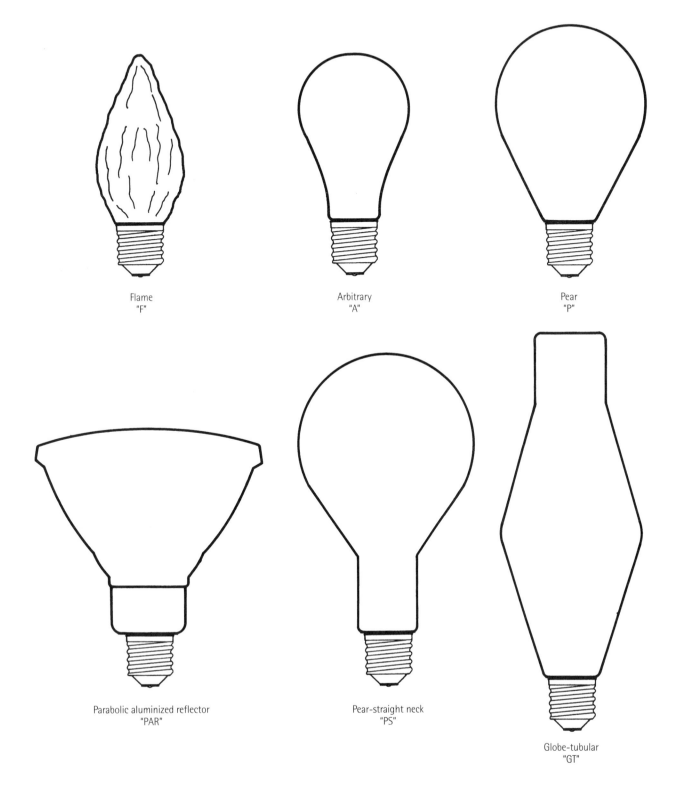

Flame
"F"

Arbitrary
"A"

Pear
"P"

Parabolic aluminized reflector
"PAR"

Pear-straight neck
"PS"

Globe-tubular
"GT"

LAMP BASES

Most incandescent lamps have a base at one end, although some tubular lamps have bases at both ends. All bases conduct current from the electrical supply into the lamp (figure 6.3); most bases also support the lamp physically, but many kinds of PAR lamps can be supported by their bulbs.

Figure 6.3 Incandescent lamp bases at ¼ actual size

The most frequently used is the medium base; its name describes its size. Smaller lamps have smaller bases, including bayonet, bipin, candelabra, inter-

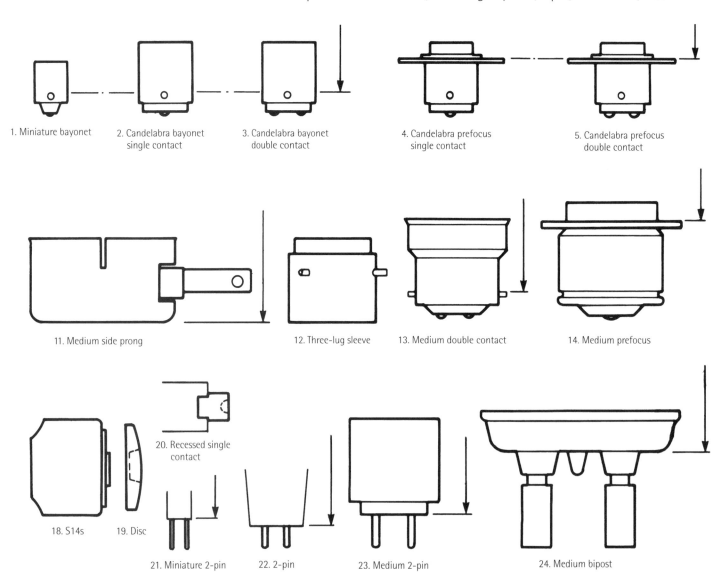

1. Miniature bayonet

2. Candelabra bayonet single contact

3. Candelabra bayonet double contact

4. Candelabra prefocus single contact

5. Candelabra prefocus double contact

11. Medium side prong

12. Three-lug sleeve

13. Medium double contact

14. Medium prefocus

18. S14s

19. Disc

20. Recessed single contact

21. Miniature 2-pin

22. 2-pin

23. Medium 2-pin

24. Medium bipost

mediate, *miniature*, *mini-candelabra ("mini-can")*, *twist-and-lock (TAL)*, and *two-pin* bases. Larger lamps have larger bases, including *mogul* screw and medium and mogul *bipost* bases. The bipin and bipost bases orient the filament position, providing rotational alignment for optical control. Bayonet and *prefocus* medium and mogul bases also locate the filament in the exact predetermined position required for optical instruments and searchlights.

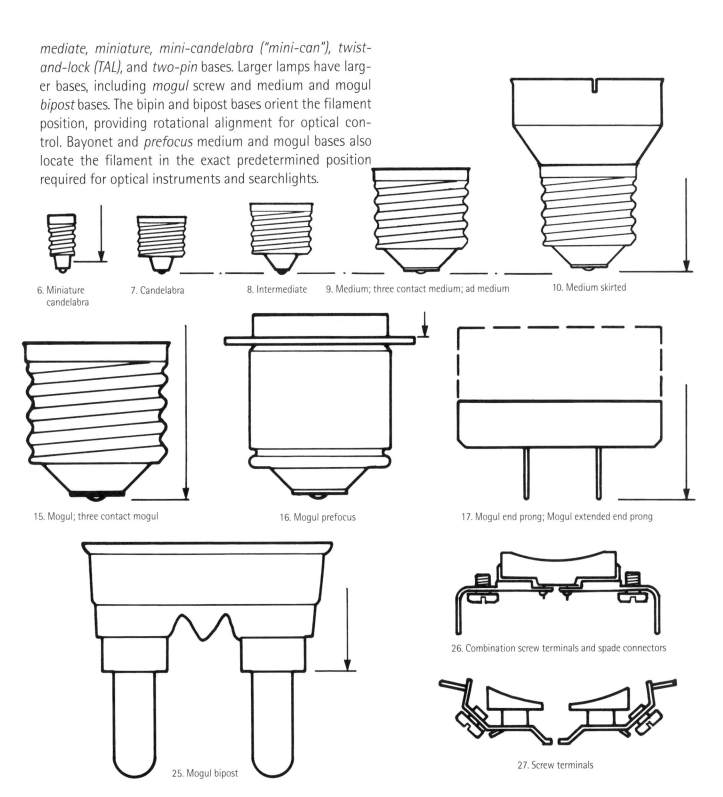

6. Miniature candelabra

7. Candelabra

8. Intermediate

9. Medium; three contact medium; ad medium

10. Medium skirted

15. Mogul; three contact mogul

16. Mogul prefocus

17. Mogul end prong; Mogul extended end prong

25. Mogul bipost

26. Combination screw terminals and spade connectors

27. Screw terminals

FILAMENTS

All incandescent lamps contain a filament, which is more or less centered within the bulb. A filament is a length of tungsten wire; tungsten is used because of its high melting temperature. Occasionally the wire is straight, but usually it is coiled to pack more length into a small envelope, concentrating light and heat and increasing efficiency. Coiled filaments are designated by the letter C. Sometimes the coil itself is coiled and designated CC for "coiled coil."

Filament design is determined by striking a balance between lamp light output and lamp life. Lamp efficiency is the ratio of light produced to electricity consumed. It is a function of filament temperature: the higher the temperature at which the filament operates or "burns," the more light it emits—and the sooner it fails or "burns out." A lamp designed for long life produces less light than a lamp of the same wattage, consuming the same current but designed for a shorter life.

LIGHT OUTPUT

Lamp bulbs do not contain air, because the incandescent tungsten will react with the oxygen in the air and quickly evaporate. Originally this was prevented by creating a vacuum in the bulb. Today, filling the bulb with an inert gas slows bulb blackening, which is caused by condensation of evaporated tungsten particles on the inner bulb wall. Argon, nitrogen, and krypton gases are used for this purpose.

Although reduced by the inert gas pressure, the filament evaporation continues throughout life; the tungsten wire becomes thinner, consumes less power, and emits less light. This light loss combined with bulb blackening causes a steady decrease in light output throughout the life of the lamp.

A reciprocal relationship exists between light output and life. Over-voltage operation results in higher wattage, higher efficiency, and higher light output, but shorter lamp life. Under-voltage burning results in lower wattage, lower efficiency, and lower light output, but longer lamp life (figure 6.4). As a

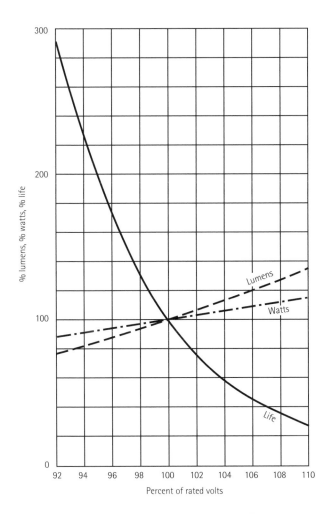

Figure 6.4 Incandescent lamp characteristics as affected by voltage. For example operating a 120-volt (V) lamp at 125V means approximately 16% more light [lumens (lm)], 7% more power [watts (W) and 42% less life [hours (hr)]. Operating a 120V lamp at 115V means approximately 15% less light (lm), 7% less power (W), and 72% more life (hrs).

rule of thumb, a given percentage reduction in wattage is accompanied by double that percentage reduction in light.

Extended-service (2500-hr) incandescent lamps achieve their longer life by a reduction in light output and efficacy. Lumen output is approximately 15 percent less than standard 750-hr and 1000-hr life lamps. These lamps are more expensive than standard ones, but their longer life is useful in locations that are difficult to relamp.

Many energy-saving or "watt saving" are simply reduced wattage lamps. The reduced power consumption is accomplished by a reduction in light output. Some energy-saving lamps have a more efficient filament design, gas fill, or reflector bulb shape to maintain light output.

Incandescent lamps are usually sold by wattage, but a watt is not a measure of light—it is a measure of energy consumed. With electric light sources, it is a measure of how much electricity the lamp uses. Lumens tell how much light a lamp gives off.

Incandescent lamps are divided into three categories according to their ability to direct light: (1) Nondirectional sources emit light in all directions; they require additional components to control their distribution, (2) Semi-directional sources give a direction to their light output; they require additional components to complete a spectral distribution, and (3) Directional sources control the distribution of emitted light; they require no additional components, being complete optical systems in themselves.

NONDIRECTIONAL SOURCES

Nondirectional lamps emit light in all directions. They include A, C, G, P, PS, S, and T shapes and decorative lamps. These lamps require external elements in the form of a lens, reflector, or shield to modify their distribution and to control their luminance (figure 6.5).

To reduce the glare from an exposed filament, many nondirectional lamps have a coating applied to the inner surface of the clear bulb. A two-bath acid etch or a light coating of electrostatically-applied white powder absorbs an insignificant amount of light, yielding a ball of light inside the bulb. This kind of lamp has lower luminance and less glare than the exposed filament. It is called an inside-frost lamp (figure 6.6).

Still greater diffusion, with a further reduction of glare and a sacrifice of about 2 percent of the light output, is achieved by a double coating of white silica powder. This gives a ball of light the size of the lamp, yielding a bulb of almost uniform luminance. It is called a soft-white lamp.

In both treatments, the outer surface of the bulb is left smooth, which makes it easy to clean. Inside-frost lamps are preferred for most luminaires to

Figure 6.5 A-lamp shapes at ¼ actual size. Maximum Overall Length (MOL): maximum end-to-end length of the bulb within tolerances stipulated by the American National Standards Institute (ANSI). Actual length may be less. Light center length (LCL): this dimension is measured from the filament to a designated point that varies with different base types.

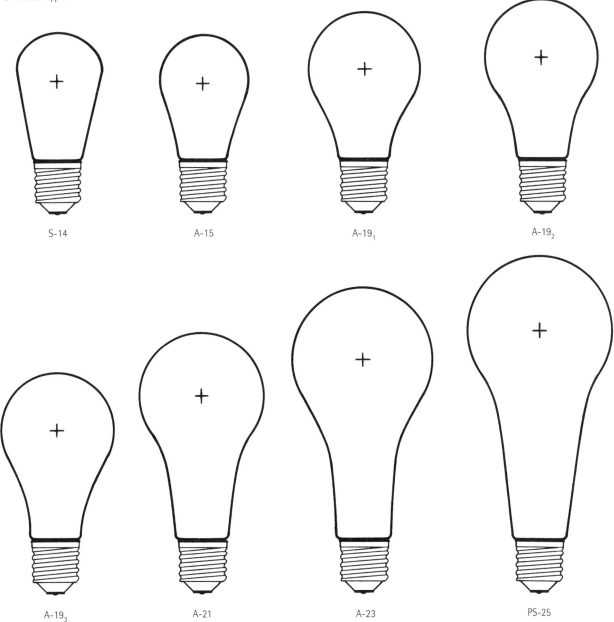

S-14   A-15   A-19$_1$ A-19$_2$

A-19$_3$ A-21   A-23   PS-25

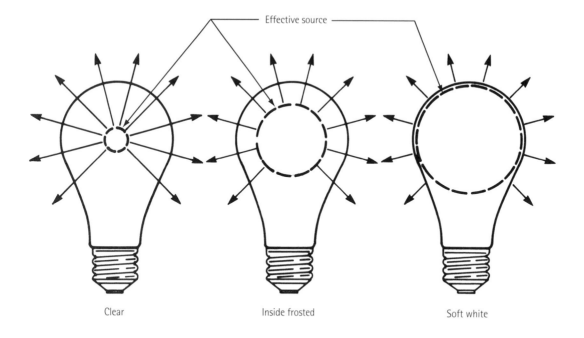

Effective source

Clear

Inside frosted

Soft white

Figure 6.6 Clear, inside frosted (acid etch), and soft white (silica coated) lamps

reduce the sharpness of shadows and the possibility of striations on nearby surfaces. Where the small point source contributes to glitter, as in the sparkle of crystal chandeliers, clear lamps are necessary.

SEMIDIRECTIONAL SOURCES

The category of semidirectional sources includes silver-bowl and white-bowl lamps. Silver bowl lamps, usually used to direct light upward, have an opaque silver coating applied to the inside of the bowl (figure 6.7). This functions as a specular reflector which remains clean, and therefore efficient, throughout the life of the lamp. Silver-bowl lamps are available in both clear and inside-frost.

When used indirectly in a suspended luminaire to light the ceiling, the upper part of the bulb must be concealed to prevent excessive luminance and glare. This is accomplished by an assemblage of circular rings around the lamps or by a shallow, diffusing glass bowl. When silver-bowl lamps are used in recessed luminaires, the upward light emitted by the lamp is redirected in a downward direction by a secondary reflector.

Figure 6.7 Silver bowl lamp

White bowl lamps, also used for indirect lighting, have a translucent white coating on the inner surface of the bulb bowl, which reduces the direct filament glare. As with silver-bowl lamps, white-bowl lamps require additional control elements.

DIRECTIONAL SOURCES

Directional sources are lamps that are complete optical systems; they include a source (the filament), a reflector, and sometimes a lens or a filament shield. Lamps in this category are **r**eflector (R), **a**luminum **r**eflector (AR), multifaceted **m**irror **r**eflector (MR), and **p**arabolic **a**luminized **r**eflector (PAR). These directional sources are available in a wide range of wattages and beamspreads, as indicated in Table 2.

   R Lamps. In *reflector* (R) lamps, the bulb is shaped into a reflecting contour; the inner surface is coated with vaporized silver. The lamps are available in spot or flood beamspreads. Spot lamps have a light frost on the inside front of the bulb; flood lamps have a heavier frosting to increase the spread of the beam.

As with nondirectional and semidirectional incandescent lamps, the glass bulbs of most R lamps are made of blown lime glass. This "soft" glass is intended only for indoor use. Some wattages are available in a "hard," heat-resistant glass for areas where contact with moisture is a possibility, but these lamps still require protection from rain.

All R lamps emit a substantial percentage of light outside the principal beam. Unless intercepted by an auxiliary reflector, this light is lost; in most luminaires R lamps are inefficient.

AR and MR lamps. See low-voltage lamps, page 82.

PAR Lamps. Parabolic aluminized reflector (PAR) lamps are made of low-expansion, borosilicate, heat-resistant glass that is pressed rather than blown. This method of construction allows great precision in shaping the reflector of the bulb and in the configuration of the lens, as well as in the positioning of the filament. The combined precision of these factors accounts for the superior beam control and greater efficiency that are characteristic of PAR lamps (figure 6.8).

PAR lamps were originally designed for outdoor applications and are sometimes still referred to as "outdoor" lamps because they are weather-resistant. Over the years their use indoors has grown rapidly wherever efficiency and precise beam control are desired.

PAR lamps are available with beamspreads that range from 3° (very narrow spot or VNSP) to 55° (very wide flood or VWFL). The initial beam is formed by the shape of the reflector and the position of the filament. The configuration of the lens modifies that beam: A light stipple smooths the narrow beam for a spot lamp; "prescription" lenses similar to those of car headlights provide the wider beam distributions of flood lamps.

In cool-beam PAR lamps, a reflective dichroic coating replaces the bright aluminum used on the reflector surface of standard PAR lamps. Visible wavelengths (light) are reflected forward into the beam while infrared wavelengths (heat) pass through the back of the bulb. About two-thirds of the heat energy in the beam is removed; light output and distribution are unchanged. These lamps were originally developed to light perishable foods (figure 6.9).

Figure 6.8 PAR and R spot and flood lamp beamspreads

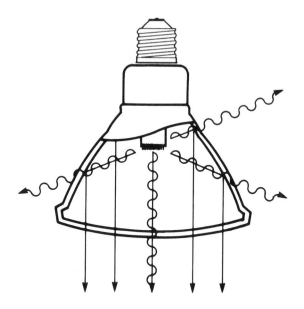

Figure 6.9 Cool-beam PAR lamp. Since the unwanted heat rays are transmitted from the back of the lamp, cool-beam lamps are to be used only in luminaires designed to allow the heat to escape.

The U.S. Energy Policy Act of 1992 established minimum average efficiency standards for certain incandescent R and PAR lamps that operate at 115 to 130 V and have medium bases and diameters larger than 2¾ in. Most common R30, R40, and PAR 38 lamps do not meet the criteria; tungsten-halogen PAR lamps do. Colored lamps and lamps for rough- and vibration-service are exempt from the efficiency standards. The Act does not prescribe standards for other kinds of incandescent lamps.

As of 31 October 1995, the following lamps are prohibited from manufacture or sale in the United States: 75R30; 75-, 100-, 120-, and 150R40; and 65-, 75-, 85-, 120-, and 150PAR38. (See Table 2.) These efficiency standards, measured in lumens-per-watt, were established according to lamp wattage. This approach, however, ignores the function of the luminaire: An inefficient R lamp with a well-designed reflector can be more efficient than the best PAR lamp in a light-wasting, multigroove-baffle downlight.

TUNGSTEN-HALOGEN LAMPS

The tungsten-halogen lamp is an incandescent lamp with a selected gas of the halogen family sealed into it. As the lamp burns, the halogen gas combines with tungsten molecules that sputter off the filament and deposits the tungsten back on the filament, rather than on the bulb wall. This keeps the bulb wall clean and at the same time builds up the filament wire to compensate for the evaporative loss that reduces its diameter, thus maintaining relative constant wattage. The result is a lamp that delivers almost its full light output throughout its life (figure 6.10).

In order for this self-cleaning cycle to occur consistently, the temperature of the lamp bulb must be a minimum of 500°C. The use of quartz rather than

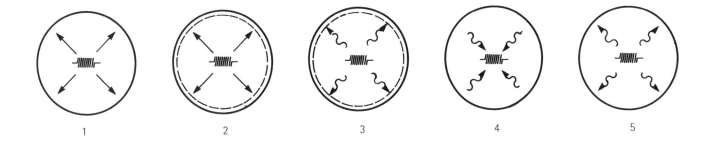

glass is dictated by this thermal requirement and the need for strength to resist high internal gas pressures. Although quartz is no longer the only material used for the enclosure of these lamps, the lamps are still sometimes referred to as "quartz-halogen."

Figure 6.10 Halogen cleaning cycle

The high internal pressure causes an explosive shattering of the bulb if it develops a fault and fails. Although this is a rare occurrence, halogen lamps must be enclosed because fragments of quartz glass are hot and can cause burns or start a fire. The halogen tube is either enclosed in an outer bulb or used in a luminaire equipped with a glass cover or fine mesh screen.

The higher the operating temperature of a filament, the higher the color temperature. Halogen lamps have a higher color temperature than conventional incandescent lamps; greater energy in the blue region of the spectrum makes them appear "whiter." They have longer life and greater efficiency; they are also more compact, permitting the use of smaller luminaires.

Halogen lamps are available in four configurations: (1) single-ended T; (2) double-ended T; (3) integral reflector AR, MR, and PAR; and (4) modified A-lamp MB and TB shapes.

Single-ended halogen lamps have bayonet, bipin, miniature screw, mini-candelabra ("mini-can"), twist-and-lock (TAL), or two-pin bases in sizes that range from T3 to T24 and wattages from 5 W to 10,000 W.

Double-ended halogen lamps have recessed single contact (RSC) bases, one at each end of the lamp. Their bulbs are of small diameter: T2½, T3, T4, T6, and T8; wattages range from 45 W to 2000 W.

Of the energy radiated by standard incandescent and halogen lamps, 85 percent is invisible infrared (heat). Infrared reflecting (IR) halogen lamps have a thin coating applied to the inner filament tube that converts some of the infrared energy to visible light. The coating allows visible light to pass through the tube wall; the infrared energy is reflected back onto the lamp filament, further heating the filament and producing more visible light.

The operating temperature for the halogen cycle is maintained with less input power, resulting in increased efficacy: the efficacy of a standard 1750 lm, 100 W, A lamp is 17.5 lm/W; conventional halogen lamps have efficacies of approximately 20 lm/W; IR halogen lamps have efficacies in excess of 30 lm/W.

Some manufacturers' line-voltage (120 V) halogen lamps have diodes. A diode is a component placed within the lamp in series with the filament that transforms the 120 V alternating current (ac) of the building to an 84 V pulsating direct current (dc). A diode causes the lamp to flicker, which is often noticeable. Because some dimming systems are incompatible with diode lamps, it is advisable to specify line-voltage halogen lamps that operate without diodes.

LOW-VOLTAGE LAMPS

Low-voltage lamps are not of magical construction—they are simply incandescent lamps which operate between 6 V and 75 V.

The wattage of all filament lamps is the product of the voltage delivered at the socket times the amperes flowing through the filament. The lower the voltage of the lamp of a given wattage, the higher the current and the larger the diameter of the filament wire required to carry it.

The increased diameter of the filament wire of low-voltage lamps allows for a more compact filament. The more compact the filament, the more precise the beam control. The main advantage of low-voltage lamps is their precise beam control.

An increase in the diameter of a filament wire raises the temperature at which it can be operated without danger of excessive evaporation. High-wattage lamps, therefore, are more efficient than low-wattage lamps of the same voltage and life rating. Lower voltage lamps, because their filament wire is of greater diameter, are also more efficient than higher-voltage lamps of the same wattage; thus, a 120 V lamp is more efficient than the 250 V lamps used in much of the rest of the world.

Low-voltage reflector lamps with narrow beamspreads are energy saving when their concentrated distribution is used to light small objects or large objects at great distances because light is confined to the lighted object without spilling past. Where wider beams are required, low-voltage lamps are often less efficient than standard lamps.

Figure 6.11 Low voltage PAR36 and low voltage PAR56 lamps

Low-voltage operation also means that the standard building current of 115 V to 125 V must be stepped down by the use of a transformer. Low-voltage luminaires with integral transformers are often larger, bulkier, and more expensive than line-voltage equipment.

The low-voltage lamps commonly used for architectural applications operate at 12 V. They include PAR, AR, and MR lamps. Low-voltage PAR lamps are manufactured in the same way as line voltage PAR lamps; the shape and diameter of the lamps may differ and the bases are always different to avoid wrong electrical connection (figure 6.11).

Many low-voltage PAR lamps are equipped with filament shields to minimize the stray light that comes directly from the filament. As a result, the lamps emit only the controlled beam from the reflector. These filament shields have the added benefit of providing glare control by preventing view of the filament.

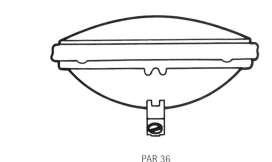

PAR 36

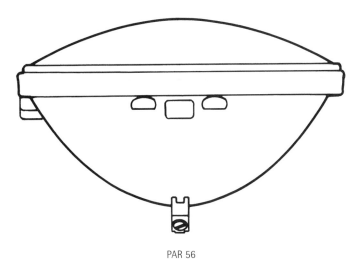

PAR 56

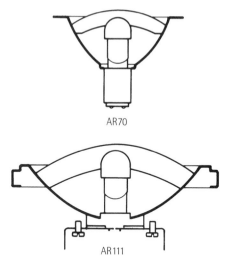

AR70

AR111

Figure 6.12 AR70 and AR111 lamps at ½ full size

Figure 6.13 MR1 and MR16 lamps

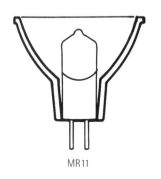

MR11

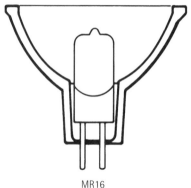

MR16

The aluminum reflector (AR) lamp consists of a prefocused axial filament lamp and faceted aluminum reflector that form an optical system. With some AR lamps the filament cap forms a grip for easy handling in addition to preventing direct glare from view. Other AR lamps have integral diffusing glass lenses to modify the beamspread.

AR lamps are available without lenses in diameters of 48mm, 70mm, and 111mm (figure 6.12) and with lenses in diameters of 37mm and 56mm. The AR111 lamp is comparable to the PAR36 lamp size and base and is used interchangeably with sealed beam PAR36 lamps. AR111 lamps also have excellently-designed reflector surfaces. AR48 and AR70 lamps are produced in two color temperatures: gold reflector lamps at 2600 K and silver reflector lamps at 3000 K.

With multifaceted mirror reflector (MR) lamps, a small halogen lamp is attached to a mirror with a surface composed of specular facets (flood) or a smooth plane (spot) (figure 6.13). The mirror is ellipsoidal in shape; the lamp's coiled filament is placed near its focus.

This combination is used acts as an optical condensing system in slide projectors, removing the need for lenses to control the light pattern. By changing the shape of the mirror or relocating the light source within the reflector, MR lamps are produced with beamspreads from 8° (very narrow spot) to 55° (wide flood).

MR lamps are available in both 1⅜ in. (MR11) and 2 in. diameters (MR16) with either a miniature bipin or bayonet base. MR11 lamps are offered in 12W, 20W, 35W, and 50W versions. MR16 lamps are offered in 20W, 35W, 42W, 50 W, 65W, and 75W versions.

Originally all MR11 and MR16 lamps had glass bulbs, two-pin bases, open fronts, and dichroic reflector coatings. These coatings remove two-thirds of the infrared heat from the projected beam and pass it through the back of the lamp, with the advantages described earlier for dichroic PAR38 cool-beam lamps.

The compact size of these lamps encouraged the design of compact luminaires. This often caused severe problems of heat build-up, however, because heat that is usually radiated from the front of the lamps now passes through the back and into the luminaire. To correct this problem, lamp manufacturers developed MR11 and MR16 lamps with an aluminum-reflector coating that substituted for the dichroic coating. This aluminum reflector coating also prevents "spill" light from the back of the lamp.

MR lamps are also available with a glass cover on the front of the lamp to protect against shattering of the halogen tube and, in some cases, to spread and smooth the beam. Other variations include reflectors made of aluminum instead of glass and bayonet and TAL bases instead of the two-pin bases. Lamps with improved dichroic coatings provide constant color over lamp life, longer lamp life, and improved lumen maintenance.

COLORED LIGHT

Colored light is commonly described in terms of hue, saturation, and brightness. Hue is the quality that is called red or green. Saturation is the strength or depth of the color—the amount by which the light appears to differ from white. A deep red light, for example, is said to be of high saturation; pink is a red of low saturation. Brightness is the perceived quantity of light, without regard to hue or saturation.

A colored or filtered incandescent lamp produces colored light by starting with white light and filtering out the undesired portions of the spectrum. Yet most colored light sources, even those that appear highly saturated, are not truly monochromatic. They emit a fairly wide band of wavelengths, often including small amounts of energy in other hue regions. The less saturated the color, the greater the content of other hues.

Color Filters

The predominant method of producing colored light is the use of color filters with a "white" light source. The white source contains all of the colors of the spectrum; the filter absorbs the unwanted parts of the spectrum and transmits the wavelengths that make up the desired color.

Color filters are usually designed for incandescent lamps. Other types of light sources, lacking a truly continuous spectrum, are seldom used with color filters. The greatest use of colored light is in retail store windows and in theatre, television, and photographic lighting.

Gelatin filters ("gels") are thin, colored, transparent plastic sheets available in a wide variety of colors as well as multicolored and diffusing sheets. Deeper saturations are obtained by using more than one thickness. Gels have a short service life because their color fades rapidly when they are transmitting intense light and heat.

Colored plastic panels are available for use with fluorescent lamps, but are unsatisfactory for use with hot incandescent filaments. Colored glass filters come in smooth, stippled, prismatic, or split–glass; they are highly stable.

Interference filters consist of one or more layers of ultrathin film coating on clear glass that reflect rather than absorb the unwanted wavelengths. The number and thickness of the film coatings determine the transmission (hue and saturation). Because unwanted wavelengths are not absorbed, interference filters remain cool.

Some interference filters are designed to reflect or transmit a portion of the spectrum: infrared or ultraviolet or both. Broad-band interference filters are often called dichroic ("two-colored") because they transmit one color and reflect the complimentary color (figure 6.14.).

It is advisable to determine the approximate spectral composition of the "white" light source before selecting a filter. If the desired wavelengths are not present in the original source, the filter will be ineffective. An extreme example is a red lamp with a green filter which will transmit no visible light.

Colored Lamps

Incandescent colored sign and decorative lamps have outside ceramic enamels, sprayed finishes, or dip coatings applied to clear bulbs to obtain colored light by the subtractive method: by absorbing the light of those colors that are undesirable.

Transparent ceramic enamels are used to coat clear glass bulbs; the finely-ground colored glass is fired into the bulb to fuse the coating into a hard, per-

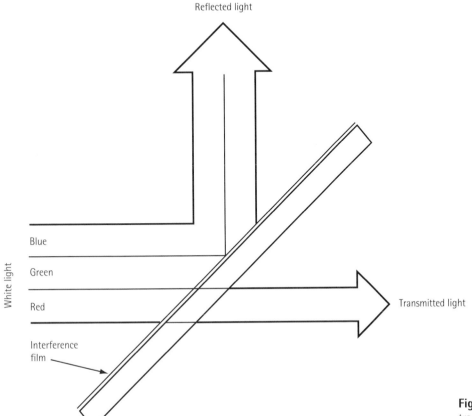

Figure 6.14 Absorbing and transmitting filters

manent finish. The coating is applied before the bulbs are made into lamps. This makes these lamps resistant to scuffing, chipping, and weather, but they are less transparent than lamps with lacquers or plastic coatings.

Sprayed finishes, usually shellacs or silicones, are applied to the completed lamp. Although these sprayed coatings have good adhesion, they lack the hardness of the ceramic enamels and have less resistance to scratches or scuffing. Sprayed lacquers are highly transparent and therefore often used when the sparkle of a visible filament is desired.

Dip coatings of transparent colors that are given an overcoat of acrylic are an improvement over the sprayed lacquers; they yield a similar result with a higher resistance to abrasion and weather. These plastic-coated lamps offer more sparkle, greater brightness, and higher saturation for any given color.

Colored 50R20, 75R30, and 150R40 lamps are manufactured with fired enamel finishes. Colored 100PAR38 lamps have a coating of dye-impregnated silicone plastic, similar to the plastic-coated sign lamps.

Colored 150PAR38 lamps have dichroic interference filters that are vacuum-deposited on the inside of the cover lens. The filter produces its specific color by transmitting only the desired wavelengths of light, with minimal heat absorption; light of other wavelengths is reflected back into the lamp. It is often more efficient than passing light through color-absorbing materials and it produces a more brilliant color than absorption methods.

CHAPTER 7

DISCHARGE LAMPS

In electric discharge lamps, light is produced by the passage of an electric current through a vapor or gas, rather than through a tungsten wire as in incandescent lamps. The electronic production by discharge sources is more efficient than the electric heating method used in filament lamps. Discharge lamps used in architectural lighting are more efficient and have a longer life.

FLUORESCENT LAMPS

A fluorescent lamp is a low-pressure mercury arc discharge source. Its operation relies on an electrical arc passing between two cathodes, one at either end of a glass tube. Flourescent lamps require a ballast to provide the proper starting voltage and regulate the lamp operating current.

When the voltage difference between the two cathodes is sufficient to strike an arc, an electric current passes through mercury vapor within the bulb. As the arc current passes through the vapor, it causes changes in the energy levels of electrons in the individual mercury ions. As the electrons change levels, they release several wavelengths of visible and ultraviolet energy. These radiations strike the tube wall, where some of them cause phosphor material to fluoresce (become luminous) and emit light (figure 7.1).

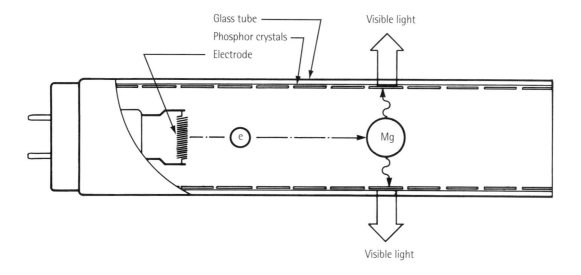

Figure 7.1 Fluorescent lamp. (1) a glass tube, internally coated with phosphors that convert ultraviolet energy into light (2) cathodes supported by a glass structure and sealed at the ends of the tube; (3) a filling gas to aid starting and operation—usually a combination of krypton, argon, and neon; (4) a small amount of mercury which vaporizes during lamp operation; (5) a base cemented on each end of the tube to connect the lamp to the lighting circuit.

Because light emanates from the phosphor, light from a fluorescent lamp is emitted from the surface of the bulb; the entire tube is the actual light source. Average luminance of the lamp is comparatively low because light is generated from a large area.

The selection of phosphors and additives determines the kind of light that is produced: ultraviolet light, colored light, or the more commonly numerous variations of "white" light.

Although operating principles are the same for all fluorescent lamps, two kinds of cathodes exist: hot-cathode and cold-cathode. (These names are misleading because the cold-cathode type dissipates more heat than the hot-cathode.)

Cold-cathode

The cold-cathode lamp is a thimble-shaped cylinder of soft iron, sometimes coated with emissive materials. This large-area source of electrons has an extremely long life. Voltage drop at the cathode is higher than with hot cathode; therefore, wattage loss is greater, more heat is developed, and lamp efficiency is lower.

Although lower in efficiency and output, cold-cathode lamps have a longer life. They are used for decorative applications and in places where inaccessibility makes lamp replacement difficult, although cold-cathode lamps are less frequently used than the hot-cathode kind.

A particular kind of small-diameter, cold-cathode lamp is called "neon;" it is easily bent to form signs and artworks. The operating principle is related to that of cold-cathode lamps; however, light is produced by ionization of the gas itself without the help of phosphors. All cold-cathode lamps provide instant starting and are easily dimmed.

Hot-cathode

Hot-cathode lamps are used for virtually all flourescent lighting. The cathode is a coiled tungsten filament at each end of the bulb impregnated with electron-emissive materials. Hot-cathode lamps are operated at a higher light output per unit length and with a higher overall efficiency than cold-cathode lamps, resulting in a lower cost for equal illuminance.

The superior efficiency and greater light output make the hot cathode ("fluorescent") lamp more suitable in almost all lighting applications; hot cathode lamps are the principal light source for lighting building interiors. Fluorescent lamps are usually identified by an "F" followed by wattage, shape, bulb diameter in eighths of an inch, and color. For example, F40T12/CWX is a 40 W, 1½ in.-diameter cool white deluxe, fluorescent lamp (figure 7.2).

Lamp-ballast Circuits

Fluorescent lamps require a ballast to regulate the electric current through the lamp. Three kinds of fluorescent lamp-ballast circuits are made: (1) preheat, (2) instant start, and (3) rapid start.

The earliest fluorescent lamps were of the preheat kind (figure 7.3). Preheat lamps have cathodes that must be heated electrically in order to make them emit electrons and thus ionize gas in the tube, making it more conductive and lowering the voltage necessary to strike the arc. The current heats the cathodes; because this occurs before the arc strikes, it is said to preheat them.

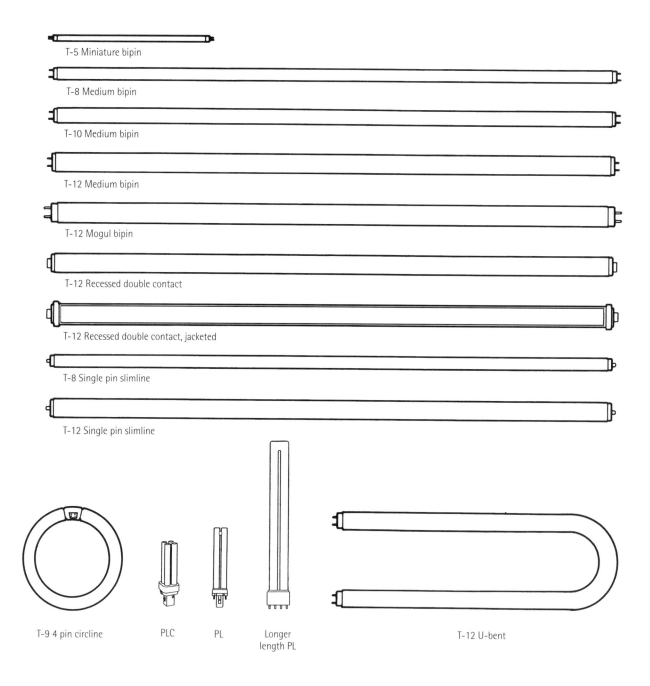

T-5 Miniature bipin

T-8 Medium bipin

T-10 Medium bipin

T-12 Medium bipin

T-12 Mogul bipin

T-12 Recessed double contact

T-12 Recessed double contact, jacketed

T-8 Single pin slimline

T-12 Single pin slimline

T-9 4 pin circline

PLC

PL

Longer length PL

T-12 U-bent

Figure 7.2 Fluorescent lamp shapes and sizes

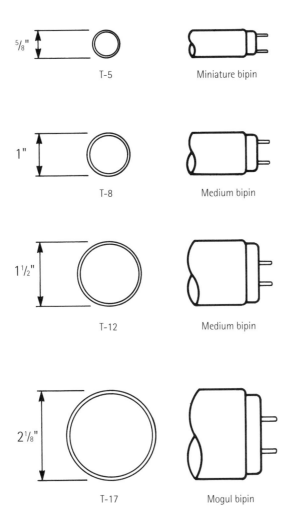

T-5   Miniature bipin

T-8   Medium bipin

T-12   Medium bipin

T-17   Mogul bipin

Figure 7.3 Preheat fluorescent lamp diameters and bases

The preheating process takes a few seconds. It is usually controlled by an automatic starter, which applies current to the cathodes of the lamp for a sufficient length of time to heat them; it then automatically shuts off, causing the voltage to be applied between the cathodes and striking the arc.

The preheating is sometimes accomplished by holding down a manual start button, as with some fluorescent desk luminaires. The button is held down for a few seconds while the cathodes heat; when the button is released, the arc strikes. Whether started manually or automatically, once the lamp is in operation, the arc maintains the cathode temperature.

Figure 7.4 Instant-start lamp diameters and bases

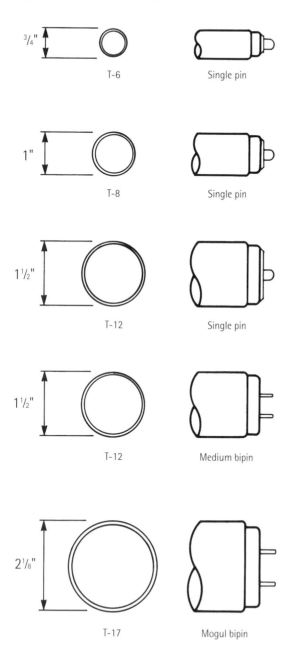

3/4" T-6   Single pin

1" T-8   Single pin

1½" T-12   Single pin

1½" T-12   Medium bipin

2⅛" T-17   Mogul bipin

Instant-start lamps are designed to operate without a starter. This simplifies the lighting system and its maintenance. The ballast provides sufficient voltage to strike the arc instantly. This is a violent action that requires cathodes which will withstand the jolt of instant starting.

Because preheating is unnecessary with instant-start lamps, only one external contact is located on each end of the lamp. Lamps with single-pin bases are called *slimline* lamps. Some instant-start lamps have bipin bases; however, in these lamps the pins are connected together inside the base (figure 7.4).

Slimline lamps can be operated at more than one current and wattage. For this reason, they are identified by length rather than lamp wattage. The number following the "F" in the designation is the nominal lamp length. For example, F96T12/CWX is a 96 in. (8 ft) 1½-in. diameter cool white deluxe slimline lamp.

Rapid-start lamps combine the features of the preheat and the instant-start circuits. Starters are unnecessary. The ballasts have separate windings that heat the cathodes continuously; the lamps start almost instantly after being switched on, but less voltage is required for starting than with instant start lamps of comparable length. Rapid-start ballasts are less expensive, smaller, and have lower power loss than instant-start ballasts (figure 7.5).

Because the cathodes of rapid start lamps are heated continuously during operation, these are the only fluorescent lamps that can be dimmed or flashed.

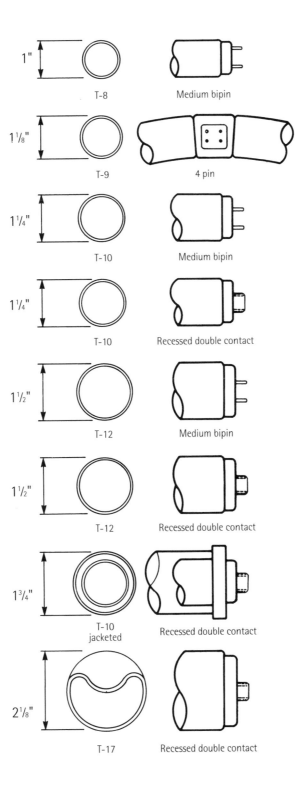

1"
T-8
Medium bipin

$1\frac{1}{8}$"
T-9
4 pin

$1\frac{1}{4}$"
T-10
Medium bipin

$1\frac{1}{4}$"
T-10
Recessed double contact

$1\frac{1}{2}$"
T-12
Medium bipin

$1\frac{1}{2}$"
T-12
Recessed double contact

$1\frac{3}{4}$"
T-10
jacketed
Recessed double contact

$2\frac{1}{8}$"
T-17
Recessed double contact

Figure 7.5 Rapid-start lamp diameters and bases

Trigger-start ballasts permit the operation of preheat fluorescent lamps up to 32 W without the use of starters. This circuit was developed prior to the rapid start circuit and is similar in operation — it provides continuous heating of the cathodes and starters are unnecessary. The lamps are made with bipin bases to permit the flow of current through the cathode filaments before the lamp starts.

For reliable starting, rapid start and trigger start lamps must be mounted within 1 inch of a 1-in.-wide grounded strip of metal, or within ½ inch of a ½-in.-wide grounded strip of metal, running the full length of the lamp. This is usually provided by a wiring channel or reflector in the luminaire housing.

T8 Lamps

Good color-rendering fluorescent lamps require the use of rare-earth phosphors, which are more expensive than standard phosphors. The smaller T8 (1-in. diameter) bulb uses only two-thirds of the phosphor quantity required by the T12 (1½-in. diameter) bulb and is therefore less expensive to produce.

In addition to better color-rendering, the rare-earth phosphors provide a substantial increase in lighting efficiency. System efficacies up to 80 lumens per watt on magnetic ballasts and up to 105 lumens per watt on electronic ballasts compare with 65 to 75 lumens per watt with T12 lamps and ordinary phosphors. The smaller diameter also increases the luminaire optical efficiency and can improve light distribution patterns.

Three kinds of rare-earth lamps are available: RE-70, RE-80, and RE-90. Color temperature is varied according to the relative balance among the phosphors. RE-70 and RE-80 lamps have three narrow-emission phosphors that produce three "peaks" of visible energy: a blue, a green, and a red (see color plates 18, 19, and 20). *RE-70* lamps contain a coat of conventional phosphors and a thin coat of the rare-earth triphosphors to produce a CRI of 70 to 79. *RE-80* lamps contain a thick coat of the rare-earth triphosphors, increasing CRI to 80 to 89 with full light output and lumen maintenance.

RE-90 lamps do not use the three narrow-emission phosphors of the other two rare-earth lamps. These quad-phosphor lamps contain four wider-emission phosphors that produce CRIs of 95 at 3000 K and 98 at 4100 K.

In addition to the four rare-earth phosphors, the RE-90 3000 K lamp has filters to reduce the quantity of blue light caused by mercury radiation, balancing the color. Light output of RE-90 lamps is reduced by one-third, but CRI is 95 with 3000 K lamps and 98 with 5000 K lamps.

Until recently, most fluorescent lamps used for architectural lighting in the U.S. were T12 bulbs with less expensive phosphors and poorer color rendering. Because energy is more expensive in Europe, governmental standards required more efficient lamps. The same government standards stipulated good color-rendering lamps. The combination of high efficiency and good color rendering made the T8 lamp the European standard.

Variations

Energy-saving or reduced-wattage lamps are interchangeable with standard lamps; they consume less power and deliver less light. Input wattage is reduced by 12 to 15 percent; lumen output is reduced by 10 to 20 percent. Energy-saving lamps are more sensitive to low temperatures than standard lamps: Minimum starting temperature is 60°F, as opposed to 50°F for standard lamps.

T12 U-bent fluorescent lamps are regular 40 W lamps bent into a "U" shape. This configuration allows two or three 4-ft lamps to be used in a 2-ft-square luminaire, with the further advantage of wiring and lampholders being conveniently located at one end of the luminaire.

T12 U-bent lamps are available in 6-in. and 3⅝-in. leg spacing, with the 6-in. leg spacing more common. T8 U-bent and T5 U-bent lamps are also available.

Circline lamps are of the rapid-start design. They operate equally well on preheat or trigger-start ballasts.

High-output (HO) rapid-start lamps operate at 800 milliAmperes (mA), compared with 425 mA for most standard rapid-start lamps. They produce about 45 percent more light than slimline lamps of corresponding physical size as a result of drawing considerably more current than the standard lamps.

High output lamps are identified by lamp length, bulb diameter, color, and the letters HO. For example, F96T12/CWX/HO is an 8-ft, 1½-in.-diameter cool white deluxe, high-output lamp. HO lamps are available in lengths from 18 in. to 96 in., with rare earth phosphors and in reduced wattage, energy-saving versions.

Very high output (VHO) lamps also operate on the rapid-start principle at 1500mA. They produce up to twice as much light as standard lamps of equal length, while using approximately three times more power. These are the most powerful fluorescent lamps available.

Reflector lamps contain an internal reflector on part of the inner surface of the tube to provide built-in directional light control. The unreflectorized portion of the tube is called the "window." Intensity of light emitted through the window is significantly increased; however, total light output is reduced. Except in special applications, regular lamps in efficient luminaires perform better (figure 7.6).

Figure 7.6 Reflector and aperture fluorescent lamps

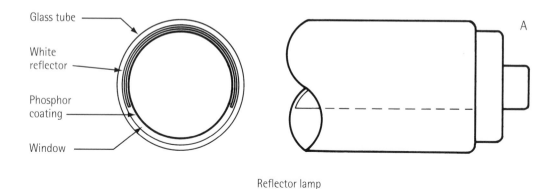

Glass tube

White reflector

Phosphor coating

Window

Reflector lamp

A

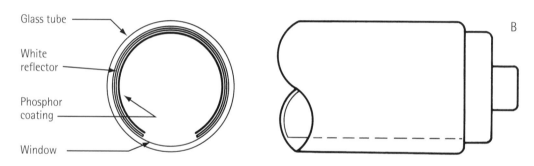

Glass tube

White reflector

Phosphor coating

Window

Aperture lamp

B

Lamp Life

Lamp life varies with the different kinds of fluorescent lamps. Rated average life of fluorescent lamps is based on the average life of a large representative group of lamps tested in a laboratory under controlled conditions; it is expressed in "burning hours." Preheat lamps have rated average lives of 7,500 to 9,000 hrs, slimline lamps 7,500 to 12,000 hrs, rapid-start lamps 18,000 to 20,000 hours, high-output lamps 9,000 to 10,000 hrs, and very-high-output lamps 10,000 hrs.

Compact Fluorescent Lamps

Compact fluorescent lamps provide high efficacy, high color rendering, and 10,000 hr. life in a single-ended fluorescent lamp. They operate in the preheat and rapid start circuit modes; many have a starter built into the lamp base (figure 7.7).

Figure 7.7 Compact fluorescent lamp

Compact fluorescent lamps have significantly higher lumen output per unit length than conventional small fluorescent lamps. This is the result of high phosphor loading, which is necessary because of their small diameter and sharp-corner, multi-tube bulb shape. As with all fluorescent lamps, compact ones require a ballast in order to start and operate properly.

The compact lamps use the same high color rendering, rare-earth phosphors as the T8 lamps mentioned earlier. Color temperature is varied according to the relative balance among the phosphors. The 2700 K color temperature is often used to simulate the color of standard incandescent lamps.

There are five major families of compact fluorescent lamps:

1. T4 1/2-in.-diameter twin-tube preheat lamps have starter devices in the 2-pin plug base of the lamp. These lamps operate on inexpensive reactor ballasts and are available from 5 to 13 W.

2. T4 or T5 5/8-in.-diameter triple-tube and quad-tube preheat lamps (including "cluster" and "four-finger") also have 2-pin plug bases and integral starters; they are available up to 32 W. Some of these

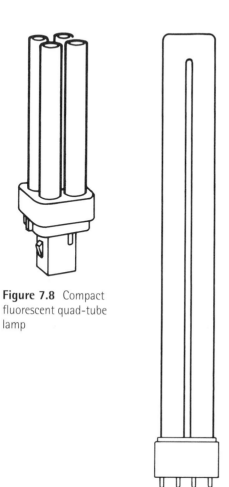

Figure 7.8 Compact fluorescent quad-tube lamp

Figure 7.9 Longer length compact flourescent lamp

lamps use reactor ballasts, others require autotransformer/reactor ballasts. Designed to be a more compact, higher lumen output variation of the twin-tube, they provide a substantial increase in light output compared to standard compact fluorescent lamps (figure 7.8). Some versions of the smaller quad-tube lamps can be dimmed. These require special dimmers and ballasts to operate properly.

3. T5 twin-tube rapid-start/preheat lamps have a 4-pin in-line base without a starter; they are used with external rapid-start and electronic ballasts. These are higher-output lamps, designed to provide the lumen output of conventional fluorescent lamps in smaller packages. They offer excellent color rendering and good efficacy (figure 7.9). These lamps can be dimmed with an electronic dimming ballast.

4. Special T4 rapid-start lamps operate without an integral starter in the base of the lamp. These are used with special dimming or low temperature ballasts.

5. Self-ballasted compact fluorescent lamps are designed to directly replace incandescent lamps, providing savings in energy and maintenance. They are a complete system, containing a double-folded compact fluorescent lamp, an instant start electronic ballast, an outer diffuser, and a medium screw base (figure 7.10). They are available in two kinds: modular (replaceable lamp) and nonmodular. The lamps consume one–fourth to one–third as much energy as their incandescent counterparts and last up to ten times longer. These compact fluorescents with medium screw base sockets are less efficient than other compact fluorescents, but offer a means of easily increasing the efficiency of an incandescent luminaire.

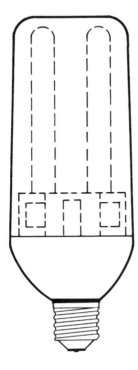

Figure 7.10 Nonmodular self-ballasted compact fluorescent lamp

Light Output

During the first 100 hrs of burning a new fluorescent lamp, the initial lumen output drops by about 5 percent; lumen reduction thereafter is less rapid. Consequently, the published "initial lumens" for fluorescent lamps is the value obtained after the first 100 hrs of burning.

The depreciation in light output during the life of the lamp is approximately 15 percent of the initial lumens. This is the result of the gradual deterioration of the phosphor powders and the evaporation of electron-emissive material from the cathodes, which causes blackening of the glass bulb adjacent to the cathodes.

The end of life is reached when the emission material on either cathode is depleted. Failed preheat lamps flash on and off or extinguish; instant-start and rapid-start lamps extinguish, flicker, or operate at reduced luminance.

Because each start further depletes the tungston cathodes, the average life of fluorescent lamps is affected by the number of lamp starts. Frequent starting shortens life; life is lengthened as the number of burning hours per start is increased. Published lamp-life ratings are based on an arbitrarily-assigned three hours of burning per start. The life of cold-cathode lamps is unaffected by the number of starts.

The starting of all fluorescent lamps is affected by the ambient temperature. Low temperatures require higher voltages for reliable starting. The majority of ballasts provide voltages that start standard lamps down to 50°F. Ballasts are available for certain kinds of lamps that can start lamps down to 0°F and down to –20°F.

The U.S. Energy Policy Act of 1992 established minimum efficiency standards for certain kinds of fluorescent lamps. The efficiency standards are a combination of minimum average lamp efficiency, measured in lumens-per-watt, and minimum color rendering index (CRI). No full-wattage F40, F40/U, F96, or F96/HO lamps can be manufactured or imported unless the lamp has a CRI of 69 or higher and meets the minimum-efficiency requirement.

Full-wattage CW, D, W, WW, and WWX lamps are now unavailable; energy-saving D and WWX lamps are unavailable. CW, D, LW, W, WW, and WWX F96T12 and F96T12/HO lamps have been prohibited from manufacture or sale in the United States since 30 April 1994. CW, D, LW, W, WW, and WWX F40T12 and F40T12/U lamps have been prohibited from manufacture or sale in the United States since 31 October 1995. See Table 2.

Lamps with a CRI of 82 or higher are exempt from these efficiency standards. In addition, aperture, cold-temperature, colored, impact-resistant, plant-growth, reflector, and ultraviolet lamps are exempt from the standards..

Colored Lamps

Colored fluorescent lamps emit only a particular portion of the spectrum; the color is determined by the selection of the phosphors used. Different mixtures of phosphor composition produce different colors of light.

In a few cases, additional filtering is required to absorb mercury radiations that will otherwise desaturate the color. For red and deep blue lamps, a filter coating is applied to the outside bulb wall.

The gold fluorescent lamp achieves its color by subtraction, because no phosphors emit mainly yellow light. A yellow filter coating on the inside of the tube absorbs the unwanted wavelengths from a warm white phosphor.

Blacklight fluorescent lamps use a special phosphor that emits primarily near-ultraviolet energy, plus a small amount of visible blue light.

Whenever subtractive filtering is used, luminous efficacy is reduced.

Colored fluorescent lamps vary widely in lumen output. For example, 25 red lamps are required to equal the lumen output of one green lamp. See Table 6.

Different colors of light have different degrees of effectiveness in attracting attention; this is independent of brightness intensity. See Table 8.

Flicker and Stroboscopic Effect

The mercury arc in a fluorescent lamp operated on a 60 Hz alternating current goes on and off 120 times per second. The light from the lamp remains visible because the phosphors have some phosphorescent or "carryover" action: They emit a reduced quantity of light for a short period of time after the arc is extinguished.

The cyclic variation in light output is known as flicker. With 60 Hz operation, the flicker rate over the length of the lamp is 120 cycles per second. At the ends of the lamp each alternate flash is relatively weak, occurring at a rate of 60 flashes per second.

The 120-cycle flicker is too fast to be visible. The 60-cycle flicker can be detected, but only by the peripheral vision of the retina. For this reason, lamp flicker is seldom noticed except when seeing the ends of lamps out of the corner of the eye.

When rapidly moving objects are observed under discharge lighting systems, blurred "ghost" images are sometimes observed. This is known as stroboscopic effect. Because of this phenomenon, an object moving at a uniform speed will appear to move in jerks. Under extreme conditions, a rotating object will seem to be standing still or even rotating in reverse direction depending on its speed of rotation and its configuration.

Stroboscopic effect rarely causes difficulty because modern phosphors have relatively long carryover periods. If a problem occurs, operating multiple ballasts on all three phases of a three-phase circuit will reduce stroboscopic effect because only one-third of the lamps operate at reduced output at a given time.

HIGH–INTENSITY–DISCHARGE (HID) LAMPS

The term high intensity discharge applies to arc-discharge sources with a high-power density. In HID lamps, light is produced by passing an electric current through a gas or vapor under high pressure, as contrasted to the low pressure in fluorescent or low-pressure sodium lamps. HID lamps used for illumination belong to three principal families: (1) mercury-vapor, (2) metal-halide, and (3) high-pressure sodium (HPS) lamps.

HID lamps consist of an arc tube enclosing two electrodes and one or more metals that are vaporized and ionized to conduct current in an electric arc from one electrode to the other. When a lamp is energized, an electric field is established between the starting electrode and the main electrode, causing individual particles of the starting gas to become electrically charged (figure 7.11). With most HID lamps, the arc tube is enclosed in an outer glass bulb.

The electrons that comprise the current stream, or arc discharge, are accelerated to tremendous speeds. When they collide with the atoms of the gas or vapor, they temporarily alter the atomic structure, and light results from the energy given off in the form of radiation as the atoms return to their normal state. The lamp warm-up process takes 3 to 7 minutes, depending on ambient temperature conditions.

Each kind of HID lamp is unique. With mercury vapor lamps, light is produced by an electric discharge through mercury vapor, resulting in poor color quality of a greenish hue. The addition of phosphor coatings on the inside of the

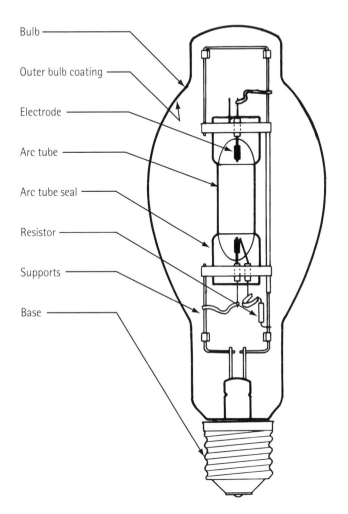

Bulb

Outer bulb coating

Electrode

Arc tube

Arc tube seal

Resistor

Supports

Base

Figure 7.11 Typical high-intensity-discharge lamp. With all HID lamps, the light-producing element is the arc tube; it contains metallic and gaseous vapors and the electrodes at the ends of the arc tube, where the arc originates and terminates. The base connects the lamp mechanically and electrically to the luminaire.

bulb improves color rendering. In metal-halide lamps, the discharge is through combined vapors of mercury and other materials, which are introduced into the arc tube as compounds of iodine. The addition of phosphor coatings provides diffusion and some color improvement. With HPS lamps, the discharge is through combined vapors of mercury and sodium, with the latter dominating the orange-tinted color familiar to us in street lighting.

High-color-rendering HID lamps have shorter lives than standard lamps and many produce lower light output, but their superior color makes them the best choice for areas where people are. Compact, metal-halide lamps offer 6,000 to 12,000-hr lives; CRIs of 80 to 93; and bipin, recessed single-contact, or mogul bipost bases to ensure accurate alignment of the light source with the optical system of the luminaire. White high-pressure-sodium lamps offer 10,000-hr lives, a CRI of 80, and some have prefocus bases to provide precise location of the source in optical systems.

Bulb Shapes

HID bulbs are produced in several incandescent bulb shapes. In addition, four shapes have been specially designed for HID service: B, BT, E, and ED. Bulb shapes (figure 7.12) include

Figure 7.12 HID lamp shapes at ¼ actual size

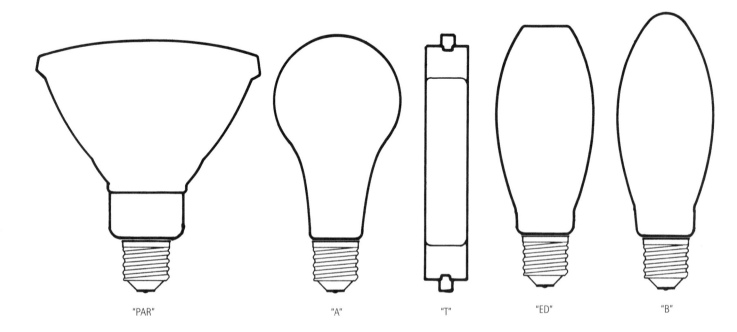

"PAR"   "A"   "T"   "ED"   "B"

A   **A**rbitrary

B   **B**ulged

BT   **B**ulged-**t**ubular

E   **E**lliptical

ED   **E**lliptical-**d**impled

PAR   **P**arabolic **a**luminized **r**eflector

R   **R**eflector

T   **T**ubular

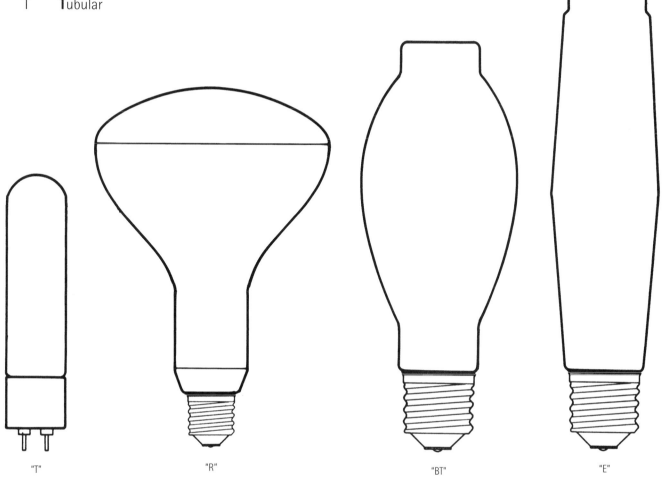

"T"   "R"   "BT"   "E"

The descriptive abbreviation of an HID lamp includes a number that represents the maximum diameter of the bulb in eighths of an inch. The American National Standards Institute (ANSI) code for description of HID lamps provides standardized nomenclature among manufacturers.

Example: M59PK–T400/U

H	mercury lamp (**H** for hydrargyrum, the Greek word for mercury, chemical symbol Hg)
M	**m**etal-halide lamp
S	high-pressure-**s**odium lamps (HPS)
B	self-**b**allasted mercury lamps
59	The numbers denote electrical properties and kind of ballast required. Lamps with the same numbers are electrically interchangeable. (Double numbers such as 43/44 indicate that the lamp will operate from more than one ballast.)
PK	Two letters identify physical properties such as clear or phosphor coated bulb. This is an arbitrary designation with no actual meaning.
T	Self-extinguishing mercury or metal-halide lamps stop operating if the outer bulb is broken to protect people from exposure to excessive UV radiation. Designation is omitted with nonself-extinguishing lamps.[1]
400	Number specifies nominal lamp wattage.
/U	Manufacturer-designated symbols appear after a slant line; these commonly identify color[2] or burning position.
/BD	Base down to horizontal ± 15°
/BU	Base up to horizontal ± 15°
/C	phosphor coated (metal halide)

---

[1] Mercury and metal halide lamps will cause serious skin burn and eye inflammation from short-wave ultraviolet radiation after only a few minutes when the outer envelope of the lamp is broken or punctured if adequate shielding is not used.
[2] Individual metal halide lamps vary somewhat more in color than mercury vapor lamps. Compact metal-halide lamps operated on electronic ballasts have more stable color.

/DX   deluxe white phosphor

/HOR base horizontal ± 45°

/T   tubular bulb

/U   universal burning position

/4   clear

For optical control clear lamps offer a relatively small "point source" of $2\frac{1}{8}$ in. to $9\frac{1}{2}$ in. in length. The phosphor-coated lamps enlarge the optical size of the source to the outer bulb wall; although the phosphor coating enhances the lamp's color-rendering ability, the increased optical size dictates the use of large reflectors for useful optical control.

Lamp Operation

As with fluorescent lamps, HID lamps require ballasts to regulate the arc current flow and to deliver the proper voltage to strike the arc. Electronic ballasts are more efficient and provide more precise control of the arc tube voltage over life, resulting in more consistent color and longer life.

Extinction of a lamp occurs in one of three ways: (1) a power interruption of more than half of a cycle; (2) a severe voltage dip of more than a few cycles; or (3) insufficient voltage maintained from the ballast.

Before the lamp will relight, it must cool sufficiently to reduce the vapor pressure to a point where the arc will restrike. The time required to cool depends partly on a luminaire's ability to dissipate heat. Typically in a luminaire, mercury vapor lamps will relight in 3 to 10 min; metal halide lamps require 10 to 20 min. HPS lamps usually restrike in approximately 1 min.

Lamp Life

Lamp life of HID lamps varies considerably depending on the kind of lamp and its burning orientation. Published lamp-life ratings are based on 10 hrs per start.

The normal mode of failure of a mercury vapor lamp is its inability to light. Almost all mercury lamps have 24,000+ hr rated average life. Rated average life of HID lamps is the point at which approximately 50 percent of the lamps in a large group have burned out and 50 percent remain burning. For mercury vapor lamps, the 50 percent "burnout" occurs in excess of 24,000 hrs, indicated by the plus sign. It is wise to relamp before reaching the point of failure, however, because the lamps continue to operate long after they are a useful light source.

Metal halide lamps have rated average lives of 7500 to 20000 hrs depending on lamp wattage. Lives of metal-halide lamps are shorter than those of other HID lamps because of inferior lumen maintenance and the presence of iodides in the arc tubes. The normal mode of failure is the inability to light because of an increased starting voltage requirement. Metal-halide lamps are particularly sensitive to frequency of starting. As with all lamps, over-wattage operation also shortens life.

Almost all HPS lamps have 24,000 hr rated average lives. Normal end of life occurs when the lamp begins to cycle on and off, the result of lamp voltage having increased to the point where the ballast voltage is insufficient to keep the lamp lighted. Over-wattage operation causes voltage to rise faster; slight under-wattage does not affect lamp life.

As with fluorescent lamps, the initial lumens rating for HID lamps is measured after the first 100 hrs of operation. This "seasoning" is necessary because the lamps depreciate rapidly during these first 100 hrs; when cleanup of impurities takes place.

Light Output

Depreciation in light output during life occurs mainly because of the escape of electron-emissive material and tungsten from the cathodes to the walls of the arc tube. This depends in part on the frequency of starting; therefore, long burning cycles increase lamp life and lumen maintenance. Other factors affecting lumen maintenance are operating current, and the current wave form produced by the ballast design.

The light output of metal-halide lamps declines more rapidly than either mercury-vapor or HPS lamps. Frequent starting is most harmful to metal-halide, less harmful to HPS, and least harmful to mercury-vapor lamps.

Dimming

It is possible to dim some HID lamps using special ballasts, but operating HID lamps at less than full output will produce color shifts and reduced lamp efficacy. As wattage decreases, the color-rendering properties of metal-halide lamps approach the color of mercury-vapor; HPS lamps approach the orange color of low–pressure sodium. Mercury-vapor lamps will retain their already inferior color properties reasonably well, but lumen maintenance and length of life are reduced.

LOW-PRESSURE SODIUM (LPS) LAMPS

Low-pressure sodium (LPS) lamps, although technically not high-intensity-discharge sources, are used in limited applications. They have high efficacies—up to 200 lumens per watt—but their extremely narrow spectral range makes these lamps unsuitable for use in interiors.

The lamp, consisting of two tubes, one inside the other, has a mixture of neon and argon gas, plus sodium metal in the inner tube and an evacuated outer bulb. Initially, the arc discharge is through the neon and argon gas and, as the sodium metal heats up and vaporizes, the yellow-amber color of sodium is produced (figure 7.13).

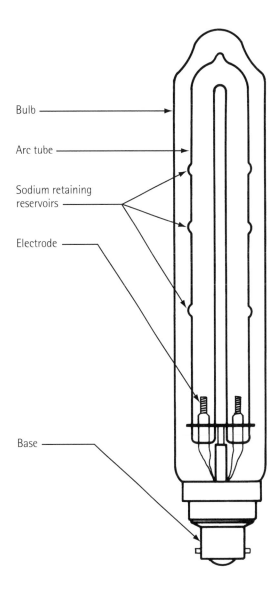

Figure 7.13 Low-pressure-sodium lamp construction

The light produced by the LPS arc, consisting only of radiation in the yellow region of the visible spectrum, is monochromatic. No mercury is present in the discharge; UV radiation emission is not a concern if the outer bulb breaks. The LPS lamps require specific ballasts; no retrofit lamps exist.

In contrast to HID sources, LPS systems maintain constant lumen output over life and light output is unaffected by changes in ambient temperature. Normal end-of-life occurs when the lamp fails to start or warm up to full light output.

CHAPTER 8

AUXILIARY CONTROLS

All discharge sources and low–voltage incandescent sources require the use of auxiliary equipment to supply the correct current or voltage or both to the source. Auxiliary equipment falls into two categories: (1) transformers and (2) ballasts. This auxiliary equipment consumes a small amount of electrical power, adding to the total amount of wattage used by the lighting system.

TRANSFORMERS

Low-voltage light sources require the use of a *transformer* to step down the standard building service of 115 V to 125 V usually to 12 V. Transformers are placed either within (*integral* to) the luminaire or in a *remote* location.

The smaller size of many low-voltage light sources allows for the design of smaller luminaires. With recessed luminaires the transformer is hidden above the ceiling and out of view. With surface- or pendant-mounted luminaires that have their transformers enclosed within the housing, however, the bulk of the luminaire is increased. Where ceiling conditions permit, surface- and pendant–mounted luminaires can be designed with the transformer recessed in the ceiling and out of view.

Track-mounted luminaires usually contain their transformer. It is also possible to provide low-voltage service to a length of track, locating the transformer in the ceiling or in an ancillary space. The high amperage of low voltage lamps strictly limits the number of track luminaires per transformer:

a 50 W, 12 V lamp draws the same amperage as a 500 W, 120 V lamp; therefore, a 20–ampere–rated track can service only four 50 W lamps. This problem is reduced by the use of 50–amp track, which permits ten 50 W, 12 V lamps to be installed on a single track circuit.

If remote transformers are used to maintain the compactness of the lighting element, the increased distance between the source and its transformer requires larger wire sizes to prevent a *voltage drop* from occurring over the longer wiring run. See Table 9 in the Appendix.

Two kinds of transformers are manufactured for low-voltage lighting: (1) Magnetic (core-and-coil) and (2) electronic (solid-state).

Magnetic transformers use copper wound around a steel core, which is *inductive* by nature. Magnetic transformers are relatively large and heavy. Properly sized for the lamp load, they have a long life expectancy. They sometimes cause a noise problem by producing an audible 60-cycle "hum. " *Toroidal* (doughnut-shaped) magnetic transformers are quieter, but they also hum when controlled by some kinds of electronic dimmers. The hum grows with the number of luminaires in a room and the luminaires if improperly designed will resonate with their transformers.

Electronic transformers use electronic circuitry, which is *capacitive* by nature. Electronic transformers are compact, lightweight, and quiet. But their life is shorter than magnetic units, premature failures are common, and they are incompatible with some dimmers. The small dimensions of electronic transformers outweigh many of these flaws, however. The lighting designer must consult the dimmer manufacturer to assure the compatibility of transformers and dimmers.

BALLASTS

All discharge sources have negative resistance characteristics. If the arc discharge is placed directly across a nonregulated voltage supply, it will draw an unlimited amount of current almost instantly and will be quickly destroyed. Therefore, a current-limiting device called a *ballast* is inserted between the discharge lamp and the power supply to limit the electric current flow through the arc discharge (figure 8.1).

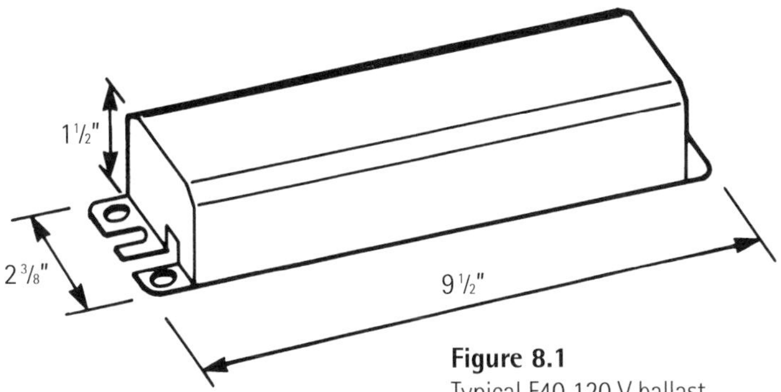

Besides limiting the current flow, the ballast also provides the correct voltage to start the arc discharge. It transforms the available line voltage to that required by the lamp.

Ballasts are not interchangeable. They are designed specifically to provide the proper operating characteristics for only one kind of lamp. For example, 175W M57 metal–halide lamps are inoperable on ballasts intended for 175W H39 mercury vapor lamps, and vice versa.

Figure 8.1
Typical F40 120 V ballast

Lamp wattage is controlled by the ballast, not by the lamp. If a 100 W HPS lamp is operated on a 400 W ballast it will operate at 400 W, to the detriment of the lamp's performance.

Unlike incandescent lamps, the rated wattage of a discharge lamp is the wattage at which it is designed to operate, not the wattage at which it will operate. Therefore, it is impossible to reduce the wattage of a discharge system simply by changing the wattage of the lamps. The ballasts must also be changed.

Two-lamp fluorescent ballasts are used frequently to reduce ballast cost and installation cost per unit of light. They are available for two-lamp series operation or two-lamp parallel operation.

Two-lamp *series* designs are the more common because they offer the lowest cost and the minimum size and weight. Only two lamp leads are supplied from the ballast. Both lamps go out when one lamp fails; the good lamp remains undamaged.

Two-lamp *parallel* designs have two independent ballast circuits and therefore are more expensive than two-lamp series designs. Three or six lamp leads are supplied from the ballast. Failure of one lamp leaves performance of the second lamp unaffected.

Electromagnetic Ballasts

Until the 1980s, discharge ballasts have been of the *electromagnetic* kind. The electromagnetic ballast consists of two copper or aluminum wire coils around a common core of steel laminations. This assembly converts electrical power into a form appropriate to start and regulate the lamp.

The ballast usually consists of a transformer and a capacitor. The transformer converts the service voltage of the lighting circuit to the starting voltage required for the lamp. The *capacitor* restricts the operating current for operation of the lamp; it is a controlling device that consumes no electrical power.

The capacitor also improves the ballast's *power factor* so that it uses energy more efficiently. An electromagnetic ballast that is equipped with a capacitor is called a *high power factor* ballast.

Power Factor

The *power factor* of a ballast is the measurement of how effectively the ballast converts the voltage and current supplied by the electrical distribution system to the power delivered by the ballast to the lamp. Perfect power utilization would result in a power factor of 100 percent.

$$\text{Power Factor} \quad = \quad \frac{\text{Input watts}}{\text{Line volts} \times \text{Line amps}}$$

The power factor of an inductive circuit is lagging (figure 8.2) and that of a capacitive circuit is leading. When discharge lamps are operated in conjunction with simple inductive ballasts, the overall power factor is 50 to 60 percent. With a capacitor, the leading current drawn by the capacitor compensates for the lagging current in the remainder of the circuit, improving the power factor.

Ballasts are classified according to one of the three following categories:

High power factor	90% or greater
Power factor corrected	80 to 89%
Low (normal) power factor	79% or less

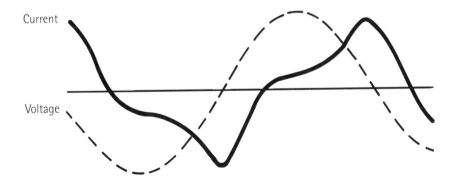

Figure 8.2 Power factor

High power factor ballasts use the lowest level of current for the specific amount of power needed; this reduces wiring costs by permitting more luminaires on branch circuits. Low power factor ballasts use higher levels of current—approximately twice the line current needed by high power factor ballasts—allowing fewer luminaires per branch circuit and increasing wiring costs.

Power factor is not an indication of the lamp–ballast system's ability to produce light; power factor measurements pertain only to the ballast's ability to use the power that is supplied. Thus, power factors are invalid as a multiplier in determining light output values.

Lamp–ballast System Efficacy

The initial lumen and mean-lumen ratings published by lamp manufacturers are based on the operation of the rated lamps by a *reference ballast.* This is a laboratory instrument that simulates the performance of a "perfect" ballast, which transfers all supplied power directly to the lamp without any power loss.

In practice, when a lamp is operated by a commercially available ballast, it provides fewer lumens than the rated amount. Because of the electrical resistance created by the passage of a current through the core and coil of an electromagnetic ballast, some power is converted to heat energy. This lost power, called *ballast loss,* is unusable for producing light from the lamp.

The disparity between light provided by the "perfect" ballast and the commercially available ballast is called the *ballast factor.* The ballast factor is the ratio of light output produced by lamps operated by a commercially available ballast to that which is theoretically supplied by lamps powered by a laboratory reference ballast.

$$\text{Ballast factor} \quad = \quad \frac{\text{Commercial ballast light output}}{\text{Perfect laboratory ballast (100\% light output)}}$$

The term "ballast factor" implies that this is a property of the ballast; it is actually a property of the lamp–ballast system. Some ballasts have different factors for different lamps. That is, they have one ballast factor for operating standard lamps and another for operating energy-saving lamps.

The *ballast efficacy factor* is a ratio of the ballast factor to the input watts of the ballast. This measurement is used to compare the efficiency of various lamp–ballast systems. Ballast efficacy factors are meaningful only for comparing different ballasts when operating the same quantity and kind of lamp.

The ballast factor is an indication of the amount of light produced by the lamp–ballast combination; the input watts are an indication of the power consumed; the ballast efficacy factor is an expression of lumens per watt, for a given lighting system.

$$\text{Ballast efficacy factor} \quad = \quad \frac{\text{Ballast factor}}{\text{Ballast input watts}}$$

For example, a ballast with a ballast factor of 0.88 using 60 W of input power has a ballast efficacy factor of 1.47 ($0.88 \times 100 \div 60 = 1.47$). Another ballast using the same input power with a ballast factor of 0.82 has a ballast efficacy of 1.37. The first ballast therefore offers the greater efficacy because it has a higher ballast efficacy factor (1.47 versus 1.37).

An electromagnetic ballast, operating from an alternating current source, produces a sound, called "hum." The degree of hum varies depending on the kind of ballast. To aid in the selection of ballasts, manufacturers give their ballasts a sound rating that ranges from *A* (the quietest, at 20 to 24 decibels) to *F* (the loudest, at 49 decibels and above).

Electronic Ballasts

The electronic ballast, based on an entirely different technology from the electromagnetic ballast, starts and regulates lamps with electronic components rather than the traditional core and coil assembly. The lighting systems they operate convert power to light more efficiently than systems run by electromagnetic ballasts.

Rather than produce more light output, electronic ballasts are usually designed to produce the same quantity of light as electromagnetic ballasts, but they use less power and thereby reduce energy costs.

The humming sound associated with electromagnetic ballasts results from the vibration of the steel laminations in the core and coil. Electronic ballasts do not have the laminated core and coil; they are 75 percent quieter than comparable *A* sound rated electromagnetic ballasts.

Electronic ballasts are smaller and lighter in weight than electromagnetic ones, typically weighing less than half as much because the electronic components are lighter than the metal components of the core and coil assembly. Electronic ballasts also operate cooler than electromagnetic ballasts. This cooler operation yields a significant savings in air conditioning costs.

Air Conditioning

The air-conditioning load caused by electric lighting derives from the total lighting system, including lamps and ballasts. Each kilowatt (kW) of electric power used by the lighting system adds 3412 British Thermal Units (BTU) to the air conditioning load.

One ton of air conditioning = 12,000 BTU. Therefore, every 3.5 kW of lighting requires one ton of air conditioning.

$$\frac{12,000}{3412} = 3.5 \text{ kW}$$

Heater–Cutout Fluorescent Ballasts

Heater-cutout electromagnetic ballasts have an electric circuit that removes the voltage supplied to the electrode heaters in rapid–start fluorescent lamps after the lamps are ignited and operating. Heater-cutout ballasts consume approximately 20 percent less input power than do standard electromagnetic energy–efficient ballasts; lumen output is reduced by approximately 12 percent.

Other Products

In addition to standard ballasts, several kinds of *energy-saving* ballasts are made. These fall into two categories: (1) ballasts that save energy by reducing wattage consumed as well as reducing light output; and (2) ballasts that, because of refinements in design, save energy chiefly by reducing wattage loss in the ballasts themselves.

Class P ballasts are equipped with automatically resetting thermal protectors. These turn off the power when the operating temperature exceeds the limits specified by Underwriters Laboratories (UL) to prevent overheating. When the ballast cools, the protector resets, restoring operating power to the ballast.

The UL symbol applied to luminaires indicates that Underwriters Laboratories has examined a sample unit and determined that it complies with appropriate safety standards. It indicates that, when properly installed, the luminaire will operate safely. The UL label is also applied to components, such as transformers and ballasts, to signify that the components meet safety requirements. (The UL label indicates overall luminaire safety when applied to the luminaire and component safety when applied to the components. Different labels and markings are used for various applications, but all make use of the trademark UL circle).

COMPARATIVE FLUORESCENT LAMP-BALLAST SYSTEM

Ballast Kind	Typical Input Power (W)	Typical Ballast Factor	System Efficiency (Lumens/W)
(2) F40T12/RS/ES lamps, 34 W each			
Electromagnetic energy-efficient	72	0.87	68
Electromagnetic heater-cutout	58	0.81	78
Electronic ballast	60	0.85	79
(2) F32T8/RS lamps, 32 W each			
Electromagnetic energy-efficient	70	0.94	78
Electromagnetic heater-cutout	61	0.86	82
Electronic ballast rapid-start	62	0.88	82
Electronic ballast instant-start	63	0.95	87

CHAPTER 9

ELECTRICITY

Knowledge of the basic principles of electricity is necessary for understanding lighting circuitry, electrical distribution, power consumption, operating costs, switch control, and dimming control.

PRINCIPLES OF ELECTRICITY

Electrically–charged particles called *electrons,* which orbit the nucleus of an atom, can be made to flow from one point to another. This is observable in objects charged by friction and in natural phenomena; lightning is a huge spark of electricity.

A flow of electricity is called an *electric current*; the rate of flow of an electric current is measured in *amperes (amps, A).* The potential of the flow of electricity is called *voltage*; it is measured in units called *volts (V).*

Water provides a helpful analogy to these concepts. The amount of pressure that moving water exerts inside a pipe is analogous to volts; amperes are similar to the "gallons per second" measurement, the rate at which water passes through the pipe. The pipe is the conductor or wire, the wall of the pipe is the insulator, the faucet is the resistance or dimmer. The larger the pipe, the greater the flow it can carry.

Figure 9.1 Complete circuit

The path through which an electric current flows is called a *circuit*. When no gap exists in the path, it is called a *complete circuit* (figure 9.1). When a gap occurs, it is called a *break in the circuit*.

Resistance impedes the flow of current and is determined by the composition of a material. This results in the production of light or heat or both. A *resistor* is a device placed in the path of an electric current to produce a specific amount of resistance. If a path of electricity is slowed by resistance or interrupted by an open switch, there will be little or no current (amps) even though the potential to produce it (volts) is high.

Wiring

Materials that electricity flows easily through are called *good conductors*. Materials through which it does not flow easily are called *poor conductors*. All metals are good conductors: Silver is the best, but it is too costly for most wiring purposes; copper is the next best and is used widely.

Almost all wire is encased within a poor conductor, which confines the current to its metallic conductor. Wire that is wrapped with a poor conductor, such as rubber or synthetic polymers, is called *insulated wire*. Before connections are made with insulated wire, the wrapping is removed from the ends of the wire.

Insulated circuit wires are sometimes covered by a mechanically–protective conduit for installation in buildings. Flexible, nonmetallic sheathed cable *(romex)* and flexible, metal sheathed cable *(BX)* are often used in single-family homes. Commercial installations use wires inserted in flexible, metal conduit *(greenfield)*, or in rigid electrical metal conduit *(EMT)* for long runs.

Circuits

Direct current (dc) is electric current that always flows in one direction. *Alternating current (ac)* also moves in a single direction; however, that direction is reversed at regular intervals. Alternating current is the prevailing electrical current in use today (figure 9.2).

A *cycle*, or hertz (Hz), is a complete set of values through which the alternating current passes. The number of times the cycle occurs each second—the *frequency* of the cycle—is 60 Hz in the U.S. and 50 Hz in most other parts of the world.

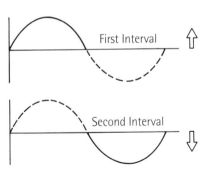

Figure 9.2 Alternating current

SERIES CIRCUIT

If one lamp fails in an inexpensive strand of Christmas tree lights, the remaining lamps in the strand go out. When the tungsten wire in one lamp breaks, it causes a break in the circuit because its filament is part of the conductive path carrying current to other lamps.

Lamps connected in this way are wired in *series*. All lamps in a series circuit must be of the same wattage; if a lamp of different wattage is substituted, the remaining lamps will grow brighter or dimmer due to the substituted lamp's resistance. A series circuit is therefore said to be *load sensitive* (figure 9.3).

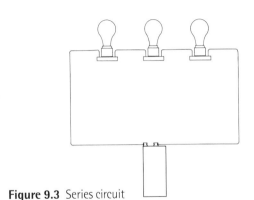

Figure 9.3 Series circuit

PARALLEL CIRCUIT

If one lamp in figure 9.4 goes off, all of the others remain lighted; the current still flows to the other lamps and the circuit remains complete. These lamps are wired in *parallel*. Since the voltage of the circuit is present across all branches of the circuit, several different *loads* (for example, a 60 W lamp and a 100 W lamp) may be connected to the same circuit. Parallel circuits are therefore not load sensitive.

A current will always follow the easiest path that is available. If the wires of a circuit are uninsulated and touch each other, the current will pass from one to the other because this is a shorter and easier path than the one intended: There will be a *short circuit*.

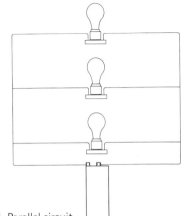

Figure 9.4 Parallel circuit

Figure 9.5 Two short circuits. The wire in these circuits is bare wire. Where the wires are twisted together, the current would flow from one to the other.

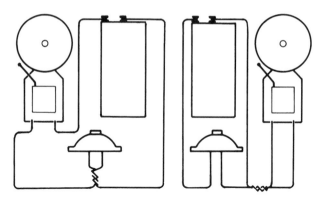

In figure 9.5, in the drawing on the left the current will take a shortcut back to the cell without going through the push button; the bell will ring continuously whether the switch is open or closed. In the drawing on the right, the bell will not ring at all; the current will take a shortcut back to the cell without going through the bell.

A short circuit allows a stronger–than–usual flow of electricity through the wires; this excessive current causes the wires to overheat. A *fuse* or *circuit breaker* is a safety device that opens the circuit before the wire becomes a fire hazard. Because the fuse is part of the circuit, it also overheats and a metal strip in the fuse melts and breaks the circuit. If the protective device is a circuit breaker, the excess current of the short circuit causes the breaker to flip open, interrupting the path of the current.

Electrical Distribution

Electric current generated and delivered by an electric utility enters a building through a *service panel*. In the U.S., three kinds of systems are common:

1. 120/240 V, single-phase, three-wire.

2. 120/208 V, three-phase, four-wire.

3. 277/480 V, three-phase, four-wire.

The 120/240 V, single-phase, three-wire system is commonly used in single-family homes and small commercial buildings. Wire conductors leading from the entrance panel distribute the power throughout the building. Because the wire has resistance, the longer the distance that power is carried, the greater the voltage *losses,* causing lights to dim and appliances to operate sluggishly. This is corrected by using larger–diameter wires, which have less resistance.

Distributing current at higher voltages reduces losses occurring because of the wire's resistance. Therefore, in large commercial buildings, 120/208 V, three-phase, four-wire and 277/480 V, three-phase, four-wire systems are used to reduce resistance losses.

In commercial buildings, running each circuit from the entrance panel will create a substantial voltage loss or require the use of large–diameter, expensive wires. To avoid voltage loss, *feeder circuits* conduct power from the entrance panel to secondary distribution panels, called *panel boards,* located throughout the building. The wires that distribute power locally between the panel board and the luminaires or receptacles are called *branch circuits.*

Power Consumption

A *watt (W)* indicates the rate at which electricity is changed into another form of power—light or heat. Power consumption in watts is calculated by multiplying volts times amps $(W = V \times A)$.

Theoretically, a 20-amp circuit operating at 120 V will handle a possible maximum load of 2400 W (that is, $20 \times 120 = 2400$). In practice, the National Electrical Code limits the possible load of a branch circuit to 80 percent of the branch circuit ampere rating: a 15 A, 120 V circuit to 1440 W; a 20 A, 120 V circuit to 1920 W; a 20 A, 277 V circuit to 4432 W.

Energy is the amount of electric power consumed over a period of time; it is measured in *kilowatthours* (kWh). One kilowatt (kW) = 1000 W. Hence, kWh = kW x hours used. For example, a 150 W lamp is equivalent to 0.15 kW. When operated for 40 hours it uses 6 kWh (0.15kW x 40 hrs = 6 kWh). Utility rates are based on monthly kWh usage.

In estimating the connected load for discharge and low voltage incandescent sources, the power consumed by the ballast or transformer must be included.

To obtain lighting *watts per square foot* for an installation, divide the total luminaire watts by the area of the space in square feet.

Life Cycle Costs

The cost of lamps and luminaires plus their installation is a minor part of the total cost over the life of a lighting system. The cost of electricity *(operating costs)* is the single largest cost in lighting. Except in homes, maintenance *(labor costs)* to replace lamps and clean luminaires is the second greatest expenditure. Lighting systems, therefore, must be evaluated in terms of *life cycle costs.*

A typical *cost analysis* will include initial lamp and luminaire costs, installation costs, electricity costs based on burning hours per year, labor costs, including those incurred because of dirt conditions, and interest costs on the original capital investment. When comparing the life–cycle costs of one system with those of another, the greater initial cost of an energy-effective system will almost always be recouped after a period of time because of the saving in energy costs. This *payback period* varies with different systems.

In comparing dissimilar systems, it is impossible to place a dollar value on the quality of light. A direct system, for example, is usually less costly than an indirect one that produces the same quantity of light on the workplane, but the *quality* of light is vastly different.

Cost comparisons are made on equal illuminance values of the equivalent quality. If there is a difference in the connected load, the additional air conditioning required to handle the larger load must also be accounted for.

SWITCH CONTROL

An electric current is the flow of electrons between two points along a path. If the path is interrupted, the current cannot flow. A *switch* breaks the flow of electricity in a circuit when it is open ("off") and it allows unimpeded flow when closed ("on").

The manually operated *toggle switch* makes contact by snapping one metal piece against another. *Mercury switches* contain a vial of mercury; contact is

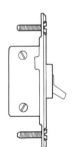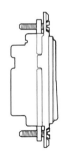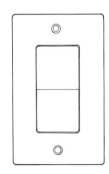

Figure 9.6 Toggle switch and rocker switch

made between two electrodes when the vial is tripped to the "on" position. These switches operate silently. The toggle designates "on" in the up position and "off" in the down position. A *rocker switch* and a *push-button switch* operate in the same manner (figure 9.6).

A *single-pole, single-throw* switch is connected at any point between the luminaire and the power supply. It opens only one side of the circuit and is therefore called a "single-pole;" it moves only between an open and a closed position and is therefore called a "single-throw." This is the switch most frequently used to control electric luminaires and wall receptacles.

A *single-pole, double-throw* switch directs the current in either of two directions. It is used to alternately turn on two different luminaires with a single switch action, such as a safelight and the general light in a darkroom. The up position will designate "on" for one luminaire, the down position "on" for the other; an optional center position will turn both "off."

A *double-pole, single-throw* switch is able to direct the current to two paths at once. It is used to control two devices simultaneously, such as a luminaire and an exhaust fan; it functions as if two separate toggle switches were operated by the same handle.

A *three-way* switch controls an electrical load from two locations. This allows the circuit to use one of two alternate paths to complete itself. (Several explanations are offered for why a switch that provides control from *two* locations is called "three-way." These explanations are hypothetical and flawed; nevertheless, the term is still customary.)

A *four-way* switch controls a circuit from three locations, a *five-way* switch controls a circuit from four locations, and so forth. For control from many different locations, a low voltage switching system is used.

DIMMING CONTROL

A *dimmer* provides variation in the intensity of an electric light source. *Full-range dimming* is the continuous variation of lighting intensity from maximum to zero without visible steps.

All dimming systems operate on one of two principles for restricting the flow of electricity to the light source: Either (1) varying the voltage, or (2) varying the length of time that the current flows during each alternating current cycle.

Historically, *resistance* dimmers were the first dimming method; they were used mainly in theaters in the early part of the century. A resistance dimmer, or "rheostat," controls voltage by introducing into the circuit a variable length of high-resistance wire. The longer the length of the wire, the greater the resistance, the lower the voltage, and the lower the intensity of the lamp.

In order to absorb a sufficient amount of energy, the resistance wire must be quite long; for this reason it is often coiled. Current flows into one end of the coil and an arm slides along the resistance wire in increments. Dimming is thus achieved in a series of steps, often a minimum of 110 to appear "flickerless."

A large drawback to this kind of dimmer is that the portion of the current that would otherwise produce light is instead converted to heat. In addition to being hot, these dimmers are bulky and consequently are no longer used.

Autotransformer dimmers avoid these problems by using an improved method of dimming. Instead of converting the unused portion of the current into heat, the autotransformer *changes* the standard-voltage current *into* low-voltage current, with only a 5 percent power loss.

A transformer has two coils of wire; the ratio of the number of turns in the two coils produces the ratio of the voltage change induced by the transformer. An autotransformer is simply a variable transformer: the primary coil remains fixed while the number of turns in the secondary coil is varied by a rotating arm that controls successive turns of the coil. Because electrical power can be drawn from different points along the secondary coil, different voltages are achieved from the same transformer.

Because autotransformers do not convert energy to heat as light intensity is reduced, they are therefore cooler and more compact than resistance dimmers. Autotransformer dimmers are widely available in sizes up to many thousands of watts.

Solid-state dimmers are predominant today; they use the second of the two methods of limiting current flow. A power control device—such as a silicon-controlled switch (SCS) under 6 kW, or a silicon-controlled rectifier (SCR), over 6 kW—allows electric current to flow at full voltage, but only for a portion of the time. This causes the lamp to dim just as if less voltage were delivered (figure 9.7).

The manner in which light output responds to changes in the control setting is called the *dimming curve*. If a change in the setting of the dimming control, from full bright to full dim, approximates the change in the amount of electricity allowed to reach the light source, the dimmer is said to have a linear curve.

The eye is more sensitive to changes in low intensities of light than to changes in high intensities. Electric lamps also respond in a nonlinear way: at 81 percent of the voltage, the light output is 50 percent. If the electrical output of a dimmer changes in a linear manner, then a light source will appear to dim faster at low intensities and slower at high intensities. To correct this, good quality dimmers feature a *square law* dimming curve. Here the dimmer control moves at constant speed, but causes the light to dim faster at high intensities and slower at low intensities. To the eye, the result is a consistent rate of change in the light intensity.

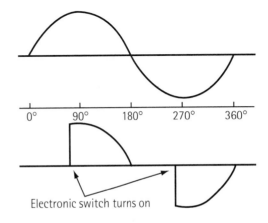

Figure 9.7 Solid state dimming control

Incandescent Lamps

Dimming incandescent sources increases the life of the lamp. Yet both incandescent and tungsten-halo-

Figure 9.8 Dimming incandescent and tungsten–halogen lamps moves light toward the warmer end of the color spectrum.

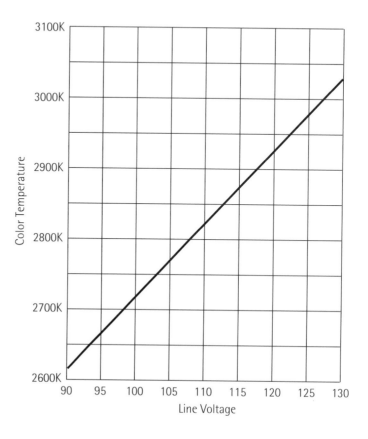

gen lamps undergo considerable shifts toward the orange-red end of the spectrum when they are dimmed. Because this increases the warm appearance of the lamps at lower light intensities, it is a positive result for people prefer warmer colors of light at lower intensities (figure 9.8).

The efficiency of an incandescent lamp is reduced when the source is operated at less than its designed voltage because the temperature of the filament is reduced. Even though the lamps are less efficient at producing light, much energy is still being saved (figure 9.9).

In some applications, normal operation of dimmers cause lamp filaments to buzz. Smaller wattage lamps, physically smaller lamps, rough service (RS)

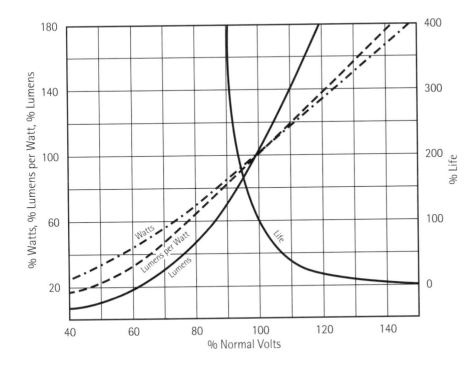

Figure 9.9 Effect of voltage variation on incandescent efficiency

lamps, low-noise stage lamps, and lamp debuzzing coils help to decrease this noise.

The lamp *debuzzing coil* is a separate component. It will hum during operation, so it should be located in an area where this noise will be acceptable.

Low Voltage Lamps

Dimmers for low-voltage luminaires are installed on the 120 V side of the low-voltage transformer. Two kinds of transformers are manufactured for low voltage lighting: (1) magnetic [core and coil] and (2) electronic [solid state].

Before selecting a dimmer control, it is necessary to determine which kind of transformer is connected to the luminaire. Each kind of transformer requires a compatible dimmer.

Magnetic-transformer, low-voltage dimmers are used for dimming luminaires equipped with magnetic transformers. They account for the dc voltages and current surges to which magnetic transformers are sensitive. Magnetic low-voltage dimmers are designed to prevent dc voltage from being applied to the transformer and to withstand voltage "spikes" and current "surges."

Electronic transformer-supplied equipment requires the use of *electronic transformer,* low-voltage dimmers. Electronic low-voltage dimmers are designed especially for electronic transformers. They eliminate the problems that occur in the interaction between the transformer and dimmer when a magnetic low-voltage dimmer is used with electronic transformers: dimmer buzz, transformer buzz, lamp flickering, and radio frequency interference.

Electronic low-voltage dimmers combined with electronic transformers have the virtue of silent operation, although these dimmers have a smaller capacity than magnetic low-voltage ones have.

Fluorescent Lamps

Dimming fluorescent lamps requires the use of special dimming ballasts, which replace the standard ballast and must be compatible with the dimming control device. Only rapid-start fluorescent lamps can be dimmed because voltage is supplied continuously to the cathodes. When dimmed, the special ballast maintains the cathode voltage so that the cathodes remain heated to ensure proper lamp operation. Because instant-start and preheat lamp electrodes are turned off after the lamps are started, they cannot be dimmed.

Fluorescent lamps cannot be dimmed all the way to "off." If they are allowed to dim too far, a flicker or spiraling light pattern becomes visible inside the tube.

Many systems dim only 3- and 4-ft lamps. It is advisable for all lamps that are controlled by a single system to be of the same length; different lengths dim at different rates.

Dimming fluorescent lamps that operate either in a cold atmosphere or in an air-handling luminaire sometimes results in variations in light output and color, which are caused by the changes in bulb wall temperature. The color shift is slight; dimmed lamps usually appear warmer in color.

Fluorescent lamp life is reduced by dimming systems. Considerings that a fluorescent lamp consumes up to 100 times its cost in energy, a slight loss in lamp life is offset greatly by the savings achieved through dimming.

HID Lamps

It is technically possible to dim high-intensity-discharge lamps over a wide range of light output. HID lamps have a shorter life as a result of dimming. As with fluorescent lamps, the shorter life is offset by energy savings achieved through dimming.

A discernible color shift occurs with dimmed HID lamps. In mercury lamps, however, this slight change will be negligible; the color is already inadequate. Clear metal halide lamps shift rapidly toward a blue-green color similar to that of a mercury lamp. Phosphor-coated metal-halide lamps exhibit the same trend, but less distinctly. HPS lamps slowly shift toward the yellow-orange color that is characteristic of LPS lamps.

Low Voltage Control Systems

Low-voltage switching and dimming control is achieved with low-voltage wires that operate a relay installed in the luminaire wiring circuit. The relay is either mounted near the luminaire or installed in a remote location. Since the low voltage wires are small and consume little electric power, it is possible to use many of them; they can be placed where needed without being enclosed in metal conduit, except where required by local codes.

With low-voltage switching systems, the branch circuit wiring goes directly to the luminaires; this eliminates costly runs of conduit to wall switch locations. Where switching occurs from three or more locations, the savings are considerable. Many switches can control a single luminaire, or one switch (a "master") can control many circuits of luminaires.

Carrier–Current Control Systems

Carrier–current switching systems are low cost, simple-to-install control systems that operate by sending a signal through the building wiring. The switch functions as a transmitter that generates the signal. A receiver located at the luminaire or electric appliance turns a circuit on or off when it senses the appropriate signal.

As long as the transmitter and the receiver are connected to the same electric service in the building, no control wiring is required. Any number of luminaires can be attached to one receiver or to any number of receivers; any number of transmitters can control any one receiver. Great flexibility is inherent in this kind of system.

Carrier-current systems, however, are subject to malfunction. Automatic garage door openers and communication systems in airplanes flying overhead may operate on the same frequency as the carrier–current system, causing luminaires and appliances to turn on and off when unintended.

Energy Management Controls

In offices of the past, lighting controls were used to provide lighting flexibility. Today, their major application is energy management. Simple controls, such as photocells, time clocks, and occupancy sensors automatically turn lights on when needed and off when unnecessary. For larger facilities, control systems are designed to integrate the lighting with other building energy systems such as those used for heating and cooling.

The key to proper application of these controls is not only the selection of the proper control device, but also the careful planning of where and when the control is needed. Two basic control strategies are available: (1) control in space by electrically positioning [switching] the light *where* it is needed and (2) control in time or supplying lighting *when* it is needed.

Daylighting controls have sensors that automatically adjust the electric lighting to preset values. When daylight is available and suitable (reaching task areas without causing glare), luminaires are dimmed or turned off.

Lumen-maintenance controls compensate for the natural deterioration of the lighting system and the room surfaces over time. They automatically increase the power to the system so that the light output is kept at a constant value.

It is advisable to use control systems for daylighting, worker area individualization, and window energy management. Individual controls in office spaces go a long way toward conserving energy, and equally important, toward giving occupants a sense of control over their immediate environment.

CHAPTER 10

LIGHT CONTROL

Directional sources, commonly called *reflector* lamps, such as AR, MR, PAR, and R lamps have built-in optical systems. All other electric light sources require external devices to modify their distributions in order to be useful in architectural applications. These modifications have two purposes: (1) to direct light to where it is wanted and (2) to block light from where it is unwanted—to shield the lamp from viewing angles that would otherwise cause glare. The control of light direction is accomplished by three methods: (1) reflection, (2) refraction, and (3) diffuse transmission.

REFLECTION

Reflection is the return of light from a surface; it occurs when a portion of the light falling on a surface is thrown back by that surface just as a ball bounces back from the floor. Three kinds of reflection are involved in the control of light: (1) specular, (2) semispecular, and (3) diffuse.

Specular Reflection

A smooth, highly polished surface like a mirror alters the direction of a beam of light without changing its form. The angle of reflection is equal to the angle of incidence—a property that makes specular materials ideal where precise beam control is desired (figure 10.1).

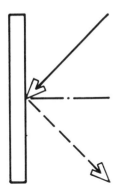

Figure 10.1 Specular reflection

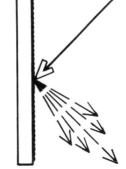

Figure 10.2 Spread reflection

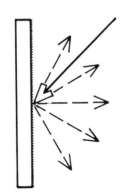

Figure 10.3 Diffuse reflection

Because these surfaces are virtually mirrors, their own surfaces are almost invisible; they may appear dark or bright, depending on the observer's position and on the luminance of the reflected image.

Semispecular Reflection

Irregular surfaces, such as those that are corrugated, hammered, brushed, sand-blasted, or etched, partially disperse the reflected beam. The greatest intensity, however, is still reflected at an angle near the angle of incidence (figure 10.2).

Semispecular materials appear with highlights or streaks of higher luminance on a background of lower luminance. In interiors, they are often used as elements of sparkle. In luminaires, semispecular materials produce a moderately controlled beam that is smooth and free from striations.

Diffuse Reflection

Rough or matte surfaces neutralize the directional nature of the incident beam. Light is reflected from each point in all directions, with maximum intensity perpendicular to the surface (figure 10.3).

Sand on the beach is an example of a diffuse reflecting surface. There are no bright spots; the surface appears the same from all angles of view. In interiors, this quality is often desirable for walls, ceilings, and work surfaces. In luminaires, diffusely reflecting materials are used to produce wide distributions of light.

REFLECTOR CONTOURS

Specular and semispecular surfaces formed into geometric contours use the law of regular reflection for beam control: the *angle of incidence* equals the *angle of reflection*. This is the same law that governs the rebound of a billiard ball off a cushion.

Specular reflection is a primary technique for modifying and controlling the direction and distribution emitted by a light source. Specular reflection takes light that would otherwise be lost or wasted within a luminaire or emitted at glaring angles and conserves it by redirecting the light into a room or onto a surface at useful angles.

In addition to this more efficient use of light, the application of properly-contoured reflectors produces predictable luminaire distributions and controlled room luminance patterns. Specular reflector contours commonly used in luminaires include actual or modified (1) ellipses, (2) parabolas, and (3) circles.

Elliptical Contour

Ellipses have two focal points; a ray of light originating at one focal point is reflected through the second focus. This produces a divergent beam; its spread depends on the distance between the two focuses. Most downlights use reflectors with exact or modified elliptical shapes. A special use of this contour produces a beam that passes through a small, inconspicuous opening flush with the ceiling plane (figure 10.4).

Parabolic Contour

The parabola is a special form of the ellipse, in which the two focuses are far apart. A ray of light originating at the exact focal point of a perfectly-shaped parabolic contour is redirected in a direction parallel to the axis of the reflector, producing a beam of parallel rays. The filament or source is never an actual point; this results in a degree of beamspread that depends on the size of the source and the diameter of the reflector (figure 10.5).

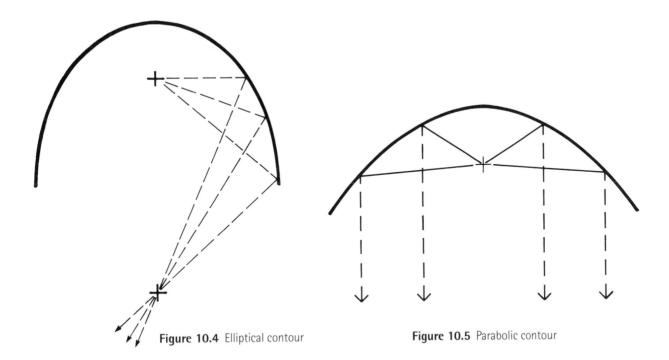

Figure 10.4 Elliptical contour   **Figure 10.5** Parabolic contour

In its pure form, the parabolic contour is used for searchlights, spotlights, and directional equipment where a concentrated beam and a limited spread of light is desired. The beam is often given additional spread by passing it through a diffusing or refracting lens, as is done with many reflector lamps.

Circular Contour

The circle is a special form of the ellipse, where both focuses are coincident; it is the opposite of the parabola. A ray of light originating at the focal point of a circular contour is reflected back through the same point. It is used separately or in combination reflectors called *compound contours* to redistribute light that would be otherwise misdirected or trapped (figure 10.6).

Other Reflector Contours

Innumerable other possible reflector contours can be mathematically defined and tailored for a particular function, such as producing uniformity of luminance from a position close to the surface being lighted; for example,

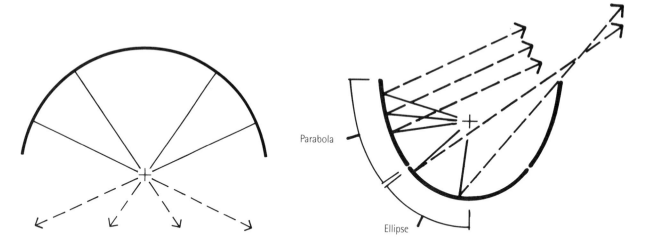

Figure 10.6 Circular contour

Figure 10.7 Compound contour for maximum beam spread (often used to produce asymmetric distribution)

to light the ceiling in a low-height room (figure 10.7). These reflectors do not have a specific focal point.

Specular Reflectors

Almost all reflector design presumes a compact "point" source of light or a linear source of light at the focus or other precise location. The most compact source is an incandescent filament in a clear bulb.

Large variations in beam control occur, however, with the use of lamps that emit light from a larger area, such as an arc tube or a phosphor-coated bulb or tube. In these cases the bulb or tube, rather than the filament, is the actual light source. This kind of lamp is both a large source displaced from the focus and a diffuse emitter. The result is a diffuse or less precisely defined beam and a reduced projection distance.

The first reflectors for electric luminaires were designed by trial and error or by "longhand" mathematics (figure 10.8). Today, computer–aided reflector design accounts for all of the characteristics of a light source and optimizes a reflector contour.

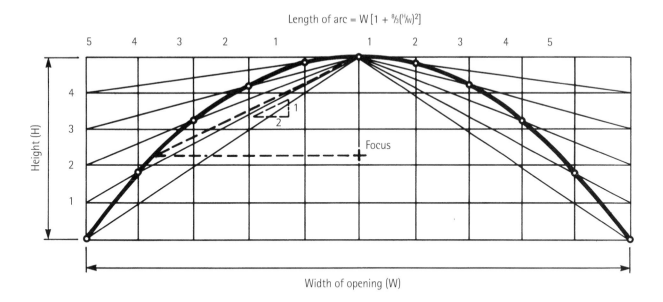

Figure 10.8 Parabolic
reflector construction guide.

Semispecular Reflectors

Although clear incandescent lamps in specular reflectors produce efficient beam control, there is often a need to smooth out irregularities in the beam. These striations are reflected images of the filament coil. They are eliminated by a slight diffusion of the beam, accomplished by using either an inside-frosted lamp, a lightly etched reflector surface, or a moderately diffusing lens in the beam path.

Diffuse Reflectors

The reflection of light from a perfectly diffuse, flat surface is multidirectional, giving a circular distribution curve; the angle of reflection is independent of the angle of incidence. With incident light dispersed in all directions, the beam is wide; because of this lack of directional control, long projection distances are impractical (figure 10.9).

The shape of a diffuse reflector has little influence on the resulting direction and distribution of light. Diffuse reflectors are often useful in luminaires that provide uniform, ambient luminance in a space.

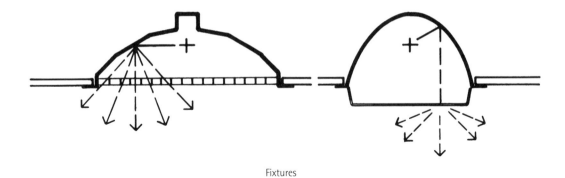

Fixtures

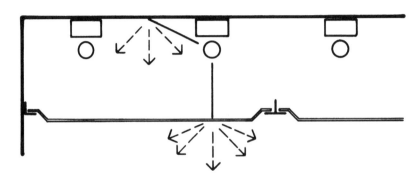

Self-luminous ceilings and walls

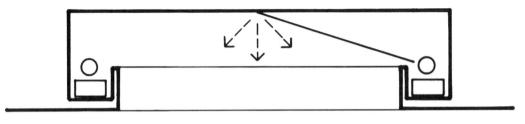

Coffers and coves

Figure 10.9 Diffuse reflector techniques

Reflector Materials

Aluminum is the material most frequently used for the fabrication of reflectors. It can be stamped, spun, hydroformed, or extruded into almost any desired shape or contour; it can be processed chemically and electrically to make it more specular; and it can be sandblasted or etched chemically to provide varying degrees of semispecular reflection.

A hard, protective surface layer of high transparency produced by the *anodizing process* prevents scratching and abrasion of specular aluminum surfaces and makes cleaning practical.

Total Internal Reflection

Total internal reflection occurs when light passes into a transparent medium, such as glass or plastic, at an appropriate angle and travels inside the medium repeatedly reflecting from side to side. Edge lighting and light transmission through rods are examples of this phenomenon.

With *fiber optics*, light entering one side of a glass or plastic fiber of optical quality is transmitted to the other end by the process of total internal reflection. Light rays that strike the core at the acceptance angle are reflected back and forth inside the core and travel to the other end of the fiber in a zigzag path of successive reflections.

In use, a single, large fiber is impractical because it lacks flexibility. To increase flexibility, a large number of fibers are clustered together in a *bundle*. In order to prevent light leaking from one fiber to another, each is coated with a transparent sheath that has a lower refractive index than the fiber. The sheathing process protects the surfaces of the fiber and allows the bundle to be embedded into other materials without loss of light from the sides (figure 10.10).

Optical fibers are combined in two kinds of bundles: coherent and incoherent. *Coherent bundles* contain fibers that are identically positioned at the point of light entrance and light exit. Because each fiber conducts a portion of the light pattern to the same point on the receiving end of a bundle, images can be transmitted through the bundle. *Incoherent bundles* contain a random arrangement of fibers that can be used to transmit light but not images.

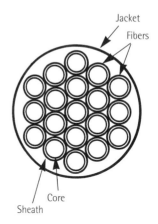

Figure 10.10 Enlarged section of fiber optic

A typical fiber-optic lighting system consists of: (1) a light projector, (2) a tungsten-halogen or metal-halide light source, (3) an optical fiber harness, (4) a fitting for each of the bundles, and (5) the bundles of optical fibers themselves. Silicone-rubber sheathing gives the bundles protection without loss of flexibility.

REFRACTION

When a straw is placed in a clear glass of water, it appears to bend at the point where it enters the water. This is because the speed of light changes when a light ray passes from air to water; the phenomenon is called *refraction*.

A similar result occurs when light passes from air to clear glass and plastics. When these transparent materials are formed into prisms or lenses, they become techniques for controlling the direction and, consequently, the distribution of light.

A beam of light is displaced at the surface of a transmitting material. If the material is formed with two parallel "faces," the displacements neutralize each other; no angular change in the direction of the beam occurs, only a slight displacement. If the opposite faces are not parallel, the unbalanced refraction permanently alters the direction of light (figure 10.11).

Light rays deviate toward the perpendicular when entering a material with a higher index of refraction and deviate away from the perpendicular when entering material with a lower index.

A *prism* is a transparent body bounded in part by two nonparallel faces. A beam of light projected through one face is emitted in a different direction through another. By providing the proper angle between prism faces, light is emitted in a desired direction (figure 10.12).

A lens may be thought of as a multiple array of prisms with a continuously-changing included angle to produce an organized distribution of light (figure 10.13). A *lens* is formed by two opposite refracting surfaces, which have a common axis. Two basic kinds of lens systems are used: (1) convex and (2) concave.

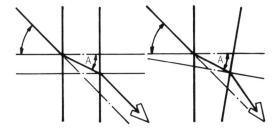

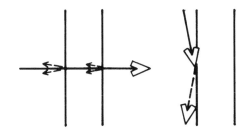

μ = Index of refraction

$\sin B = \left(\dfrac{\mu_A}{\mu_B}\right) \sin A$

Figure 10.11 Index of refraction

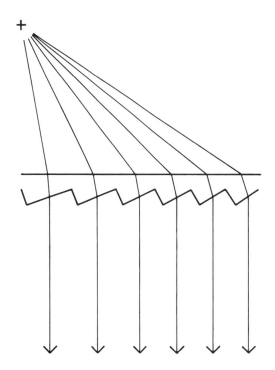

Figure 10.12 Prismatic action

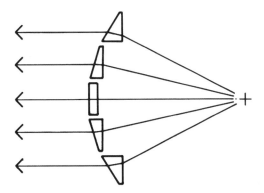

Figure 10.13 A lens is a system of prisms

The *convex (positive or converging) lens* is thicker in the middle than it is at the edges. Its focal point lies on the axis, at the point where the diverging rays from the source are refracted to produce a parallel beam of light (figure 10.14).

The *concave (negative* or *diverging) lens* is thinner in the middle than it is at the edges. This causes a parallel beam of light to diverge. The focus is called a *virtual* focal point; it is the artificial point at which the diverging rays would meet if they were traced backward as straight lines through the lens (figure 10.15).

Figure 10.14 Convex lens

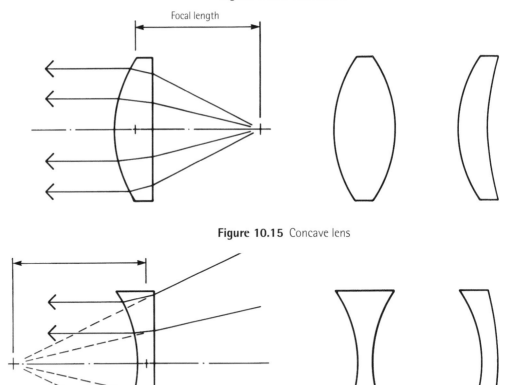

Figure 10.15 Concave lens

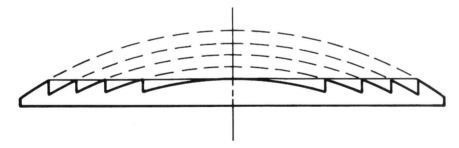

Figure 10.16 Fresnel lens

Because refraction takes place at the surface of the material, with the direction of the ray unchanged between surfaces, part of this transmitting material can be removed without affecting the optical control. A convex lens with sections of the glass removed produces a lens that is thinner and lighter in weight. The *Fresnel lens,* which is based on this principle, consists of a series of concentric lens sections regressed into a planar array (figure 10.16).

When the light source is positioned at points other than the primary focus of the optical system, the lamp–refractor combination produces an asymmetric or spread distribution (figure 10.17).

Figure 10.17 Distribution of light through Fresnel lens.

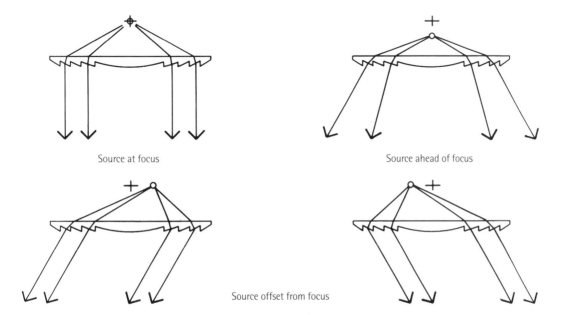

Source at focus

Source ahead of focus

Source offset from focus

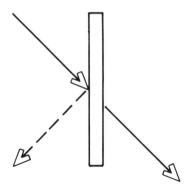

Figure 10.18 Direct transmission

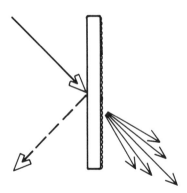

Figure 10.19 Spread transmission

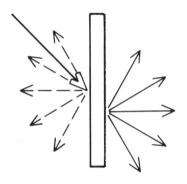

Figure 10.20 Diffuse transmission

TRANSMISSION

Transmission of light through a material is affected by two things. (1) the reflections at each surface of the material and (2) the absorption and reflection within the material. As a continuous spread of reflection exists from mirrored, fully-specular surfaces to matte, fully-diffusing surfaces, a similar, continuous spread of transmission exists from fully-transparent, clear materials to fully-diffusing translucent ones.

Direct Transmission

Transparent materials leave the light distribution unchanged. They are used as protective covers for absorbing or reflecting infrared or ultraviolet radiation or where change in the color of light is desired while maintaining the light distribution produced by reflecting contours. Because the light remains visible, materials such as clear glass and plastic are ineffective for glare control (figure 10.18).

Semidiffuse Transmission

Translucent materials emit light at wider angles because of configurations on at least one side of the material. A slight redirection of the transmitted beam is achieved by minor surface irregularities, such as shallow facets or flutes, which smooth out imperfections and striations. A greater degree of diffusion is achieved by etches, sandblasts, and matting aerosol sprays. Semidiffuse materials provide lamp concealment and glare control (figure 10.19).

Diffuse Transmission

Diffuse transmission disperses light in all directions and eliminates the directional quality of the beam. Full diffusion is achieved by using opal glasses and plastics that incorporate microscopic particles and remove all directionality from the transmitted beam (figure 10.20).

GLARE CONTROL

Sometimes the lens or reflector that is providing the light control is also used to achieve concurrent glare control and lamp concealment. At other times separate elements are used.

Baffles and Louvers

Baffles and louvers shield glare at normal viewing angles, thereby contributing to visual comfort.

Baffles provide shielding in one direction, along a single axis. For small aperture luminaires, a baffle around the perimeter provides shielding from all directions (figure 10.21).

Louvers are a series of baffles or shielding elements placed in a geometric pattern to provide shielding from many directions with minimum interference to the desired beam distribution (figure 10.22).

Figure 10.21 Baffles

Figure 10.22 Louvers

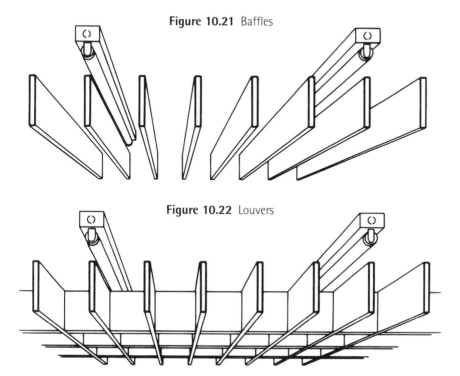

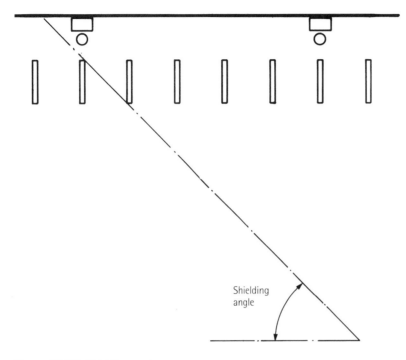

Figure 10.23 Shielding angle

Figure 10.24 Shielding as an aspect of contour design

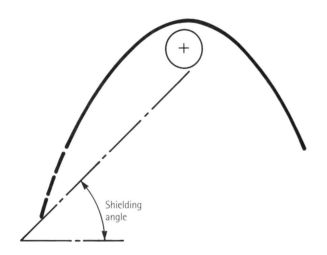

Shielding surface

Shielding conceals the lamp and controls glare within a zone called the *shielding angle*. This is the maximum angle that the eye is raised above horizontal without seeing the light source beyond the shielding system (figure 10.23).

Although baffles and louvers conceal the light source from direct view within this specified zone, horizontal work surfaces are still directly exposed to the source. The mirrored image of the light source becomes a source of *reflected* glare from glossy paper, photographs, objects behind glass, and polished table tops (figure 10.24).

Baffles and louvers may be black or made from reflective and transmitting materials. The intensity of light directed toward the eye is determined by the luminance of these surfaces . The choice of materials is based on various considerations including visual comfort and design harmony with the space (figure 10.25).

To achieve concurrent glare control and lamp concealment with minimal change in the diffuse beam, use open louvers or plastic or glass with a slight degree of diffusion. Whether the beam is modified by diffuse reflection or by diffuse transmission, the distribution of light is the same.

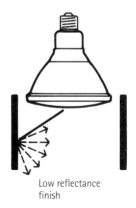

Material transmittance

High reflectance finish

Low reflectance finish

Surface reflectance

Reflectors

An opaque, concave reflector also functions as a baffle, which shields the light source. Additionally, the reflector's shape affects the appearance of the visible interior surface. If light is redirected toward the eye, the result is high luminance and unpleasant direct glare. If light is directed downward and away from the eye, luminance is reduced and glare is avoided.

In the most efficient reflector designs, source shielding is incorporated into the contour design. This involves extending the reflector surface to provide the necessary shielding (figure 10.26).

As reflector depth is increased, total efficiency is reduced because of absorption losses at the reflector surface. Because a greater portion of the emitted light is brought under control and redirected, candlepower and useful lumens increase.

Parabolic reflectors are often used for glare control. Little reflected luminance occurs in the cross view of these reflectors because most of the light is directed downward with minimal light directed toward the eye; this gives an impression of low luminance from normal angles of view (figure 10.27).

Figure 10.25 Transmitting materials: translucent white and colored plastic or glass, perforated metal. High reflectance finish: lightly etched metal, light wood,. light color paint. Low reflectance finish: matte black finish,. dark wood finish, dark color paint.

Figure 10.26 Parabolic reflector used for luminance control

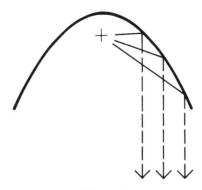

Reflector action

Figure 10.27 Parabolic reflector design for louvers and baffles

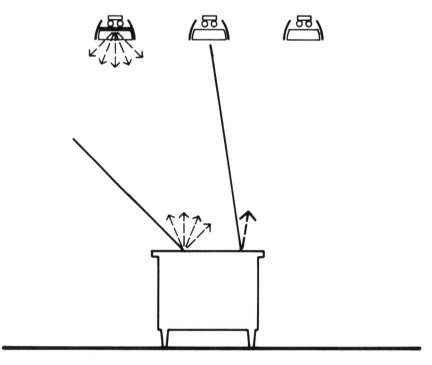

1. Reduce glossiness of work surface
2. Add diffuse transmitting material to increase the diffusion of the light source
3. Locate lighting equipment outside of the reflected field of view

Figure 10.28 Corrective solutions

Diffusion causes more light to be directed toward the eye. As a result, luminance is increased when reflector surfaces are etched or brushed.

Parabolic reflector design is applied to both reflectors and baffles. Figure 10.28 shows the pattern of light reflections for light rays originating above the louver. Ideally, light is reflected at an angle equal to the shielding angle.

Well-designed specular parabolic louvers provide equal or superior glare control to matte black or gray louvers, with greater system efficiency because of the reduced absorption of light.

CHAPTER 11

PHOTOMETRICS

MEASUREMENT OF LIGHT

Photometry is the science that measures light. Five terms are commonly used to quantify light: intensity, flux, illuminance, luminance, and exitance.

1. Intensity is the light emitted in a specific direction by a source. Properly called *luminous intensity* or "flux per solid angle in a given direction," it is measured in candelas (cd). Intensity in a succession of directions is plotted on a distribution curve or polar graph.

2. Flux is the light emitted in all directions by a source. Properly called *luminous flux* or "time rate flow of light," it is measured in lumens (lm).

3. Illuminance is the density of light on a surface. Properly defined as "density of flux incident on a surface measured perpendicular to the surface," it is measured in footcandles (fc).

4. Luminance is the accepted term for light that is reflected from a surface in a given direction (back towards the eyes). Properly defined as "intensity of flux leaving a surface in a given direction," it is measured in candelas per square foot (cd/ft^2).

5. Exitance is the total quantity of light emitted, reflected, or transmitted in all directions from a surface. Properly defined as "density of flux leaving a surface," it is measured in lumens per square foot (lm/ft^2).

Shortcomings

Illuminance is frequently used to measure the quantity of light in architectural space because it is the easiest and least expensive unit to measure. Yet it is impossible to *see* a footcandle.

What is seen is *luminance*, which is a function of the amount of light falling on a surface and the reflectance of that surface (its ability to reflect light). One sees an object or surface only when light is reflected from that object or surface back toward the eyes, or when it is emitting light itself ("self–luminous").

Brightness is what we perceive. It is a subjective attribute perceived in varying degrees of intensity. This phenomenon used to be measured in *footlamberts (fL)*, an expression that is now deprecated by the Illuminating Engineering Society (IES) because they are difficult to measure with accuracy. Once a convenient measure of perceived luminance becomes available, it will be far better to calculate perceived surface luminance values—which will account for the aesthetic, psychological, and physiological variables of the visual process—than to calculate footcandle values—which account for none of these factors.

The perception of surface luminance is based largely on the eye's ability to *adapt.* The iris *dilates* (opens) when illuminance is low and *contracts* (closes) when illuminance is high. It takes the eye longer to adapt from light to dark than from dark to light. When one enters a dark theater on a sunny day, it takes 20 to 30 minutes for the eyes to adapt completely to the lower illuminance. When one leaves the theater and returns to daylight, it takes sometimes only seconds for the eyes to adapt to the higher luminance.

In a more subtle way, the eyes are continually adapting as one moves in and through variously lighted spaces or looks around and at objects of varying illuminances. Even measured luminance, expressed in cd/ft^2, does not indicate the *apparent* brightness because of the eye's ability to adapt. Measured luminance, then, provides a poor indication of the perceived brightness, which is modified by the surrounding conditions and the adaptation of the eyes.

It is the *balance* of these relative luminances, *not* the quantity of illumi-nance received on a surface, that determines successful lighting design. Therefore, the illuminance measurements that follow are *not* to be used as a starting point for a design. They are to be used only as a back-up to check a completed design.

Candlepower Distribution Curve

The candlepower distribution curve represents the amount of luminous intensity (cd) generated in each direction by a light source in a plane through the center of the source. Consequently the candlepower curve gives a picture of the total light pattern produced by a source.

Candlepower distribution curves are available from the luminaire manufac-turer and are often found on the back of the manufacturer's product data sheet. A *polar graph* is used to represent the distributional intensity of a luminaire, and a *rectilinear* or *Cartesian graph* to represent the distributional intensity of a directional lamp.

In the polar graph (figure 11.1), the luminaire is located at the center of the radiating lines. The radiating lines represent specific degrees of angular rota-tion from the 0° axis (*nadir*) of the luminaire. The concentric circles represent graduating intensity expressed in candelas, with values entered along the vertical scale.

To determine the candlepower of this luminaire at 30°, find the appropriate angled line drawn from the center of the luminaire. Follow the line until it meets the polar curve, then follow the circular line originating at that point and read the candlepower on the vertical scale. In figure 11.1, the luminaire produces 1850 cd at 30° from nadir.

For luminaires with symmetrical light distributions, a single curve fully describes the luminaire's distribution. Often only one side of the polar graph is shown, since the other side is an identical, mirror image.

A luminaire with an asymmetrical distribution, such as a linear fluorescent downlight, requires curves in a number of planes to adequately represent its

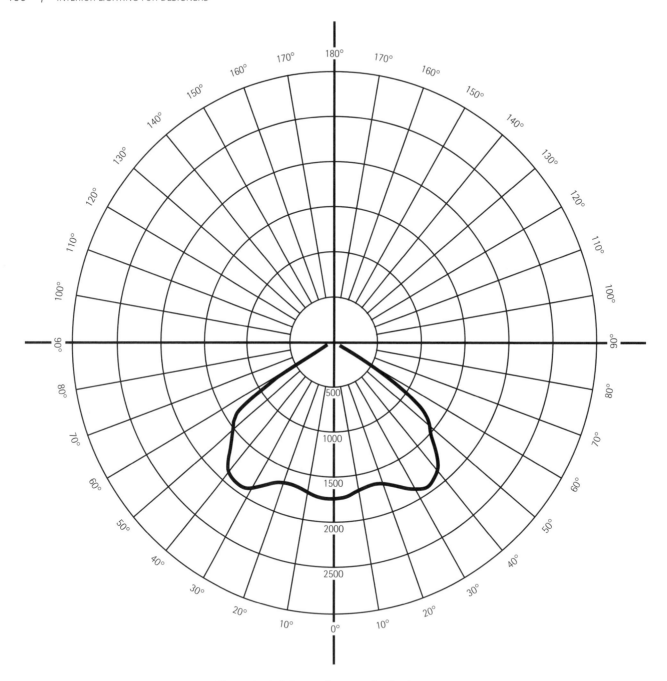

Figure 11.1 Polar candlepower distribution curve

distribution. Typically, one curve is parallel to the luminaire, another is perpendicular to the luminaire, and either a third plane at 45° or three planes at 22½° intervals are added (figure 11.2).

Luminaires or reflector lamp sources with directional distributions and abrupt cutoffs, where the light intensity changes rapidly within a small angular area, give values that are difficult to read on a polar graph. Consequently, a rectilinear or Cartesian graph is substituted to portray the candlepower distribution (figure 11.3).

On this graph, the horizontal scale represents the degrees from the beam axis and the vertical scale represents the intensity in candelas. In figure 11.3, approximately 3000 cd are produced by the light source at 10° from the beam center.

When selecting luminaires for a lighting application, be sure that the proposed luminaire *and its source* are precisely those showing the manufacturer's photometric test data. It is inaccurate to extrapolate from one source or reflector finish to another, unless the photometric report includes multipliers for various tested sources.

RECOMMENDED ILLUMINANCE VALUES

Illuminance value recommendations are published as footcandles (fc) at the *workplane*. For almost all commercial and industrial activities, this surface is a horizontal plane 2' 6" above the floor—standard desk height—even though the space may be a corridor or a basketball court with no desk in sight.

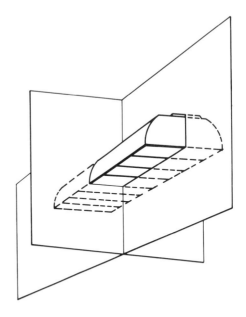

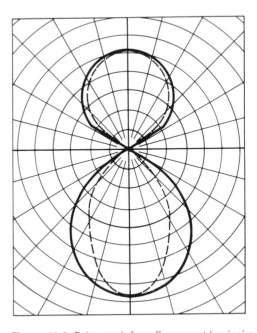

Figure 11.2 Polar graph for a fluorescent luminaire

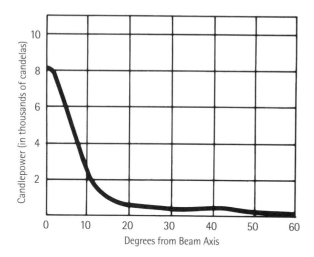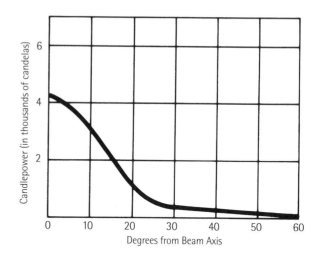

Figure 11.3 Rectilinear candlepower distribution curve

Remember that these values refer to illuminance on the horizontal work surface only; they have limited significance to us when we interpret the actual environment. Such factors as wall lighting, luminance accents, shadow, sparkle, and color have a greater influence on emotional reaction. These factors are particularly important in areas involving casual seeing where low recommended illuminance values may be misleading because a dull or gloomy environment is unsatisfactory.

True illuminance requirements vary with the visual difficulty of the work task, the age and eyes of the worker, and the importance of speed and accuracy in the completion of the task. Typical illuminance values are shown in Table 16. At best, these values provide a *guide* to the quantity of illuminance needed on the work surface for accurate and comfortable seeing.

A consolidated listing of the IES illuminance recommendations appears in Table 17. It covers illuminance ranges for a variety of categories of tasks.

Categories *A*, *B*, and *C* include casual activities that take place over the entire area of a space. For example, in a circulation space such as a hotel lobby or office building corridor, the visual task of circulation is a constant throughout the space, and an illuminance range of 5–7½–10 fc is recommended.

Categories *D, E,* and *F* refer to tasks that remain fixed at one or more particular locations; these values are to be applied only to the appropriate task area, recognizing that several different kinds of tasks may occur in the same room. The IES recommends a value of 20 fc as the minimum illuminance on the horizontal work surface for the "nontask" parts of the room where less demanding visual work is performed.

Categories *G, H,* and *I* are for visually difficult tasks. The lighting system for these tasks requires careful analysis.

Table 18 provides the *weighting factors* used to select a specific design illuminance value from the range provided in Table 17 for categories D through I. These weighting factors consider the age of the users, the reflectance of the task background (such as paper or chalkboard), and the degree of demand for speed and accuracy (such as casual reading of newspaper headlines at one extreme compared with a pharmacist reading prescription notes at the other).

When the sum of the weighting factors is -3 or -2, use the lowest value; when it is -1 to +1, use the middle value; and when it is +2 or +3, use the highest value.

> **Example** College students reading in a library are performing many visual tasks; the average is probably of medium contrast or small size. Therefore, use illuminance category E on Table 17, 50–75–100 fc. The weighting factors are found from Table 18, as follows:
>
> *Workers' Ages:* Students are typically under age 40.   *–1*
>
> *Speed/Accuracy:* Working on tasks where accuracy is important.   *0*
>
> *Reflectance of Task Background:* More than 70% for books printed in black ink on white paper.   *–1*
>
> *Calculation:* $(-1)+(0)+(-1)=(-2)$

Thus, use the lowest value in illuminance range E: 50 fc.

For more complete information, refer to the current edition of the *IES Lighting Handbook* under "Illuminance Selection."

ILLUMINANCE CALCULATIONS

Although people see not footcandles but luminance contrast, the question of how much light is necessary must still be answered. Following are descriptions of calculation methods, with examples for determining illuminance at a specific point as well as the average illuminance on a specific plane.

Illuminance at a Point

To find the value of incident illuminance at a specific point produced from a compact source, the *inverse–square method* is used. This method closely approximates the illumination where the distance from the source is at least five times the maximum dimension of the source.

SOURCE AIMED AT TARGET

Illuminance is proportional to the candlepower of the source in the given direction, and inversely proportional to the square of the distance from the source. To calculate illuminance (fc) from a source aimed at a surface:

$$fc = \frac{I}{D^2}$$

where *I* is the candlepower of the source in candelas in the direction of the point and *D* is the distance from the source to the point (figure 11.4).

> Example. A 90PAR/H/SP10° lamp is aimed at a point on a surface 6 ft away. From a candlepower distribution chart, find that the 90PAR/H/SP10° lamp produces 16,000 cd at 0°:

$$fc = \frac{16,000}{(6)^2} = 444$$

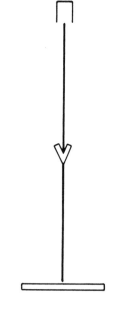

Figure 11.4
Illuminance on a surface perpendicular to the source

SOURCE AIMED AT ANGLE TO HORIZONTAL SURFACE

If the source is aimed at an angle toward the target instead of being perpendicular to the target, the light will spread over a greater area, reducing the illuminance at a specific point. For a horizontal surface, the reduction is equal to the *cosine* of the angle of incidence or tilt.

To calculate illuminance from a source at an angle to a horizontal surface:

$$fc = \frac{I}{D^2} \times \cos \Theta$$

where I is the candlepower of the source in the direction of the light ray, Θ is the angle of tilt between the light ray and a perpendicular to the target, and D is the *distance* from the source to the target surface (figure 11.5).

In figure 11.5, H is the vertical mounting *h*eight of the light source above the target of measurement, and R is the horizontal distance (*r*un) from the light source to the target.

> **Example** A 90PAR/H/SP10° lamp is tilted at a 30° from nadir (straight down) to cast light on a horizontal surface 6 ft away (D). To determine illuminance on the surface, follow these steps:
>
> 1. From a candlepower distribution chart, find that the 90PAR/H/SP10° lamp produces 16,000 cd at 0° (the direction of the ray)
>
> 2. From the table of trigonometric functions (Table 10), find that the cosine of 30° is 0.866
>
> $$fc = \frac{(16,000)}{(6)^2} \times 0.866 = 385$$

SOURCE AT NADIR, TARGET TO SIDE ON HORIZONTAL SURFACE

If the source is aimed straight down but the target is located to one side of the central ray, the illuminance at the target on a horizontal surface will be the intensity of the beam at nadir reduced by the cosine of the angle from the source to the target.

To calculate illuminance from a source at nadir to a target off to one side on a horizontal surface, the same formula is used:

$$fc = \frac{I}{D^2} \times \cos \Theta$$

where *I* is the candlepower of the source *in the direction of the light ray*, Θ is the angle between nadir and the target, and *D* is the distance from the source to the target surface (figure 11.6).

Example   A 90PAR/H/FL30° lamp is pointed straight down. To determine the illuminance at a target that is 10° to one side of nadir on a horizontal surface 6 ft away, follow these steps:

1. From a candlepower distribution chart, find that the 90PAR/H/FL30° lamp produces 2800 cd at 10° (the direction of the ray).

2. From the table of trigonometric functions (Table 10), find that the cosine of 10° is 0.985

$$fc = \frac{(2800)}{(6)^2} \times 0.985 = 77$$

SOURCE AIMED AT ANGLE TO VERTICAL SURFACE

If the source is aimed at an angle toward a target on a *vertical* surface, the reduction in illuminance at the target is equal to the *sine* of the angle of incidence or tilt.

$$fc = \frac{I}{D^2} \times \sin \Theta$$

where *I* is the candlepower of the source in the direction of the light ray, Θ is the angle of tilt between the light ray and the target, and *D* is the distance from the source to the target (figure 11.7).

In figure 11.7, *H* is the vertical mounting height of the light source above the target and *R* is the horizontal distance (run) from the light source to the target.

Example   A 90PAR/H/SP10° lamp is tilted at a 30° from nadir to cast light on a vertical surface 6 ft away. To determine illuminance on the surface, follow these steps:

1. From a candlepower distribution chart, find that the 90PAR/H/SP10° lamp produces 16,000 cd at 0° (the direction of the ray).

2. From the table of trigonometric functions (Table 10), find that the sine of 30° is 0.500

$$fc = \frac{(16,000)}{(6)^2} \times 0.500 = 222$$

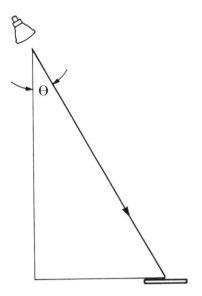

Figure 11.5 Illuminance on a horizontal surface—source at an angle

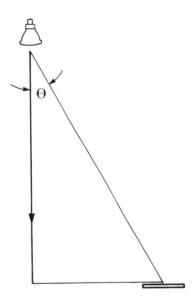

Figure 11.6 Illuminance on a horizontal surface—target located to one side of a source at nadir

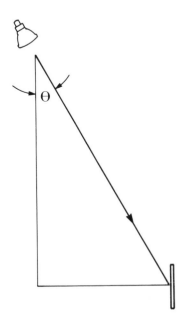

Figure 11.7 Illuminance on a vertical surface—source at an angle

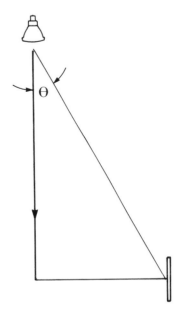

Figure 11.8 Illuminance on a vertical surface—target located to one side of a source at nadir

SOURCE AT NADIR, TARGET TO SIDE ON VERTICAL SURFACE

If the source is aimed straight down but the vertical target is located to one side of the light ray, the illuminance at the target on a vertical surface will be reduced by the sine of the angle between nadir and the target.

To calculate illuminance from a source at nadir to a target off to one side on a vertical surface, the same formula is used:

$$fc = \frac{I}{D^2} \times \sin \Theta$$

where *I* is the candlepower of the source *in the direction of the light ray*, Θ is the angle between nadir and the target (to one side), and *D* is the distance from the source to the target surface (figure 11.8).

> Example   A 90PAR/H/FL30° lamp is pointed straight down. To determine the illuminance at a target that is 10° to one side of nadir on a vertical surface 6 ft away, follow these steps:
>
> 1. From a candlepower distribution chart, find that the 90PAR/H/FL30° lamp produces 2800 cd at 10° (the direction of the ray).
>
> 2. From the table of trigonometric functions (Table 10), find that the sine of 10° is 0.174.

$$fc = \frac{(2800)}{(6)^2} \times 0.174 = 14$$

Shortcomings

The inverse square method yields only a rough idea of what is perceived. Its chief use is for comparison, as when establishing the ratio between an object and its surround. Even here, the inverse–square method fails to account for any interreflections within the space. And more significantly, perceived luminance depends on the reflectance of the surface and the position of the observer.

Average Illuminance Calculations

To assure that adequate illuminance is provided over a large area, the *lumen method,* or *zonal cavity calculation,* is used. This calculation is performed by hand or generated by computer; it predicts the *average* illuminance incident on a horizontal work surface, usually the workplane.

For a rough estimate of the average illuminance on a horizontal surface, the abbreviated version of the lumen method described below will suffice. It considers both the interreflections of light from room surfaces and the contributions of several light sources. It corrects for *maintained* illuminance, accounting for typical depreciation in lamp lumens over the life of the source and for dirt accumulation on the luminaire surfaces.

To calculate the average maintained illuminance falling on a horizontal surface,

$$fc = \frac{\text{Number of Lamps} \times \text{Initial Lamp Lumens} \times \text{LLF} \times \text{CU}}{\text{Area}}$$

Number of Lamps For single-lamp luminaires, the number of lamps equals the quantity of luminaires in a given area. If the luminaires contain more than one lamp, count the number of luminaires and multiply by the number of lamps per luminaire.

Initial Lamp Lumens The initial lamp lumens are published by the lamp manufacturers in their large lamp catalogs.

LLF LLF is an abbreviation for *light loss factor.* As a system ages, a natural depreciation in light output occurs. (With tungsten–halogen lamps, the loss is negligible.) Also, dust and dirt accumulate on room and luminaire surfaces. Other light loss factors such as ambient temperature, actual input voltage, ballast factor, HID lamp position, and lamp burnouts influence the illuminance in a space; for this quick method, only two are considered: LLD and LDD.

- *LLD* is an abbreviation for *lamp lumen depreciation.* This is the amount of light output that is reduced over the life of the lamp because of filament evaporation, tungsten deposits on the bulb wall, and phosphor degradation.

A list of lamp lumen depreciation for many sources is found in Table 12. When mean lamp lumens ("design lumens") are listed in the lamp catalog, this value may be used directly in the formula without the LLD factor.

- *LDD* is an abbreviation for *luminaire dirt depreciation*. This is the reduction of light output over time owing to the accumulation of dust and dirt on the reflecting and transmitting surfaces of the luminaire. This figure is dependent on the cleanliness of the space, the frequency of luminaire cleanings, and the luminaire's tendency to collect dirt (for example, open-top luminaires have a greater ability to collect dirt than closed-top luminaires; some luminaires have a ventilation pattern designed so that the flow of air slows the accumulation of dust.). See Tables 13 and 14.

With this method, LLF = LLD × LDD. Typical light loss factors for open light shielding systems (such as louvers) are 0.85 for very clean spaces, 0.75 for clean spaces, 0.65 for medium spaces, and 0.55 for dirty spaces.

CU   CU stands for the coefficient of *utilization*. The CU is an expression of the percentage of light output that is expected from a specific luminaire in a room. It accounts for the efficiency of the luminaire: its ability to deliver light to the work surface compared to the lumens supplied by the lamp(s). This is the amount of light that is not trapped and lost inside the luminaire.

The CU also accounts for the efficiency of the room in redirecting and inter-reflecting the incident light that strikes its surfaces. This is affected by the room's proportions as well as its reflectances. A large, low room is more efficient than a tall, narrow one. In the large, low room little incident light is interrupted by the walls; almost all of the light is received directly by the workplane. In a high, narrow room much of the incident light strikes the walls at least once before reaching the workplane, sometimes being reflected between several surfaces before reaching the task.

These variables produce an infinite number of CU's for each luminaire. For practical purposes, they are reduced to a group of figures for typical room proportions and reflectances.

Room Cavity Ratio   The CU is found by checking the manufacturer's coefficient of utilization table, which is usually published on the back of a product data sheet. In order to use the CU table, it is first necessary to calculate the *room cavity ratio.*

The room cavity ratio provides an expression of the efficiency of room proportions. To determine this ratio,

$$RCR = \frac{5(h)\,(l+w)}{l \times w}$$

where *h* is the height of the ceiling above the task surface; the task surface is usually considered to be 2'6" *AFF* (above finished floor).

A sample coefficient of utilization table for a compact fluorescent open reflector downlight is shown in Table 15.

EXAMPLE

Calculate the average maintained illuminance on the workplane in a small 10 ft x 20 ft office with a regular arrangement of eight luminaires where each luminaire uses two 26 W compact fluorescent lamps.

$$fc = \frac{\text{Number of lamps} \times \text{Initial Lamp Lumens} \times \text{LLF} \times \text{CU}}{\text{Area}}$$

The number of lamps (2 lamps per luminaire $\times$ 8 luminaires) is 16. From a large lamp catalog, find that the initial lumens for a PL–C 26 W lamp is 1800 lm. LLF = LLD $\times$ LDD: The LLD is found in Table 11 under fluorescent, compact, quad tube—lamp lumen depreciation factor is 0.85. The LDD requires Table 13, where it is found that a direct downlight with an opaque unapertured top enclosure and without a bottom enclosure is maintenance category IV. Table 14 yields a LDD of 0.96 for a very clean room that will have its luminaires cleaned every 6 months: $0.85 \times 0.96 = 0.82$.

To find the coefficient of utilization, first calculate the room cavity ratio:

$$RCR = \frac{5(h)\,(l+w)}{l \times w} = \frac{(5)\,(5.5)\,(10+20)}{(10)\,(20)} = 4.1$$

Here, h = ceiling height of 8'0" minus desk height of 2'6" = 5'6".

In Table 15, which is supplied by the manufacturer of this open reflector downlight, find that for a space with 80 percent ceiling reflectance, 50 percent wall reflectance, 20 percent floor reflectance, and an RCR of 4, the CU is 0.63.

$$fc = \frac{(16)(1800)(0.82)(0.63)}{(10)(20)} = 74$$

This small office, lighted by eight two-lamp 26 W compact–fluorescent, open reflector downlights, will have an average maintained illuminance of 74 fc on the desk. Although the lumen method does not demonstrate it, in all spaces the illuminance value is higher in the center of the room and drops off near the walls.

COMPUTER ASSISTANCE

The more complete *zonal cavity method* is found in the current edition of the *IES Lighting Handbook* and is available on disc from several software companies for use with a personal computer.

Computer-generated point calculations yield illuminance at selected points throughout a room. They also provide average, maximum, minimum, and standard deviation of illuminance values; room surface luminances; and lighting power density (watts/ft^2). Output is usually a chart of calculated values, an isofootcandle plot, or a shaded plan with gray scales representing the range of illuminance values.

Computer-generated ray-tracing calculations are the most accurate method of computing illuminance. By tracing each "ray" of light, realistic depictions of illuminance patterns on room surfaces, partitions, furniture, and artwork are displayed. Output is in the form of renderings or video images. Hardware requirements for this kind of program are greater than for other methods; at a minimum, a microcomputer with powerful graphics capabilities is necessary.

The IES publishes an annual survey of lighting software in its magazine, *Lighting Design + Application*. Products are reviewed for analysis features, applications, outputs, user features, hardware requirements, and costs.

Shortcomings

Whether executed by hand or calculated by computer, the lumen method fails to provide the *range* of light intensity in a room and *where* differences in illuminance values occur. It is, therefore, inaccurate for nonuniform and task-ambient lighting systems.

This method is also unable to provide information about lighting quality, visual comfort, and luminance patterns. The lumen method is useful mainly for predicting horizontal illuminance with general lighting systems.

SURFACE REFLECTANCE

Although interior surfaces are not light control devices, their reflectance properties are fundamental to the lighting design. The quantity and direction of light reflected from these surfaces affect both the efficiency of the initial light distribution and one's perception of surface luminance.

Wall, ceiling, and floor surfaces are large-area "reflectors" that redistribute light in the room. High-reflectance finishes, such as white, and off-white, promote maximum use of the available light; increasingly darker finishes intercept and absorb increasingly greater proportions of the light.

Because a useful amount of light reaches the workplane after reflection from the walls and the ceiling, the efficiency of the lighting system depends in part on the reflectance of room surfaces and finishes. This is particularly true of ambient-diffuse and indirect systems, where a large portion of the light is initially directed toward the ceiling or the walls or both.

In task-oriented spaces such as offices, factories, or cafeterias (where the "task" is seeing the food and the people), the following surface reflectances are recommended for the efficient use of light:

20% to 50%	Floor
50% to 70%	Wall
70% to 90%	Ceiling

The illuminance values in Tables 16 and 17 presume that commercial reflectances are:

20%	Floor
50%	Wall
80%	Ceiling

and presume that industrial reflectances are:

20%	Floor
50%	Wall
50%	Ceiling

The recommended reflectance for furniture, machinery, partitions, and work surfaces are the following:

25% to 45%	Furniture and machinery
25% to 50%	Work surfaces

Room surface finish reflectances are obtained from the manufacturers of paints, wall coverings, ceiling tiles, floor coverings, furniture, and machinery. The following *room reflectances* are a guide:

White, off white, gray, light tints of blue or brown	75% to 90%
Medium green, yellow, brown, or gray	30% to 60%
Dark gray, medium blue	10% to 20%
Dark blue, brown, dark green, and many wood finishes	5% to 10%

CHAPTER 12

LUMINAIRES

A luminaire provides physical support, electrical connection, and light control for an electric lamp. Almost all lamps require a method to curtail glare; in addition, many need a method to modify distribution. Ideally, the luminaire directs light to where it is needed while shielding the lamp from the eyes at normal angles of view.

Luminaires are composed of several parts that provide these different functions: the housing, the light-controlling element, and the glare-controlling element. Depending on the design requirements and optical control desired, some of these functions may be combined.

HOUSINGS

The electrical connection and physical support for the light source, and its electrical auxiliary equipment, when required, are provided by the luminaire housing. Housings are divided into four categories based on how they are supported: (1) recessed, (2) surface mounted, (3) pendant mounted, and (4) track mounted.

Recessed housings are mounted above the finished ceiling, are entirely hidden from view, and have an aperture (opening) at the ceiling plane to allow light to pass through. Semirecessed housings are mounted partially above the ceiling with the remainder visible from below. Some recessed housings are designed to be mounted into the wall, the floor, or the ground.

The electrical connection between the building wiring and the luminaire is made at the junction box, which is often attached to the housing (figure 12.1). UL standards require that the "splices" of luminaire wires to branch circuit wires be accessible for field inspection after the lighting fixture is installed. This access is usually accomplished through the aperture of the luminaire.

Surface-mounted housings are mounted to the surface of a ceiling, a wall, or, in rare cases, a floor. If the ceiling or wall construction permits, the junction box is recessed into the mounting surface, giving a cleaner appearance; otherwise, the junction box is mounted against the surface of the ceiling or wall.

Figure 12.1 Recessed incandescent downlight with junction box

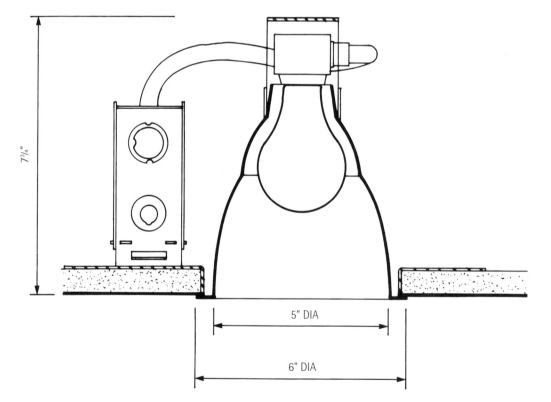

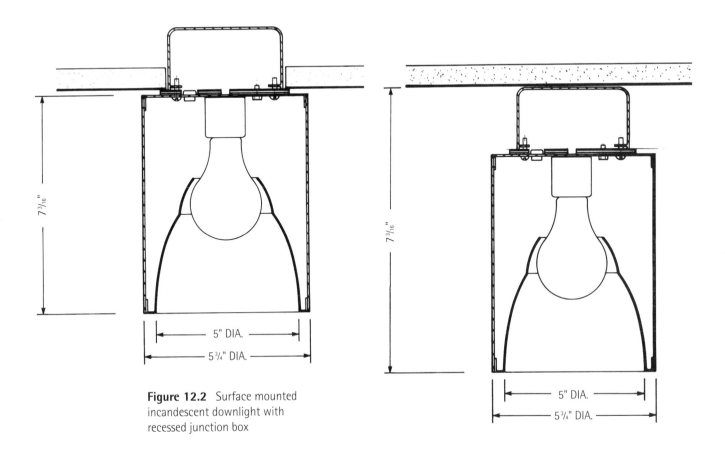

Figure 12.2 Surface mounted incandescent downlight with recessed junction box

Figure 12.3 Surface mounted incandescent downlight with surface mounted junction box

In both cases, the housing serves to partially or entirely conceal the junction box (figures 12.2 and 12.3). Because the housing of a surface-mounted luminaire is visible, it becomes a design element in the space.

Pendant-mounted housings also make use of a recessed or surface-mounted junction box located at the ceiling for electrical supply connection, but the luminaire is separated from the ceiling surface by a pendant such as a stem, chain, or cord. The junction box is concealed by a canopy (figure 12.4).

Pendant-mounted luminaires are used to provide uplight on the ceiling plane or to bring the light source closer to the task or activity in the space. At other times pendant-mounted luminaires are selected for decorative impact, as with a chandelier.

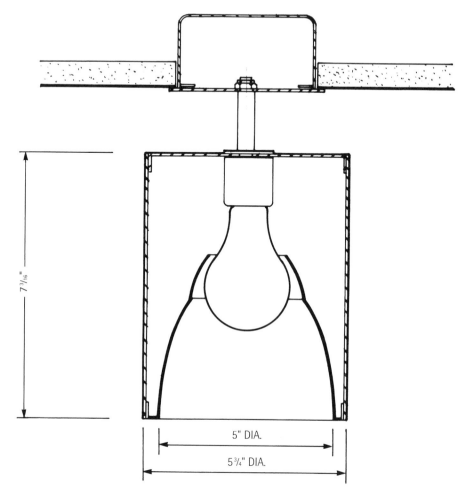

Figure 12.4 Pendant mounted incandescent downlight
with recessed junction box covered by a canopy

In high ceiling spaces, bringing the light source down closer to the floor is often unnecessary. Instead of suspending the lighting element down into the space where it becomes visually dominant, a more concentrated source at the ceiling plane is less conspicuous.

With track-mounted luminaires, a recessed, surface-mounted, or pendant-mounted lighting track provides both physical support and electrical connection through an adapter on the luminaire.

The main advantage of track is its flexibility. Track is often used where surfaces and objects to be lighted will be frequently or occasionally changed, or added or deleted, as in a museum or gallery. It also serves as an inexpensive way to bring electrical power to where it is needed in renovation and remodeling projects.

Luminaires can be divided into five categories that describe their lighting function: (1) downlights, (2) wash lights, (3) object lights, (4) task lights, and (5) multidirectional lights.

DOWNLIGHTS

Downlights, also called direct luminaires, produce a downward light distribution which is usually symmetrical. They are used in multiples to provide ambient light in a large space or for providing focal glow on a horizontal surface such as the floor or workplane (figure 12.5).

Figure 12.5 Side-mounted A lamp shallow depth downlight

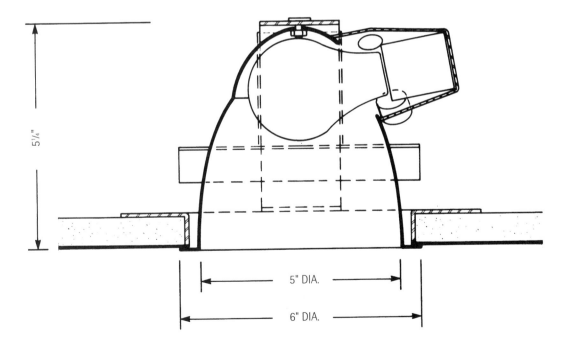

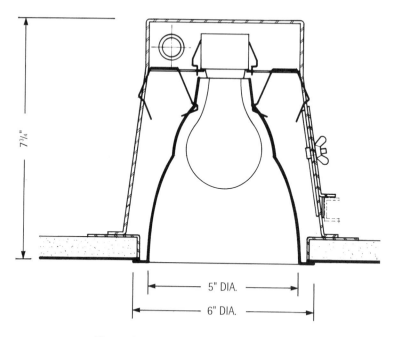

Figure 12.6 5-inch aperture incandescent downlight

Point Source Downlights

A nondirectional, concentrated light source is often mounted in a reflector to control its distribution and luminance because the source would otherwise emit light in all directions. In an open reflector downlight, a reflector made from spun or hydroformed aluminum accomplishes both purposes. A-lamp downlights allow for efficient use of inexpensive and readily available A-lamps (figure 12.6).

Tungsten-halogen (figure 12.7), compact-fluorescent (figure 12.8), and HID open-reflector downlights (figure 12.9) operate under the same principle as the A-lamp downlight. Fluorescent and HID apertures are larger because the source is larger. For a given source, the larger the aperture, the greater the efficiency of the luminaire.

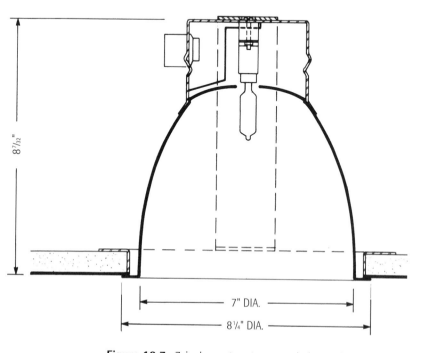

Figure 12.7 7-inch aperture tungsten-halogen downlight

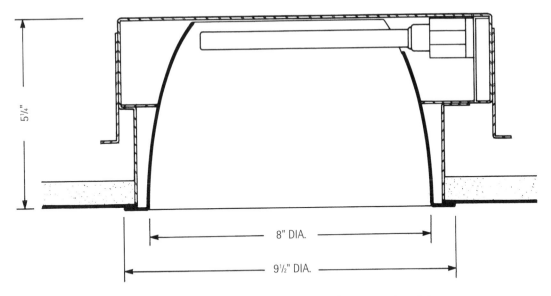

Figure 12.8 8-inch aperture compact-fluorescent downlight

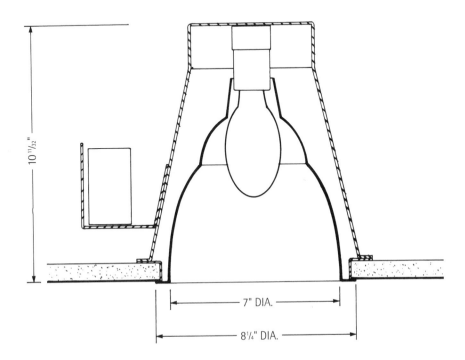

Figure 12.9 7-inch aperture low-wattage metal-halide downlight

Economy versions of the open reflector downlight, often called "high hats" or "cans," use an imprecise reflector to direct light downward and either a black multigroove baffle or a white splay ring for luminance control. These luminaires usually provide too much glare for visual comfort and are inefficient at directing light down to the horizontal surface. Although they are less expensive initially they provide only short-term value: More watts are used to achieve an equivalent quantity of light.

Figure 12.10 Ellipsoidal downlight

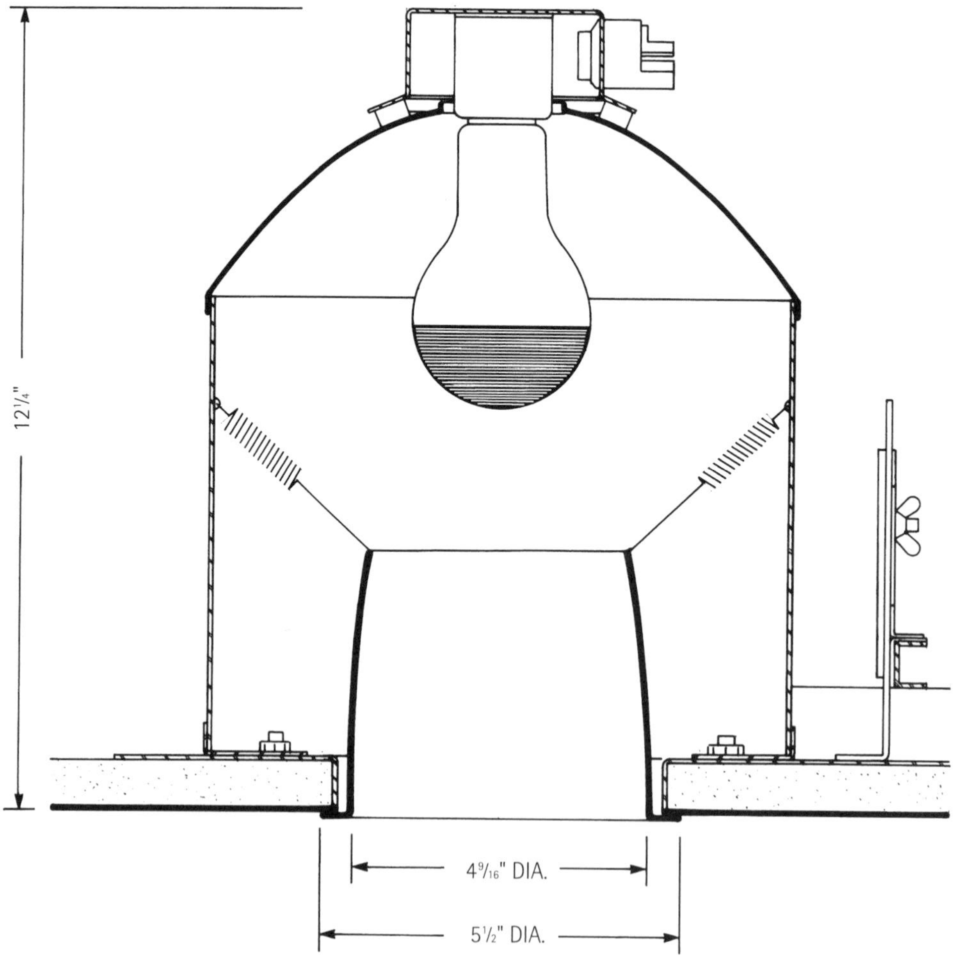

Ellipsoidal downlights were early attempts at controlling the luminance of the source and providing a wide, soft distribution. They sometimes used silver-bowl lamps and were excellent at reducing the luminance of the aperture; they were, however, inefficient at directing light downward. These luminaires were large because the elliptical reflector is larger than the parabolic contour; today they are used infrequently (figure 12.10).

Shallow-contour, silver-bowl, open-reflector downlights are used for a general diffusion of light combined with sparkle at the ceiling plane, which is provided by the luminaire's "pebbled"-surface aluminum reflector. The reflecting bowl of the lamp throws light up into the luminaire reflector which, in turn, redirects the light in a controlled downward beam (figure 12.11).

Figure 12.11 Shallow-contour silver-bowl open-reflector downlight

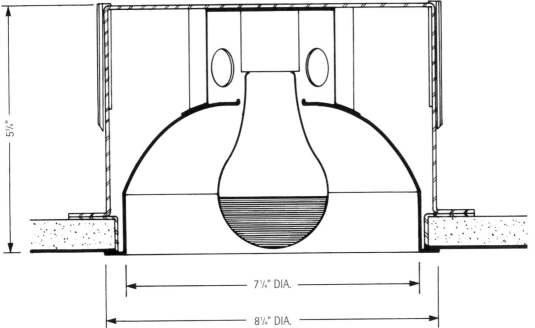

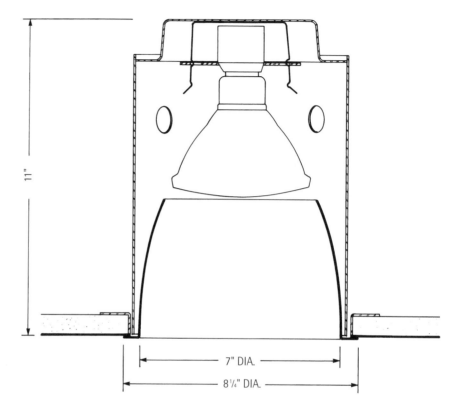

Figure 12.12 Open reflector PAR downlight

Reflectorized-lamp downlights do not require a light-controlling element because the AR, MR, PAR, or R lamp provides that function. Luminaires for these sources require only a luminance-controlling element; the most efficient is the open parabolic reflector. These luminaires are relatively easy to maintain: Very little dirt collects on the underside of the lamp, and every time the lamp is changed, the entire optical system is replaced (figure 12.12).

R14 or R20 downlights are sometimes used with spot lamps when a narrow beam of light is desired from a small aperture (figure 12.13), but PAR16 and PAR20 lamps are more efficient. R30 and R40 downlights are infrequently used; the wide spread of the R flood lamp is available from an A-lamp downlight, which is more efficient and uses a source that costs approximately one-fifth as much (figure 12.14).

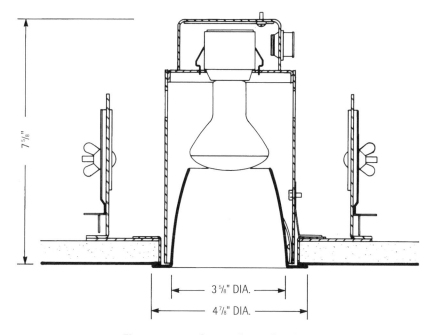

Figure 12.13 Open-reflector R20 downlight

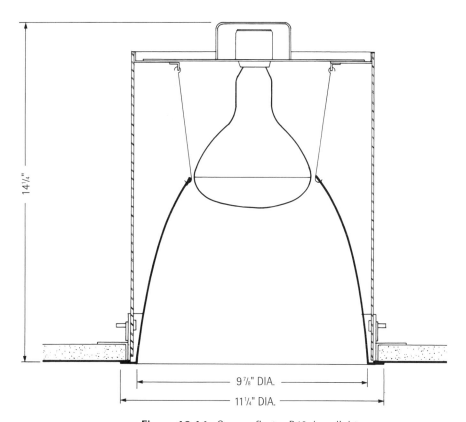

Figure 12.14 Open-reflector R40 downlight

When more concentrated beams are desired, PAR lamps are more efficient, delivering more light at a given wattage, for the same cost. PAR lamp downlights are used for greater emphasis on the horizontal plane (called "punch") than is usually produced by other downlights.

Almost all open reflector downlights have round apertures. Reflectors are available with either an overlap flange or a flush ceiling detail. The overlap flange is used in gypsum board and acoustical tile ceilings to conceal the uneven edge at the ceiling opening. Flush details are used in plaster ceilings to create a neat, finished appearance; the ceiling is plastered directly to the edge of a plaster ring or frame (figure 12.15).

Figure 12.15 Flush detail reflector

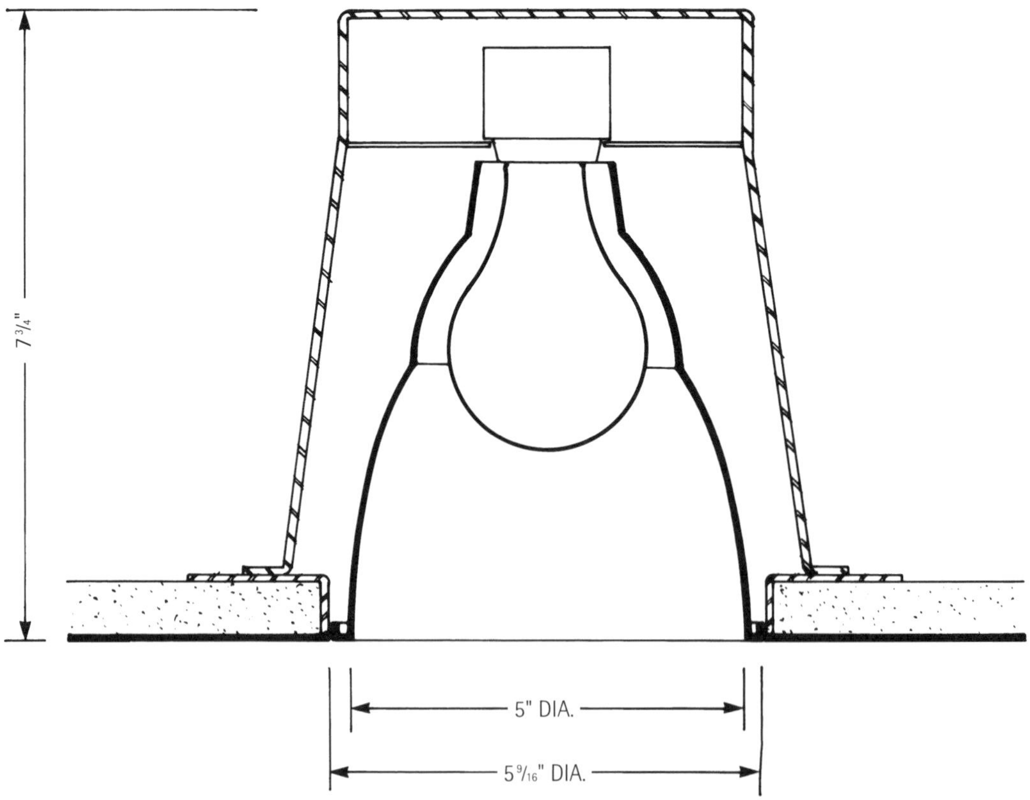

Specular aluminum reflectors should be treated like fine glassware. Dirt, fingerprints, and scratches spoil the appearance and diminish the performance of reflectors. It is advisable to handle reflectors carefully during construction; once installed they may be cleaned with a soft cloth and glass cleaner or removed and cleaned in a dishwasher or industrial washing machine.

Rectilinear Fluorescent Downlights

Fluorescent downlights are based on the same principles as the incandescent downlight. They typically use either rapid start T8, T12, or long compact fluorescent sources.

Common sizes for rapid start fluorescent downlights, also called troffers, are 1 ft × 4 ft, 2 ft × 4 ft, and 2 ft × 2 ft; the latter are used when a nondirectional (square) ceiling element is desired. Because these luminaires take up such a large portion of the ceiling surface (as compared to a round aperture downlight), they are significant factors in the design and appearance of the ceiling plane.

Suspended ceiling systems frequently use 2 ft × 4 ft fluorescent downlights because they integrate easily. Square 1 ft × 1 ft and 1.5 ft × 1.5 ft luminaires with compact fluorescent sources take up a smaller portion of the ceiling surface, providing energy-effective luminaires in compact sizes.

With all fluorescent downlights, the shielding material is the critical component, because this element is most prominent in the direct field of view. The purpose of diffusers, lenses, louvers, reflectors, and other shielding materials used in fluorescent downlight luminaires is to redirect light from the glare zone down toward work surfaces.

- Prismatic lenses incorporate a pattern of small prisms or other refractive elements to reduce the luminance of the luminaire and inhibit direct glare. But almost all fluorescent luminaire lenses fail to reduce their luminance sufficiently to provide the visual comfort and prevent bright images in VDT screens. The excessive contrast between the lens and the ceiling plane also creates distracting reflections.

- Egg-crate louvers are made of intersecting straight-sided blades that reduce luminance by blocking light rays that otherwise would emerge at glare angles. They are made of translucent or opaque plastic or painted metal. Egg-crate louvers are inefficient in transmitting light, controlling glare and preventing VDT screen reflections.

- Parabolic louvers control luminance precisely; they consist of multiple cells with parabolic reflectors, and a specular or semispecular finish. The cells range in size from $\frac{1}{2}$ in. $\times$ $\frac{1}{2}$ in. to 1 ft $\times$ 1 ft.

- Small-cell parabolic louvers reduce luminance, but are inefficient in light output. To maximize efficiency, they often have a highly specular finish, which may cause such a low luminance at the ceiling plane that the room seems dim and depressing.

- Deep-cell, open parabolic louvers offer the best combination of shielding and efficiency.

To avoid reflected glare in VDT screens, it is recommended that average luminaire luminance be less than

850 cd/m^2 at 55° from vertical

350 cd/m^2 at 65° from vertical

175 cd/m^2 at 75° from vertical

A manufacturer's luminaire photometric report should include a luminance summary that tabulates brightness values at angles above 45° from nadir. This summary may be used to evaluate the suitability of direct luminaires in offices with VDTs.

Luminous Ceilings

A luminous ceiling also provides direct, downward distribution. It consists of a plane of translucent glass or plastic—often the size of the entire room—suspended below a regular grid of fluorescent lamps. The suspended element becomes the finished ceiling. This technique, popular in the 1950s and 1960s, provides uniform, diffuse, ambient light (figure 12.16).

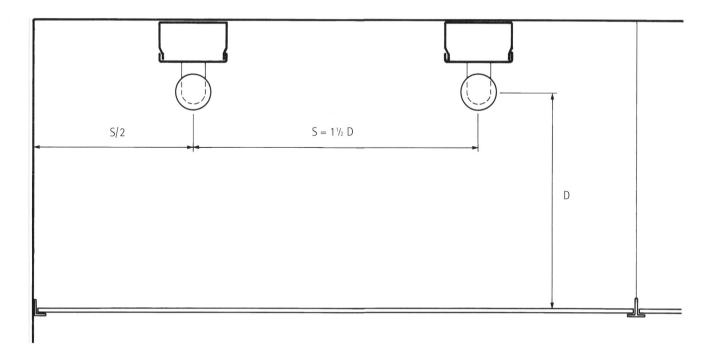

The cavity above the luminous plane must be free of obstructions and all surfaces are to be finished with a high-reflectance (80 to 90 percent), matte-white paint. Luminous ceilings share the same drawback as indirect lighting—they light everything from all directions, with no shadows or modeling, giving the gloomy effect of an overcast sky.

Figure 12.16 Typical luminous ceiling

WASH LIGHTS

In rooms of moderate size, walls are often the major element in the field of view; washing walls with light has properly become a major technique in the practice of creative illumination. Walls are lighted in two ways: (1) by using closely-spaced directional sources mounted in a continuous slot adjacent to the wall, or (2) by using a row of asymmetric-distribution luminaires placed parallel to the wall at a distance of about one-third the height of the wall, and with the individual units spaced about the same distance apart from each other as they are away from the wall.

WALLWASHERS

Wash lights are luminaires that provide an even "wash" of relatively uniform brightness, usually on a wall but occasionally on a ceiling. *Wallwashers* are used for lighting walls, sometimes to light artwork, and occasionally to create ambient light in a space.

All kinds of wallwashers use reflectors or reflectorized lamps or both, frequently combined with lenses to spread the light sideways and smooth the beam. They fall into three categories: (1) downlight/wallwashers, (2) lensed wallwashers and (3) open-reflector wallwashers.

The combination *downlight/wallwasher* is a special kind of wallwasher. It consists of an open-reflector downlight with an added elliptical reflector, sometimes called a "kicker." This additional reflector "kicks" light up toward the top of the wall, eliminating the parabolic scallop that is created by the normal, conical light pattern when it is intersected by a wall.

The downlight/wallwasher looks identical to the same-size aperture open-reflector downlight. This makes it possible to use downlights (without kickers) for general room illumination and to then add downlight/wallwashers adjacent to the walls, usually on closer centers for uniformity of illumination. Downlight/wallwash luminaires are available for incandescent A, tungsten-halogen, compact-fluorescent, mercury, metal-halide, and HPS lamps.

Variations of the downlight/wallwash have been developed to light adjacent walls forming a corner (*downlight/corner wallwasher)*, to light opposite sides of a corridor (*downlight/double wallwasher)*, and to light the wall next to a door without spilling through the doorway and causing glare (*downlight/half wallwasher*) (figure 12.17). These luminaires have downlight distributions in three directions virtually unchanged by the kicker reflector. The lighted vertical surface is moderately lighted; the horizontal and vertical planes seem to have a relatively equal emphasis (figure 12.18).

A greater emphasis on the vertical surface is provided by luminaires that light only the walls without any significant downward distribution. Reflector wallwashers with or without lenses make use of sophisticated optical systems to provide distribution and luminance control.

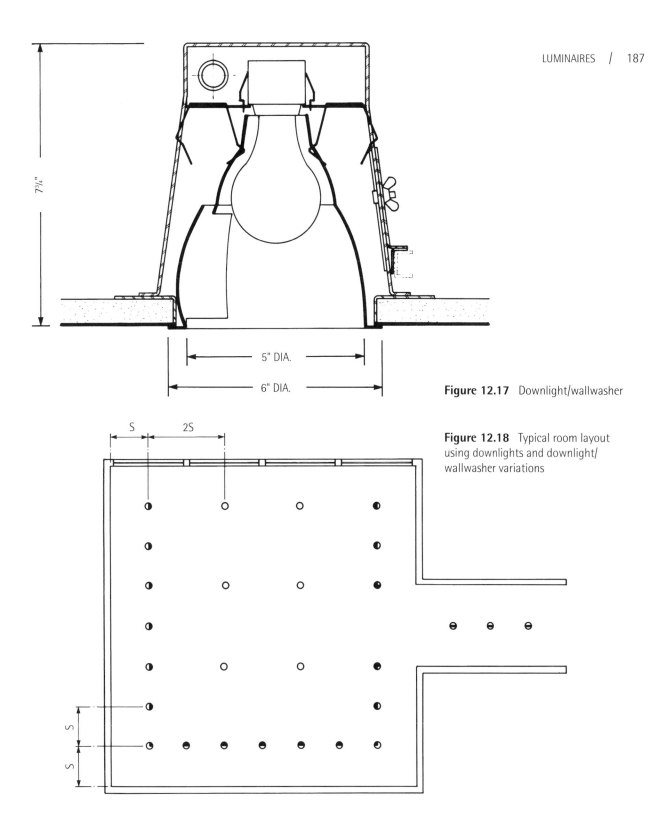

7³/₄"

5" DIA.

6" DIA.

Figure 12.17 Downlight/wallwasher

S   2S

S

S

Figure 12.18 Typical room layout using downlights and downlight/ wallwasher variations

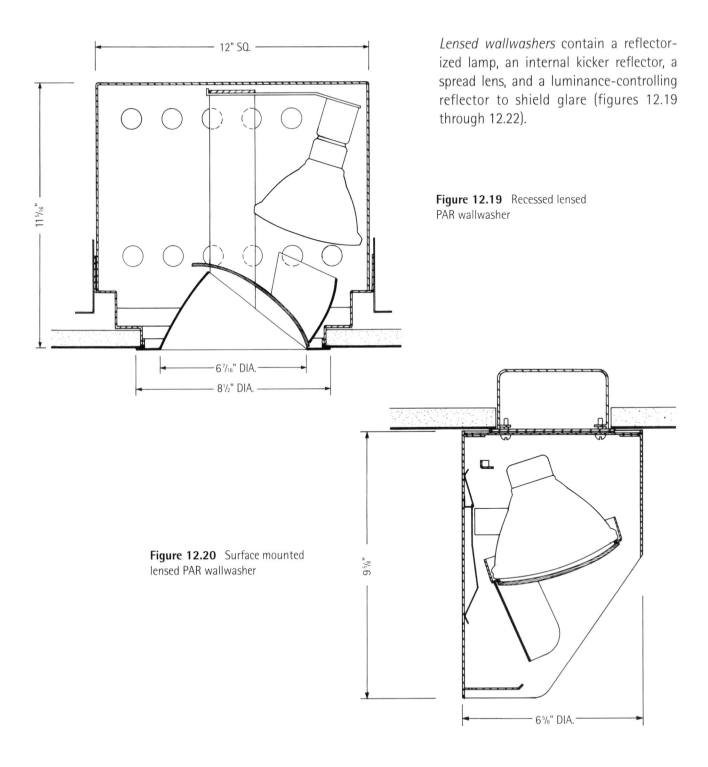

Lensed wallwashers contain a reflector-ized lamp, an internal kicker reflector, a spread lens, and a luminance-controlling reflector to shield glare (figures 12.19 through 12.22).

Figure 12.19 Recessed lensed PAR wallwasher

Figure 12.20 Surface mounted lensed PAR wallwasher

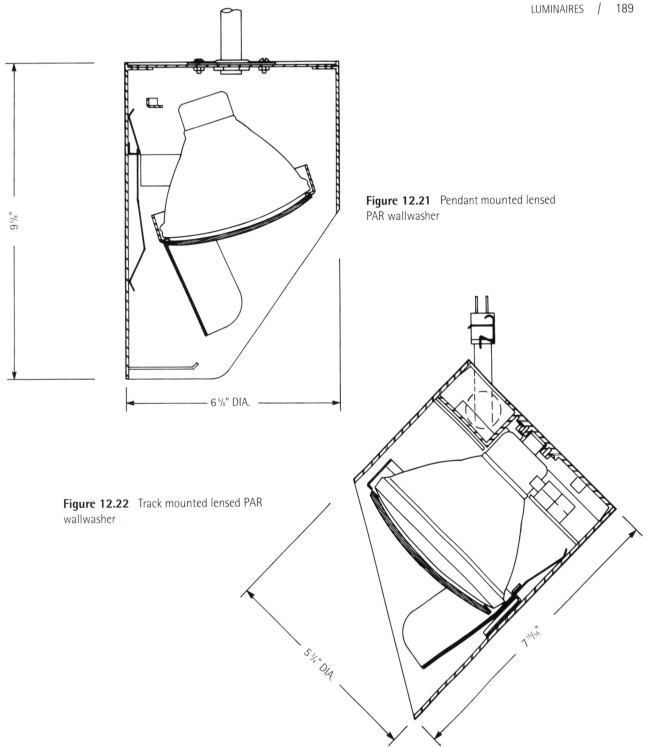

Figure 12.21 Pendant mounted lensed PAR wallwasher

Figure 12.22 Track mounted lensed PAR wallwasher

Reflectors that are not circular, parabolic, elliptical, or hyperbolic are called nonfocal reflectors. Open-reflector wallwashers have a reflector shape that combines an ellipse with a parabola (figures 12.23 through 12.25) or use nonfocal shapes.

Lensed and open-reflector wallwashers used without downlights provide a shadowless, low-contrast setting. When people are distant from the lighted wall they are seen as flat-featured; people next to the lighted wall are seen as silhouettes. These problems are avoided by adding downlights. The combination downlight/wallwashers work well in small rooms, such as a 10-ft-wide office where opposite walls are lighted; the downlight component provides good modeling of faces throughout the room.

Figure 12.23   Recessed T4 tungsten halogen wallwasher

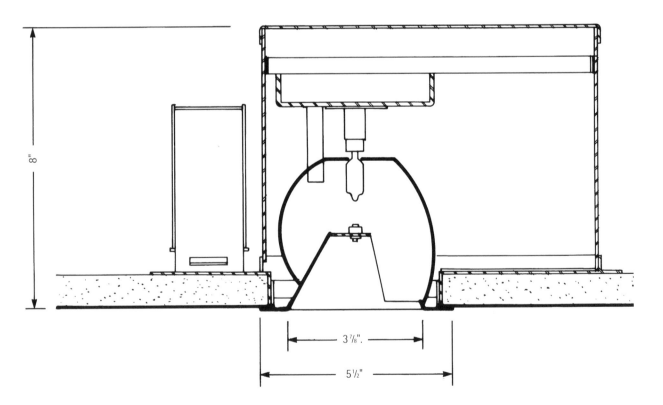

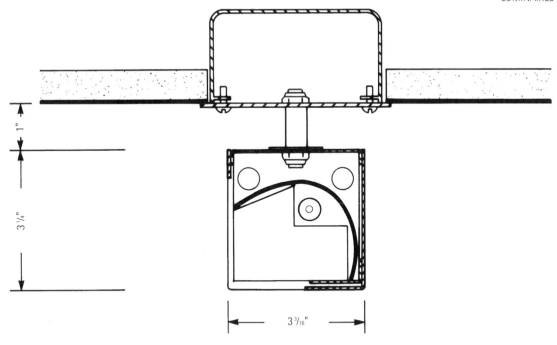

Figure 12.24 Surface (stem) mounted T4 tungsten halogen wallwasher

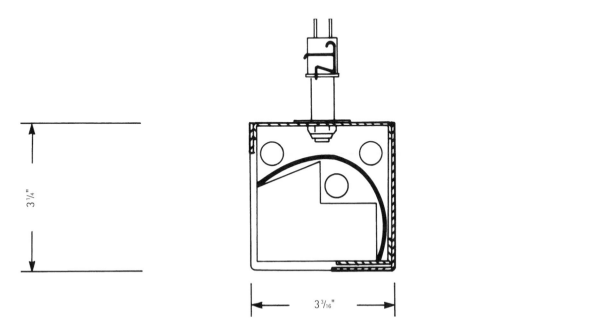

Figure 12.25 Track mounted T4 tungsten halogen wallwasher

Wallwashing is also produced by diffuse-source, fluorescent-lamp wallwash systems. The inability of a diffuse source to project a high intensity toward the bottom of a wall usually results in a bright area at the top of the wall and a rapid falloff of luminance thereafter. Sophisticated reflector systems with a wide aperture help to solve this problem. Fluorescent wallwash systems are more energy-effective than their incandescent counterparts (figure 12.26).

Figure 12.26 Fluorescent perimeter wallwash luminaire

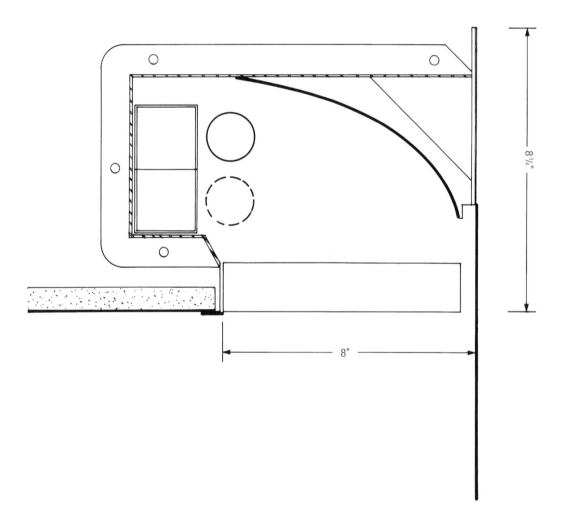

Continuous slots

Continuous slots are located in the ceiling next to the wall and can enclose other kinds of wallwash luminaires (figure 12.27). The ceiling is deemphasized, while vertical surfaces such as walls, murals, and draperies are given prominence.

Figure 12.27 Lighted cornice

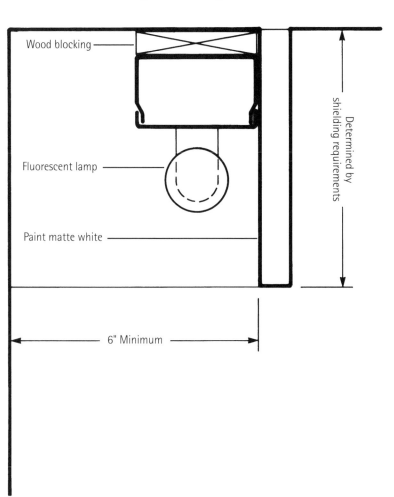

Wood blocking

Fluorescent lamp

Paint matte white

Determined by shielding requirements

6" Minimum

INCANDESCENT

Wallwashing may also be provided by individual directional lamps mounted in a continuous linear raceway. These systems require the use of a directional point source that is able to project its light over the length of the wall (figures 12.28 and 12.29).

Figure 12.28 Typical incandescent raceway wallwasher: architectural construction

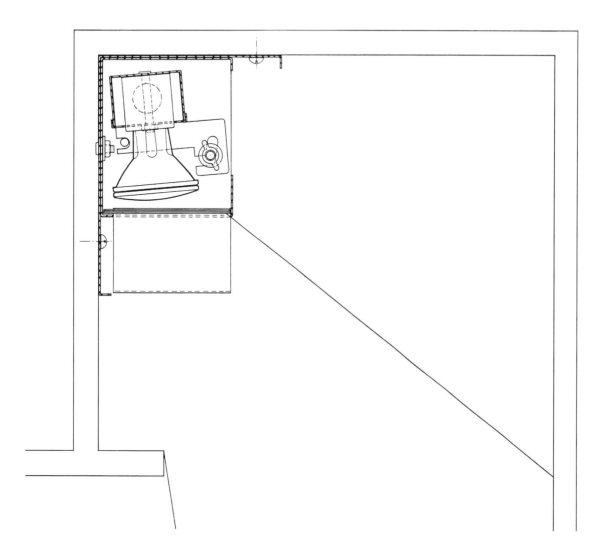

Lamps are typically mounted close to the surface being lighted. The distance from the lamps to the wall and the distance between the lamps is determined by a full-size mock-up. Excessive lamp spacing will cause scallops. To minimize scallops, the following maximum lamp spacing serves as a guide:

for PAR flood lamps: maximum spacing is 0.8 x the distance to the wall

for R flood lamps: maximum spacing is 1.0 x the distance to the wall

Figure 12.29 Typical incandescent raceway wallwasher: manufactured product includes linear spread lens to distribute evenly across the wall and baffle to shield the view of the lamps along the length of the trough

FLUORESCENT

To provide approximate visual uniformity when using fluorescent lamps to light walls, display boards, or draperies, place the channels in a 1:4 ratio of distance away from the lighted surface to the distance apart from each other (figure 12.30). Luminance at the bottom will be about one-tenth the luminance at the top. For many applications, the resulting perception of near uniformity is adequate.

Figure 12.30 Uniformity is slightly improved when the floor has a high reflectance source or has a high reflectance border at the wall. (The minimum discernible variation luminance is approximately 2 to 1.)

Figure 12.31 Illumination from vertical light strips

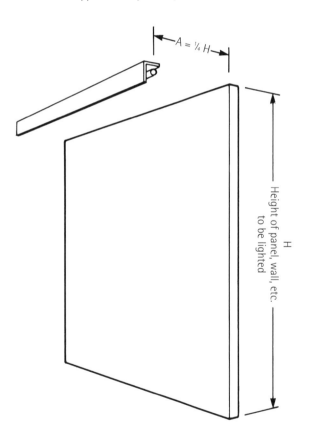

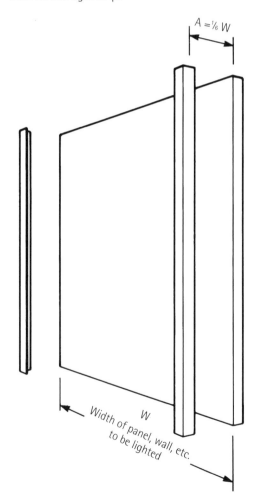

To minimize specular reflections near the top of lighted vertical surfaces, a matte (diffuse) finish is essential. Specular surfaces such as mirrors and highly-polished marble cannot be lighted, because the light received on the surface is reflected down to the floor and no impression of brightness is created.

Luminaires placed closer than the 1 to 4 ratio, called grazing light, emphasize surface texture and low sculptural relief. But this may also increase the awareness of irregularities and lack of flatness of the lighted surface. Additional frontal light, direct or indirect, reduces this problem by filling in the minute shadows cast by the irregularities.

Vertical light strips are used for wash light when the ceiling height is low and the placement of overhead equipment is difficult (figure 12.31), but great care must be taken to avoid glare.

When fluorescent lamps are used, the cross-section dimension of the luminaire can be made smaller by locating the ballasts remotely. The shielding angle for blocking the view of the vertical light source is even more critical than it is for horizontal slots and valances (figure 12.32).

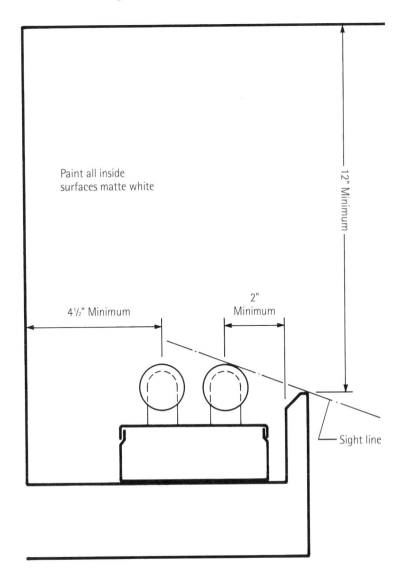

Figure 12.32 Shielding angle for vertical light strips

Fluorescent continuous slots and vertical light strips are useful wallwashing techniques only when nonuniformity of luminance is acceptable. The close placement of the light source to the wall that is usually required makes the luminance on the wall much higher near the source.

Indirect Luminaires

"Washing" with light has come to mean the use of a continuous row of lighting devices located at the edge of the "washed" surface. Ceilings are usually not "washed;" they are lighted by devices known as indirect luminaires or uplights (figure 12.33). These are suspended from the ceiling by stems or cables, mounted on top of furniture that is at least head-high, attached to walls, columns, or the tops of floor stands. Some provide indirect light only; others, usually stem-mounted, also have a downlight component.

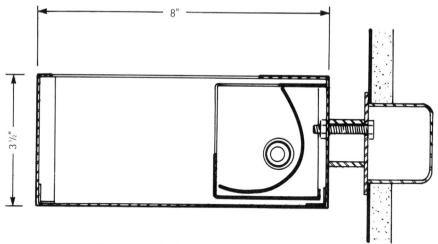

Figure 12.33 Typical tungsten halogen uplight

Compact-source indirect luminaires often use linear sources, such as T3 and T4 tungsten-halogen lamps, ED18 and T18 metal-halide lamps, and E18 and E25 HPS lamps. Diffuse-source indirect luminaires use compact, T8 and T12 fluorescent lamps.

Indirect fluorescent luminaires were developed primarily to provide an evenly-illuminated ceiling similar to the recessed luminous ceiling (figure 12.34). The intent is the same: to create an evenly illuminated ceiling plane without variations in luminance on the ceiling surface.

Indirect luminaires are especially suitable for high ceiling rooms which permit the luminaires to be far enough below the ceiling to avoid "hot spots." If they are mounted too close to the ceiling surface, the variations in light and dark will often be unpleasant and disturbing; the ceiling surface will become a series of hot spots and dark shadows instead of an evenly illuminated plane.

People perceive a greater quantity of light in a given area when they can see where the light is coming from. Pendant-mounted fluorescent uplights that provide a source of luminance from below give an impression of increased illuminance. Uplights that are completely opaque (dark) from below yield an impression of lower illuminance.

Furniture-mounted indirect luminaires incorporate an indirect lighting element onto the top of furniture or free-standing partitions (figure 12.35). They are usually mounted with their apertures above average eye height (5 ft 8 in.) in order to avoid glare. Furniture and partition layouts must accommodate the luminaire spacing required to achieve uniform ceiling luminance.

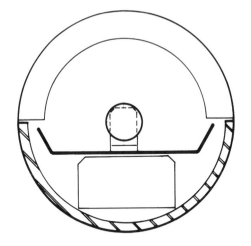

Figure 12.34 Typical fluorescent indirect luminaire

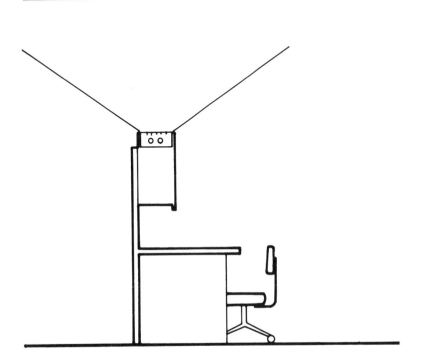

Figure 12.35 Furniture-mounted indirect luminaire

Wall- or ceiling-mounted indirect luminaires are mounted to walls and columns (figure 12.36). Like wallwashers, they have an asymmetric light distribution that produces a sweep of light across the ceiling and avoids hot spots and spills on adjacent surfaces.

Coves

Coves are another method of providing ambient light in high ceiling rooms. Their luminaires direct light toward the ceiling plane which, like a washed wall, becomes a large-area diffusing source. Coves are useful to supplement more energy-effective lighting methods, such as recessed downlighting systems.

Figure 12.36 Column-mounted indirect luminaire

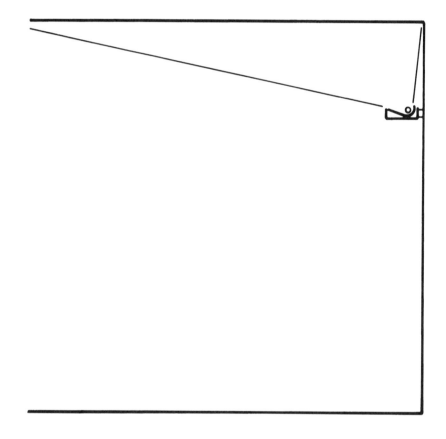

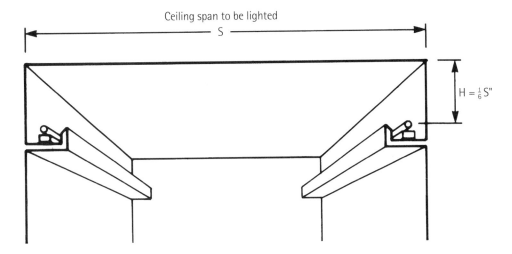

Ceiling span to be lighted

S

$H = \frac{1}{6}S''$

Figure 12.37 A 1:4 placement ratio is applicable when light is from one side only. A 1:6 ratio is applicable when light is from two or four sides.

The placement ratios in figure 12.37 are intended to produce approximate visual uniformity. Specular reflections are minimized if the ceiling surface is a high-reflectance matte or satin finish.

Custom-built coves are constructed of wood, plastic, or metal. A glass or plastic bottom is sometimes used to introduce a downward component of light for sparkle.

Fluorescent lamps or cold-cathode tubes are commonly used in coves because they are energy-efficient, linear sources. All lamps must be of the same color and it is best that they are of the same tube diameter and have the same manufacturer to prevent color variations on the lighted surfaces. Lamps of similar light output per foot of length are also desirable to avoid noticeable variations in luminance on the illuminated surfaces.

When the lamp mounting channels are placed end-to-end, a noticeable gap in light occurs because the lampholders take up space and the lamps emit less light near their ends. The shadows caused by this gap may be avoided by staggering the mounting channels so that they overlap by at least three inches. Prefabricated staggered channels with overlapping lamps achieve the same result (figure 12.38).

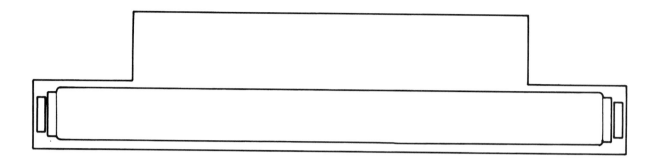

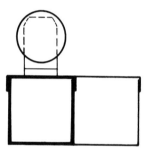

Figure 12.38 One-lamp fluorescent staggered channel

When space limits the cove design so that the source is too close to the adjacent wall and ceiling, then these surfaces will appear excessively bright. Shields can be incorporated into the design to intercept some of the light and prevent it from reaching the upper wall. The upper wall will be lighted by reflection from the cove lip and ceiling, reducing the light gradients (figure 12.39).

To insure uniformity on the ceiling plane, the distance from the centerline of the lamp to the ceiling must be a minimum of 12 in. for rapid-start lamps and 18 in. for HO and VHO lamps. Curved transitions between adjacent surfaces will produce more gradual, softer gradients.

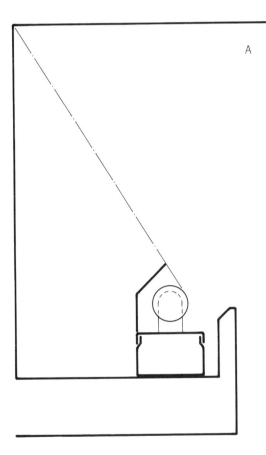

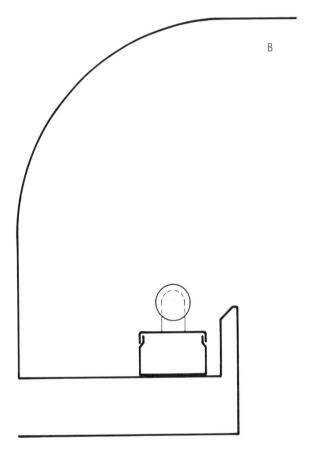

Figure 12.39 A. External shield
B. Curved contour

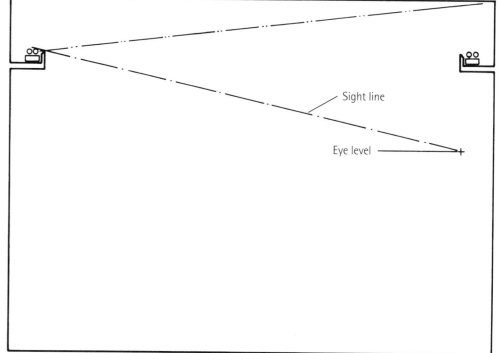

Sight line

Eye level ——+

Figure 12.40 Cove shielding

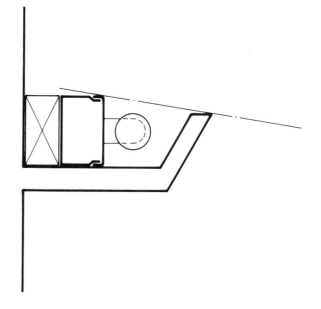

Figure 12.41 Typical cove

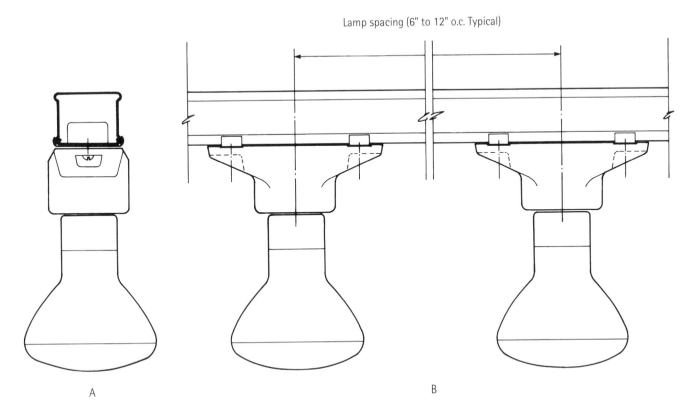

Lamp spacing (6" to 12" o.c. Typical)

A

B

Figure 12.42 Typical incandescent lamp raceway

A sightline analysis determines the dimensions of the cove lip and the placement of the lamps. On a section drawing through the cove, draw a line between a viewer's eye, located at the farthest viewing point, and the edge of the cove lip. The lip of the cove is designed to shield the lamp at normal viewing angles but must not interfere with the distribution of light across the ceiling (figures 12.40 and 12.41).

When incandescent directional sources are used in a linear array, the beam axis is aimed at a point two-thirds of the way across the lighted surface. This provides relative uniformity of illumination (figure 12.42).

OBJECT LIGHTS

Adjustable object lights, also called *accent lights,* provide a symmetric distribution of light aimed at one or several objects. They use a directional source such as AR, MR, or PAR lamps. These "spot lights" are used to provide focal glow and add contrast to a setting.

Recessed adjustable object lights may have a horizontal rotation stop to prevent wires from tangling as the lamp is rotated. Vertical adjustment is from 0° to between 35° and 45°. The best track-mounted adjustable object lights are designed to rotate slightly more than 360°; inferior luminaires have a "blind spot" with rotation limited to between 300° and 350°. Track luminaires have a greater range of vertical adjustment than recessed equipment (figures 12.43 through 12.45).

Figure 12.43 Recessed incandescent adjustable object light

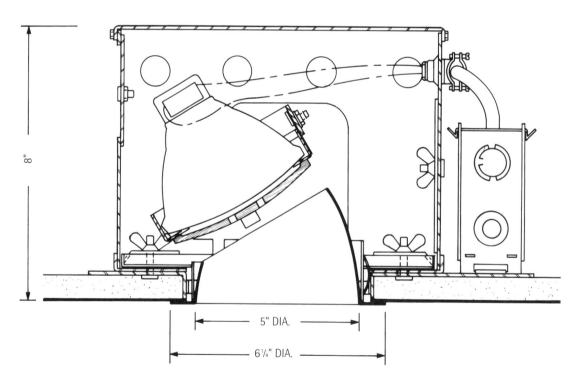

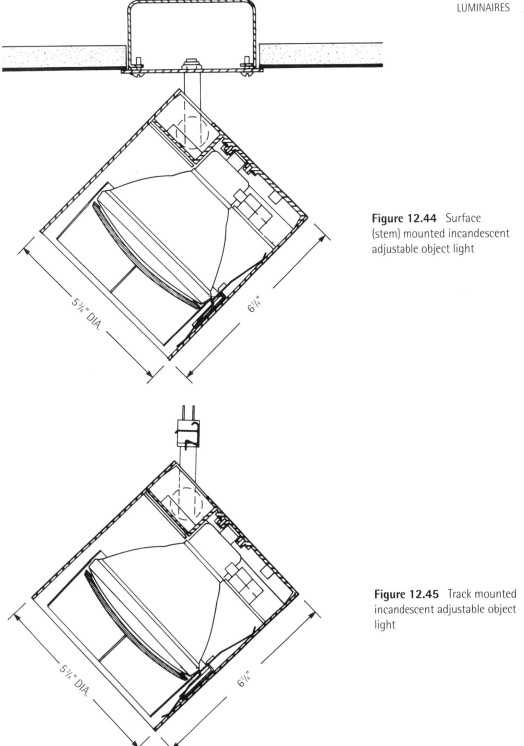

Figure 12.44 Surface (stem) mounted incandescent adjustable object light

Figure 12.45 Track mounted incandescent adjustable object light

Whether surface-, pendant-, track-mounted, or recessed, adjustable object light housings are usually designed to avoid undue interference with the beam pattern of reflectorized-lamp sources.

The least expensive luminaires may lack any luminance control, and the source glare can be uncomfortable. Better-quality lighting fixtures provide greater degrees of luminance control, typically using an open reflector in recessed equipment and baffles or cube-cell louvers in surface-, pendant-, and track-mounted luminaires.

Louvers intercept some of the light in the beam. Cross-baffles are a more efficient method of shielding lamps from the eyes because of less light loss. Cube-cell louvers reduce light output as much as 50 percent.

When used for artwork and larger objects, object lights are also supplied with a linear spread lens to modify the distribution and soften the edge of the beam. Linear spread lenses are typically made of borosilicate glass with a fluted pattern; they usually are designed to spread the beam in one direction only and are rotated as required during focusing. Without the spread lens, the same directional light source provides a symmetrical concentrated beam-spread suited to smaller objects and those that require "punch."

Object lights contribute to a moderate to high contrast setting because they introduce nonuniform illumination. Medium- to wide-beam lamps give moderate contrast; narrow-beam lamps give high contrast.

TASK LIGHTS

Task luminaires bring the light source close to the surface being lighted. They are useful for work surfaces of systems-furniture, which may receive insufficient light from an overall lighting system because of shadows from vertical partitions and furniture-mounted high shelves and cabinets.

Local-task luminaires are often energy-effective and useful for reducing reflections in VDTs. Task lighting uses less power because the source is closer to the surface being lighted. Task luminaires can provide the illuminance required for paper-based visual tasks while allowing the ambient light to be of a lower illuminance and decreasing the chances of distracting VDT screen reflections.

Task luminaires are often mounted under a cabinet or shelf that is directly over the work station (figure 12.46). This location is in the offending zone, however, producing veiling reflections on the work surface. This is eliminated by using optical lenses that block the perpendicular light rays and convert them to rays that fall on the task from the side and do not cause veiling reflections.

Adjustable task luminaires are usually mounted at one side of the task. An adjustable arm permits positioning the luminaire to suit the task, maximizing task visibility. An asymmetric light distribution is sometimes incorporated to direct light more uniformly over the task area.

Figure 12.46 Sometimes undercabinet or undershelf task luminaires cause veiling reflections. This is eliminated by using a lateral lens.

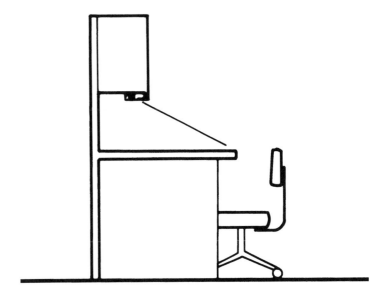

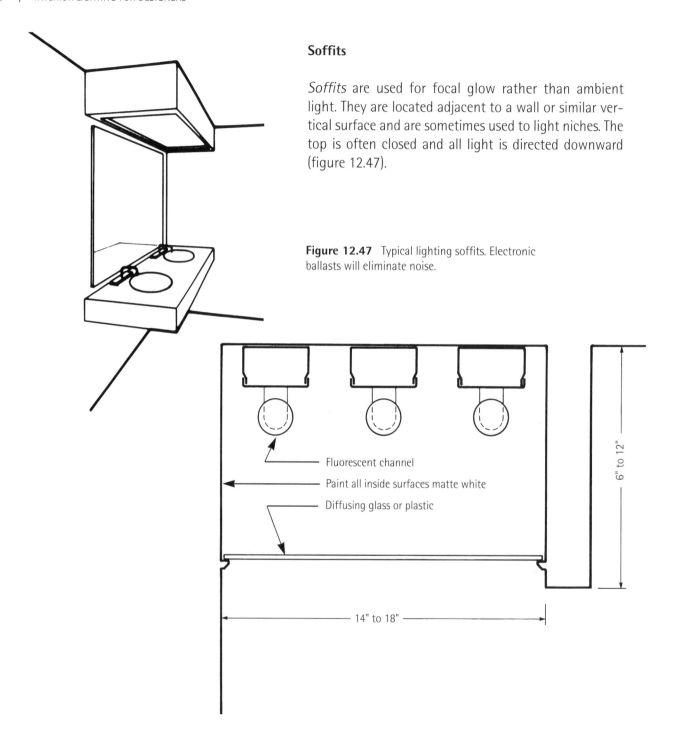

Soffits

Soffits are used for focal glow rather than ambient light. They are located adjacent to a wall or similar vertical surface and are sometimes used to light niches. The top is often closed and all light is directed downward (figure 12.47).

Figure 12.47 Typical lighting soffits. Electronic ballasts will eliminate noise.

Fluorescent channel

Paint all inside surfaces matte white

Diffusing glass or plastic

6" to 12"

14" to 18"

Over work areas, reflectors increase the use of light; open louvers or lightly etched plastic or glass perform best. Matte finishes for work surfaces minimize specular reflections.

For make-up and grooming areas, a translucent diffusing panel lights faces from many directions, minimizing harsh shadows. A light-colored counter top is of further help as it reflects light back toward the face.

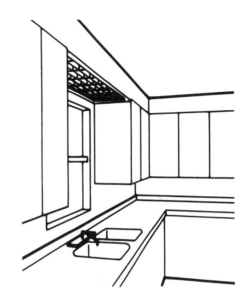

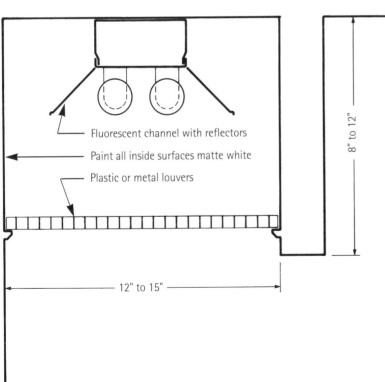

Fluorescent channel with reflectors

Paint all inside surfaces matte white

Plastic or metal louvers

8" to 12"

12" to 15"

Low Brackets

Low brackets are used for lighting special task areas such as counter tops and writing or reading surfaces (figure 12.48).

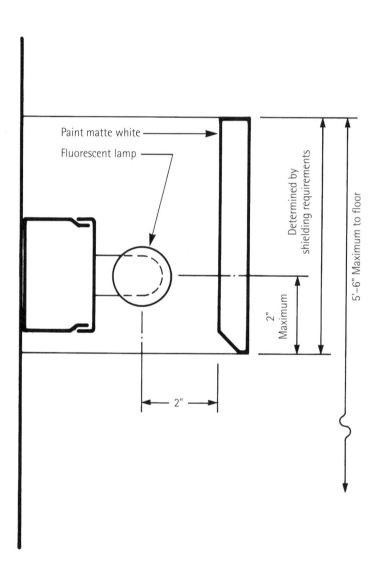

Figure 12.48 Lighted low bracket

MULTIDIRECTIONAL LUMINAIRES

Direct-indirect Luminaires

Direct-indirect luminaires provide a combination of direct lighting and indirect lighting, with all of the attributes of both systems. The sharper shadows created by direct systems are softened by the diffuse indirect light. The increased ceiling luminance creates a greater diffusion of light in the space. Interreflections reduce ceiling plane luminance variations and the resulting VDT screen reflections.

Valances

Valances are used over windows, usually combined with draperies. They provide indirect uplight that reflects off the ceiling for ambient illumination and provide "washing" downlight for the drapery or artwork (figure 12.49).

Figure 12.49 Lighted valance

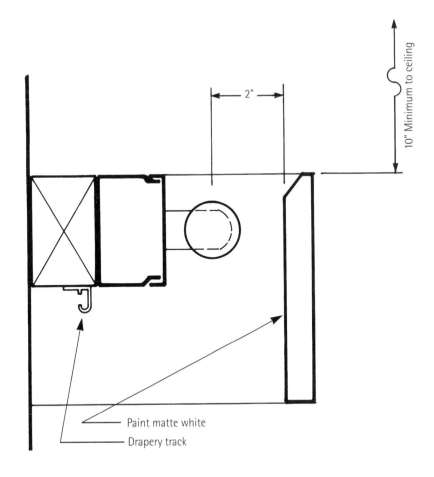

2"

10" Minimum to ceiling

Paint matte white
Drapery track

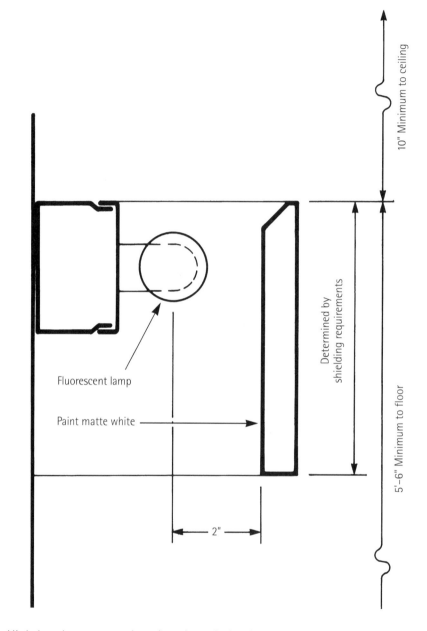

Figure 12.50 Lighted high bracket

Fluorescent lamp

Paint matte white

10" Minimum to ceiling

Determined by shielding requirements

5'–6" Minimum to floor

2"

High brackets are used on interior windowless walls. They provide both up- and downlight for ambient illuminance or specific emphasis on surfaces and artwork (figure 12.51).

Decorative Luminaires

Decorative luminaires are used to provide ambient lighting in areas where their appearance contributes to the design harmony of the space. They are available as ceiling-mounted globes and diffusers, suspended chandeliers and pendants, wall-mounted lanterns and sconces, and floor-mounted torchères.

The majority of decorative luminaires produces multidirectional distribution. Some have optical control hidden inside their decorative exteriors to provide a specific distribution of light.

CHAPTER 13

DESIGN

Lighting design is a process. Specifically, it is the process of integrating light into the fabric of architecture.

Successful lighting is integrated into both the architectural concept and the physical structure. The lighting concept is integrated into the architectural concept in two ways: (1) by reinforcing the activity in the space and (2) by highlighting areas to be prominent and deemphasizing areas to be subdued.

Lighting equipment is integrated into the physical structure of the building in three ways: (1) by selecting visible elements that harmonize with the design motif, (2) by incorporating hidden elements with the architectural forms and surfaces, and (3) by coordinating electrical systems with the other mechanical systems of the building.

VISUAL CLARITY

People search for simplification of their visual fields when faced with demanding tasks and activities. In an environment that is used for complex activities, too many visual stimuli or too many patterns will result in an overload condition. One becomes tense and frustrated and has a diminished ability to perform a complex task.

When reading with music playing nearby, the sound competes yet allows comprehension of simpler passages. At a complex portion of the material,

Figure 13.1 Clutter in the visual field is analogous to
noise or static in acoustical design.

where the reading task becomes more absorbing, one instinctively turns the
volume down or off. In doing so, the amount of information that is compet-
ing for attention is reduced.

Meaningless or confusing luminances in a space are similarly distracting. The
brain becomes overstimulated, spending additional time and energy sorting
out conflicting information. This is called *visual clutter* (figure 13.1); it is
analogous to *noise* or *static* in acoustical design.

As the activity or task becomes more complex—more loaded—visual clutter
becomes more distracting. Visual clarity affects worker performance, particularly when the worker is faced with demanding—more stimulating—tasks.

Visual clutter undermines long-term performance of complex tasks. It is the lighting designer's role to simplify the visual process and the environmental background so that distortions and irrelevant clutter are minimized. The goal is to reduce distractions so that the environment assists one's concentration and conserves one's energy for more productive tasks and activity demands.

People define the environment through a process of additive perception. Information is gathered by scanning the boundaries of a space, thereby forming a concept of direction and limits. When the lighting system is designed to establish the physical boundaries of a space, it helps people to maintain a sense of direction and an understanding of spatial form with minimal distraction from the environment.

Carefully organized luminance patterns and repetitive luminaire layouts are useful techniques for simplifying the processes of orientation and activity comprehension. Organized luminaire patterns of matching-size apertures with matching-luminance reflectors further reduce confusion.

An irregular luminaire pattern on the ceiling confuses orientation and spatial understanding. One reacts negatively not because tasks are poorly illuminated or because glare produces discomfort, but because of the distractions produced by the luminaire placement. When the luminaire pattern directs attention to the ceiling, one must overcome the distraction and consciously focus attention on the more meaningful visual stimuli in the room and on the activities.

In addition to creating organized patterns, it is desirable to have all of the luminaire apertures be of the same dimension and of the same finish. This kind of environment reduces the effort required to discover in it or impose upon it regularity or meaning. A greater certainty is felt in an organized environment and therefore less attention is paid to it.

Lighting designers are ceiling designers. Lighting layout drawings include locations of luminaires, sprinkler heads, air diffusers, return grills, smoke detectors, loudspeakers, and so forth. To prevent visual clutter, these ceiling elements are organized in an invisible "grid."

Figure 13.2 Scallops

ARCHITECTURAL SURFACES

Lighting helps to define and separate the major surfaces of a space if the shape of the light distribution relates to the form of the surface. For example, a wall or ceiling lighted with a "wash" of light will approximate the form and dimension of that surface.

Scallop patterns and similar irregularities are to be minimized. Except for special situations, a lighted surface is not intended to be perceived as a form or a surface that is intersected by arbitrary patterns of light; it is intended to be perceived as a unified form.

Scallops of light are incompatible with the plane form of the wall surface. Because the eye is involuntarily attracted to areas that contrast with the ambient luminance, the result is a disorienting pattern of superimposed light that confuses perception of the visual form of the wall (figure 13.2).

Figure 13.3 Linear wash of light.

A linear wash of light facilitates clear visual separation of the wall and ceiling surfaces—borders. The evenly lighted wall is perceived as an integrated visual form (figure 13.3). The same is true of the evenly lighted ceiling plane.

Reliance upon formulas to provide a specific value of illuminance on the horizontal plane disregards the importance of vertical surfaces. Consequently, luminaires used for ambient illumination cast unanticipated or undesired light patterns on the vertical surfaces or leave them in relative darkness. The result is often monotonous and uninteresting.

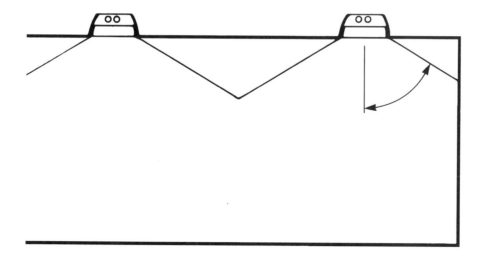

Figure 13.4 Sharp cut-off luminaires produce shadows along the top of an adjacent wall.

When luminaires are placed in a nonuniform pattern, it is helpful to antici-pate where light will intersect adjacent wall surfaces. In some installations, specific wall areas have a higher or lower luminance than the rest of the space. It then becomes advisable to adjust the wall finish to conform with the overall design intent or to provide supplemental wall lighting.

Fluorescent downlights with sharp luminance cutoff show a sharp cutoff on adjacent walls. This results in a shadow line along the top of the wall which often causes a space to be perceived as dimly lighted (figure 13.4). Wallwashers or a continuous perimeter trough system will fill in this shadow. A similar result is achieved by using a high–reflectance wall finish in the shadow area with a darker finish below it.

To alleviate scallops when using open reflector downlights, use down-light/wallwash reflectors at the perimeter as indicated in figure 12.18.

Irregular patterns of light are sometimes desirable. A shaft of sunlight has intrinsic value, as do some electric light patterns that avoid a relationship to the physical form of a space. The value of these irregular patterns of light is that they serve as a temporary visual stimulant.

Irregular light patterns are also successful when they relate to an appealing attribute of the physical space, such as a painting, sculpture, plant, or architectural detail. Unless specifically intended, however, it is desirable to avoid these irregular light patterns.

LIGHTING VERTICAL SURFACES

The primary emphasis of lighted space is to be within the visual field, establishing patterns that are directly related to one's priorities for defining space (orientation) and for defining activities (participation) (figure 13.5).

Figure 13.5 Low-brightness louvers minimize clutter on the ceiling and establish the primary focus in the activity portions of the visual field.

Vertical surfaces require special attention: They are the first surfaces that are seen upon entering a space. Vertical surfaces define the boundaries of the space; they are used for displaying works of art and communicating a message. Clear perception of the vertical surfaces contributes to the overall impact of the design.

Matte Surfaces

Three kinds of lighting systems are available for *uniform* vertical surface illumination: (1) point–source wallwash, (2) point–source continuous linear wallwash, and (3) diffuse–source continuous linear wallwash.

Point–source wallwash luminaires. The greater the ceiling height, the farther from the wall that luminaires are located to provide uniform illumination from top to bottom. For uniform lighting from side to side, the "square rule" applies: Luminaires are located on centers closer than or equal to their distance from the wall. The center-to-center spacing varies with the ceiling height and the light intensity desired on the surface.

Point–source continuous linear wallwash systems. Uniform lighting is also provided by a *grazing* light from luminaires located close to the surface being illuminated. A line voltage incandescent or HID lamp is used for this application. Low–voltage incandescent lamps will work, but with their tighter beamspreads, more lamps are required for uniform lighting.

The same "square rule" applies: The lamps need to be spaced on centers closer than or equal to their distance from the wall. Again, the center-to-center spacing varies with the ceiling height and the light intensity desired on the wall surface. The goal is also the same: to provide even illuminance both horizontally across the wall and vertically from top to bottom.

A full scale mock-up is advised to test for the following:

1. Beamspread overlap (spot beamspreads usually require a spread lens).
2. The optimum distance away from the wall and on-center spacing.
3. The trough height, depth, and finishes required.

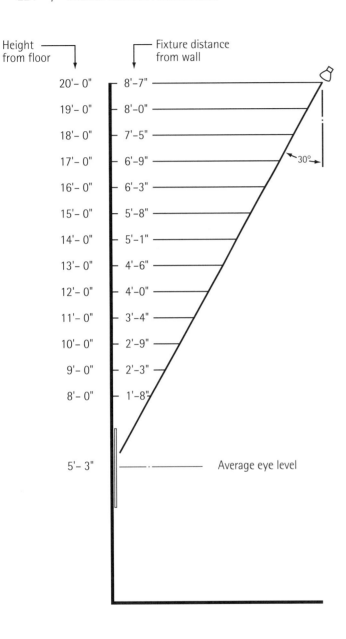

Height from floor — Fixture distance from wall

Height from floor	Fixture distance from wall
20'- 0"	8'-7"
19'- 0"	8'-0"
18'- 0"	7'-5"
17'- 0"	6'-9"
16'- 0"	6'-3"
15'- 0"	5'-8"
14'- 0"	5'-1"
13'- 0"	4'-6"
12'- 0"	4'-0"
11'- 0"	3'-4"
10'- 0"	2'-9"
9'- 0"	2'-3"
8'- 0"	1'-8"
5'- 3"	Average eye level

30°

Figure 13.6 Typical luminaire mounting locations with 30° aiming angle

4. The necessity of baffles to shield the lamps from view along the length of the trough.

A full size mock-up is the only way to ensure that the finished installation will achieve the desired illuminance value and avoid scallops and striations at the top of the wall.

Diffuse-source continuous wallwash systems. The diffuse fluorescent source is good at providing even lighting across the wall in the horizontal direction, but is inadequate at providing even illuminance vertically from top to bottom. Reflectors help to mitigate the problem, but fail to solve it. The use of a fluorescent wallwash system is reserved for low ceiling areas with heights from 8 ft to 10 ft.

For *nonuniform* wall lighting, point-source object lights are ideal. When more than one luminaire is required because of the size of the object to be lighted, the "square rule" applies once again: The luminaires are spaced on centers closer than or equal to the distance away from the wall. The distance from the wall varies with the ceiling height (figure 13.6).

Specular Surfaces

When providing light for glossy surfaces, such as glass, marble, high-gloss enamels, and varnishes, specular reflections complicate the placement of lighting equipment. Careful location and shielding of the source is necessary to prevent distracting reflections and veiling images.

The glossy surface is thought of as a mirror, with high luminance minimized in the reflected field of view. To reduce reflected images, remove bright elements in the reflected field of view or shield them with properly located baffles or screens.

People, objects, and other surfaces in the room become "secondary light sources." If they are located in the reflected field of view, they cause distracting or veiling reflections in glossy surfaces. In some cases, the perception of varnished or glass-covered paintings, or of marble and other specular materials, is partially or completely obscured by such reflected images.

Luminance Balance

It is desirable to light opposite walls in a space, establishing luminance balance. *Balance* is different from *symmetry:* Lighting the opposing walls in the same manner is unnecessary, although one may choose to do so. For example, one wall will be uniformly illuminated with a wallwash system and the other will be nonuniformly illuminated with object lights.

It is also desirable to balance the perimeter of a space with its center. If a room's breadth is greater than its height, it is impossible to light it successfully solely from the walls. When diffusely lighted walls are distant from each other in a low ceiling space and they are the only source of illumination, the resulting environment is bland and gloomy. Downlighting is added to the center, otherwise all persons and objects in the center of the space will be in silhouette.

TASK LIGHTING

Lighting systems in the workplace provide for accurate perception at a specific task area (a desk, counter, machine, or workbench). This is achieved by using one of two lighting methods: (1) a general-ambient approach or (2) a task-ambient approach.

- *General-ambient systems* provide a uniform quantity of light throughout a space. When the task location is apt to vary widely or when the

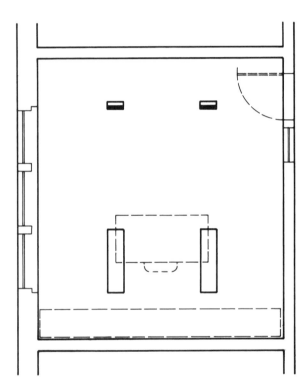

Figure 13.7 Nonuniform office lighting layout

space is apt to be reconfigured frequently, this approach is often used.

- *Task-ambient systems* are more energy-effective. Higher values of *task* illuminance are provided for the workplane while lower values of *ambient* illuminance are provided for surrounding areas.

Task-ambient systems are appropriate in rooms where task areas are permanently located, such as private offices, factories, laboratories, and stores. Task lighting is provided where needed, with the remaining space lighted for more casual activities (figure 13.7).

Typically, an ambient (direct, uniform) lighting system that provides lower illuminance is supplemented by task-oriented luminaires mounted on or near the furniture. Areas surrounding visual tasks need less illuminance than the visual tasks. It is recommended that the ambient illuminance be at least 33 percent of the task illuminance for comfort and ease of adaptation.

With the task-ambient approach, it is critical to design for the task *first* (focal glow), *then* supplement the task lighting with the ambient room lighting.

VDTs

Ambient lighting causes visibility problems in the VDT screen. Almost all VDT screens have a dark, glossy or satin surface that reflects images of the surrounding space; the operator will see luminaires, ceilings, walls, or windows as elements of excessive luminance reflected in the screen (figure 13.8).

VDT tasks often require an almost horizontal line of sight when viewing the screen. Because of this, a large area of the ceiling will be in the field of view in large open offices. It is critical to minimize variation in luminance on the ceiling plane in order to prevent discomfort glare (figure 13.9).

Paper-based Tasks

Almost all office work involves paper-based tasks. Paper documents are referenced for word processing, order entry, information retrieval, and computer-aided design. In addition to the lighting requirements for VDT tasks, lighting for paper-based visual tasks must also be considered.

Ambient lighting provides overall illumination for circulation, provides balance between the VDT task luminance and its surround, and provides a part or all of the illuminance for paper-based tasks.

With well-designed direct luminaires, the luminance of the aperture will be equivalent to the luminance of the ceiling. The result is a lack of luminance contrast between the reflected image of the luminaire and the ceiling.

In a well-designed indirect lighting system, the light received on the ceiling plane will exhibit an even luminance; this yields a lack of luminance contrast in the VDT screen. As long as the luminance seen in the VDT is uniform across the screen, minimal interference will occur in the discerning of screen characters.

The two systems differ in their illuminance and chances of veiling reflections on paper-based visual tasks. Office partitions block some overhead

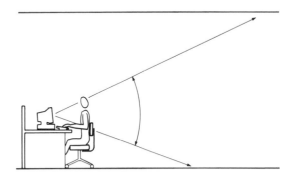

Figure 13.8 Normal range for reflected line of sight angles 65° to 110° from vertical

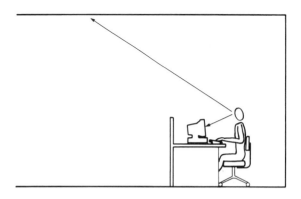

Figure 13.9 A large area of the ceiling is within the field of view when viewing a VDT

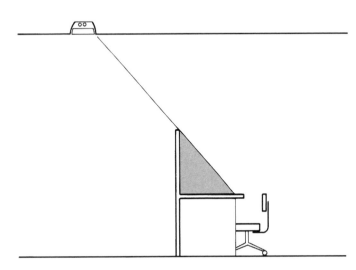

Figure 13.10 Some areas have noticeable shadows from office partitions, especially when partitions are located on three sides of the work surface

light, preventing it from reaching work surfaces. Depending on the location of direct luminaires, some areas will be left in shadow (figure 13.10). Well-designed indirect lighting, because it produces even illuminance overhead, softens and reduces this shadowing.

AMBIENT LIGHTING

Ambient lighting is provided by two basic methods: (1) direct lighting, where overhead luminaires provide a downward light distribution, and (2) indirect lighting, where pendant luminaires provide upward light that is then reflected from the ceiling.

Direct Lighting

With *direct lighting*, luminaires are arranged according to the ambient lighting requirements for either uniform or nonuniform distribution over the horizontal workplane.

For direct ambient lighting, the *spacing criteria,* or *spacing to mounting height ratio (S/MH)* provided by the luminaire manufacturer gives the maximum recommended spacing between luminaires to achieve uniform, ambient lighting.

S/MH is the center-to-center distance between luminaires ("spacing") based on their mounting height above the workplane. For example, if the S/MH = 2, then for an 8 ft ceiling height,

MH = 8'0"– 2'6" to the workplane = 5'6"

S = 5'6" × 2 = 11 ft center-to-center maximum spacing from the center of one luminaire to the center of the next (figure 13.11).

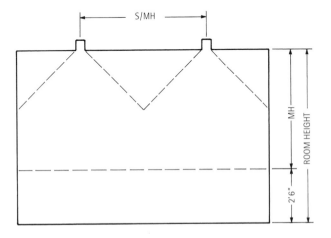

Figure 13.11 Spacing to mounting height ratio

For rectilinear luminaires, S/MH is expressed as "parallel" or "perpendicular," indicating the spacing–to–mounting–height ratio in either the direction parallel or the direction perpendicular to the length of the luminaires.

To maintain uniformity of light intensity over a large work area, avoid exceeding the manufacturer's recommended maximum S/MH. Maximum distance from the last row of luminaires to the wall is to be one-half to one-third the spacing in the room to prevent a falloff in illuminance near the walls (figures 13.12 to 13.14).

Even with this reduced spacing, work surface illuminance near the walls is often only half that measured in the center of the room because of wall surface absorption. In critical seeing areas, supplementary luminaires are used (figure 13.15).

Luminaire Patterns

Whether providing uniform or nonuniform lighting, it is advisable to organize luminaires in a *pattern* based upon an invisible grid that is related to the architecture. If the S/MH yields a 10'0" dimension, for example, and the room is 78'0" long, a good solution is eight equal spaces measured to the center line of each luminaire (figure 13.16). A halfspace at either end will ensure adequate illuminance at the walls. In the other direction, which is 36'0", four equal spaces work well.

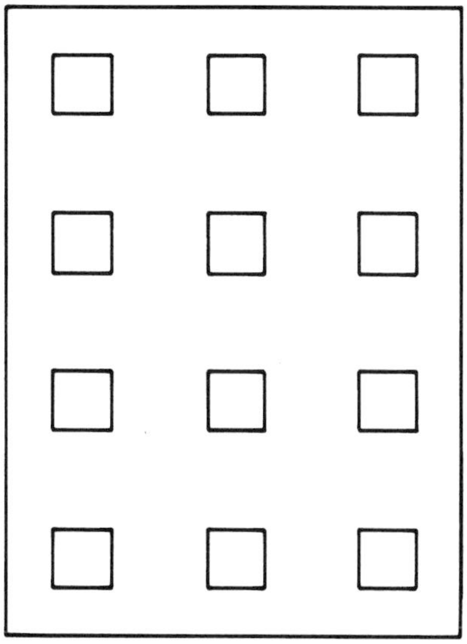

It is unnecessary to fill each cross-point of the invisible grid in order to maintain the order supplied by that pattern. Note that with round-aperture luminaires, spacing at the perimeter is half the

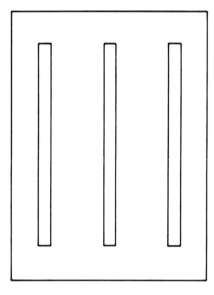

Figure 13.12 Linear pattern, rectilinear luminaire

Figure 13.13 Regular pattern, rectilinear luminaire

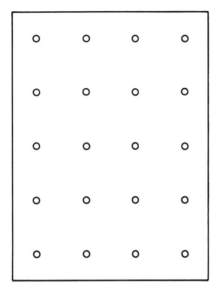

Figure 13.14 Regular pattern, round aperture luminaire

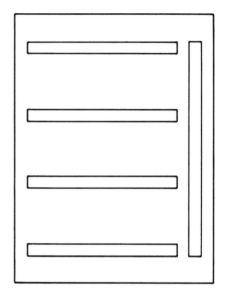

Figure 13.15 Supplementary illumination near the wall

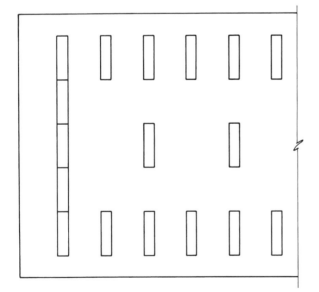

Figure 13.16 1 x 4 luminaire pattern

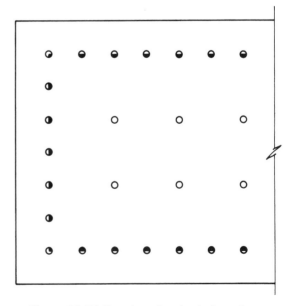

Figure 13.17 Round aperture luminaire pattern

spacing of the room to provide uniform wall lighting with combination downlight/wallwash luminaires (figure 13.17).

Indirect Lighting

The primary use of indirect lighting is to create evenly luminous ceilings that reduce VDT screen reflections. For indirect lighting to be successful, luminance differences must be minimal. If bright patches of higher luminance occur, they are reflected in the VDT screen, causing a distracting background.

A well-designed indirect luminaire has a wide distribution. Multiple luminaires are located so that their light output will be evenly distributed across the ceiling without "hot spots" or areas of high luminance (figure 13.18).

To avoid distracting luminance variation in VDT screens, the recommended variation in ceiling luminance is a ratio of less than 4 to 1. Additionally, the average luminance of any 2 ft by 2 ft area of the ceiling is less than 850 cd/m^2 measured at any angle. This same limit applies to windows, walls, and partitions that will be reflected in the VDT screen.

Figure 13.18 Above, properly located indirect luminaires with wide distributions produce even luminance; below, improperly located indirect luminaires with narrow distributions produce areas of uneven luminance

The goal is uniform ceiling luminance, where luminances and luminance ratios are consistent throughout the space.

The diffuse light from indirect systems, however, reduces one's sense of visual clarity, depth perception, and sense of orientation. The lack of highlight and shadow is mitigated by a greater use of surface color, wall lighting or object lighting; these techniques add visual interest, thus improving perception of the environment.

Some indirect luminaires incorporate a luminous element that is visible from below. This allows people to identify the source of light, which increases the perception of luminance in a space and introduces visual highlight into a shadowless environment.

In a small office only part of the ceiling will be reflected in the VDT screen. Here, it is advisable that the walls of the space have sufficient luminance to avoid noticeable contrast between the walls and the ceiling, a condition that will cause distracting contrast in VDT screens.

The appearance of a low-luminance direct lighting system and an indirect lighting system differs considerably. The direct system produces negligible luminance on the ceiling plane and provides great emphasis on the horizontal work surface, furniture, and floor coverings. The indirect system places luminance emphasis on the ceiling plane and deemphasizes the surfaces in the lower half of the room. The direct–indirect system accomplishes both.

Luminance Ratios

In offices, it is advisable to control the luminance variations within limits to ensure good visibility. Within these limits, variation is desirable and will make the office environment more pleasing. Luminance differences are specified in terms of the ratio between one luminance and the other (figure 13.19).

It is undesirable to maintain these ratios throughout the entire environment, however. For visual interest and distant eye focus (for eye muscle relaxation periodically throughout the day), small areas that exceed the lumi-

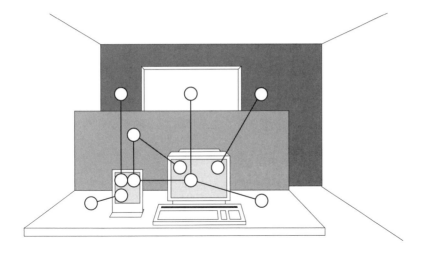

Figure 13.19 Maximum lumi-nance ratios recommended for a VDT work station.

nance ratio recommendations are advantageous. These include artwork, accent finishes on walls or floors, accent finishes on chairs and accessories, and focal lighting.

The perception of luminance depends on surface reflectance as much as it does on illuminance. Consideration of surface finish reflectances is just as important as the lighting design.

LIGHTING ART

The two principal methods for lighting art are (1) uniform illumination and (2) nonuniform illumination.

Providing *uniform* lighting for all vertical surfaces that will receive art gives prominence to the architecture; no hierarchy is established among the individual works of art, allowing viewers to select their own focus. It is possible to change objects without readjusting the lighting equipment (figure 13.20).

Providing *nonuniform* lighting focuses light on individual objects while leaving the surround in comparative darkness. This gives prominence to the art over the architecture, creating a more dramatic environment. Every time the art changes, the lighting equipment needs to be readjusted (figure 13.21).

In a space that will have frequently changing artwork or exhibits and nonuniform illumination, a flexible lighting system is appropriate. Track systems are often selected because it is easy to locate and to aim the track luminaires as needed. The track itself also serves as the wireway, providing a simple method of power distribution.

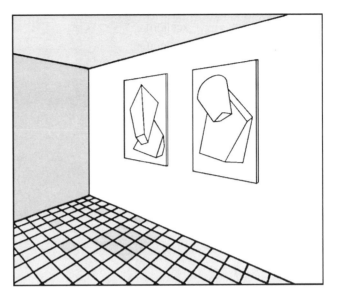

Figure 13.20 Uniform illumination for art.

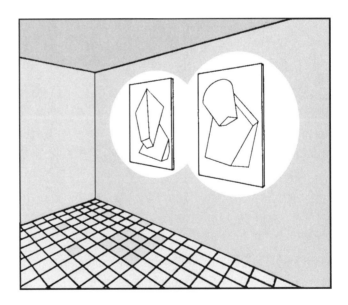

Figure 13.21 Nonuniform illumination for art

With either method for lighting art, excellent color rendering is essential for the proper appreciation of the objects. Continuous spectrum, high–color–rendering sources allow the art to be viewed under spectral distribution conditions similar to those under which it was created.

The medium, surface texture, kind of frame and enclosure (glass or plastic) of an object are considered. For flat works mounted on a horizontal surface, the optimum placement for a light source is usually at an angle of 30° from nadir (straight down) to eye level (5'6" AFF, average) (figure 13.22).

An aiming angle of less than 30° (more nearly vertical) causes disturbing shadows from the frame and distortion of the object because of exaggeration of the texture. An aiming angle greater than 30° (more nearly horizontal) results in reflected glare from the surface of the object, washing out the detail. This greater angle will also cause viewers to be standing in their own shadow and will cause the luminaire to be a source of glare to others moving through the space.

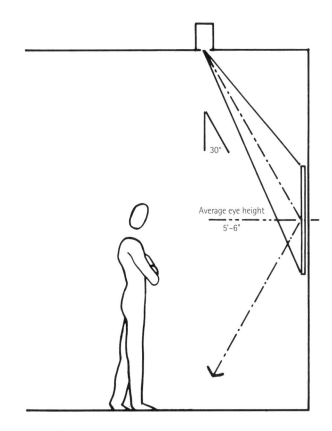

Figure 13.22 Optimum placement for lighting art

The way three-dimensional objects are lighted also affects the viewer's perception of the piece. Concentrated beams create higher contrast and deeper shadows, emphasizing form and texture. Frontal lighting between 30° to 45° from horizontal and between 30° to 45° from vertical models objects in a manner that best replicates sunlight.

Lighting a vertical surface behind an object provides a luminous backdrop to separate the object visually from its background (figure 13.23). Lighting the object from the side as well as from above provides added dimension to the piece.

Figure 13.23 Lighting vertical surface behind object

Perception is disturbed by reversing the expected relationship of highlight and shadow and lighting an object from a less conventional angle. Uplighting creates an ominous, ghoulish impression. Backlighting leaves an object in silhouette.

Conservation of Materials

Conservation of materials is a fundamental concern in the lighting of art. All organic material is susceptible to pigment change and weakening of strength from exposure to light and its accompanying heat. In the museum environment, these materials include paper, cotton, linen, parchment, leather, silk, wool, feathers, hair, dyes, oils, glues, gums, and resins — and because of similarities in chemical structure, almost all synthetic dyes and plastics.

Damage is related to wavelength. Ultraviolet (UV) radiation causes more damage, but much less UV than visible radiation is present in all light sources, including daylight. A material that is fairly *fast* (more stable) but nevertheless susceptible to damage, such as the oil in paintings, will be changed mainly by UV radiation. But more sensitive dyes and pigments, which are damaged by either UV or visible radiation, will be changed mainly by the visible radiation since it is more plentiful. In the museum environment, it is necessary to address both UV and visible radiation.

First, evaluate the daylight because it contains a much higher proportion of UV than do electric sources. The highest-quality UV filters for daylight are made of acrylic and other plastics formulated to eliminate the transmission of UV but allow the passage of visible light. They are available as self-supporting sheets used in place of glass, thin acetate applied to glass, and varnish.

White paint is also a good UV absorber. If all light entering a room is reflected at least once from a white surface, the UV problem will be solved. Titanium dioxide pigment is optimal for this purpose, but lead and zinc white are also good absorbers.

Second, evaluate the fluorescent and HID lamps. Although they emit UV radiation less strongly than daylight, all discharge lamps require UV filters. Plastic sheets of UV-absorbing material are available from manufacturers of color filters.

Incandescent lamps emit too little UV to require a filter. UV radiation from almost all incandescent lamps is less than 0.1 percent of the input wattage. Tungsten–halogen lamps emit slightly more UV below 300 nm. This is still an insignificant amount and fortunately ordinary glass, transparent to longer-wavelength UV, completely blocks this extra-short emission.

It is more difficult to limit visible radiation than to limit UV radiation because the artwork will then be left in darkness. Museum practice suggests that for oil and tempera paintings, oriental lacquer, undyed leather, horn, bone, and ivory, maximum maintained illuminance is to be 15 fc on the surface. For objects especially sensitive to light, such as drawings, prints, watercolors, tapestries, textiles, costumes, manuscripts, and almost all natural history exhibits, maximum maintained illuminance is to be 5 fc.

With the quantity of light maintained at 5 fc to 15 fc, radiant heat is also controlled to reasonable limits. Lamps should be located outside exhibition cases and ventilated with air that avoids traveling directly past the exhibits. Dichroic "cool beam" lamps are useful. Their color appearance is somewhat cooler than standard sources; however, the color rendering is undisturbed.

Time of exposure is another critical factor. *Exposure* is the simple product of illuminance and time. The same amount of damage will be produced by a large quantity of illuminance for a short time or a small quantity of illuminance for a long time. If the illuminance is halved, the rate of damage is halved. The optimal strategy is to reduce both illuminance and time of exposure.

With low illuminance values, "warm" versus "cool" colors of light are preferred. The low quantity of light is less important to the viewer than the balance of luminance between the works of art and the surround (the remaining space). The viewer's eyes must be adapted to the illuminance before the viewer enters the room.

APPENDIX

TABLE 1 Typical Color Rendering Indexes

Lamp Description	Color Rendering Index (CRI)	Kelvin Color Temperature (K)
Incandescent and Tungsten Halogen		
Incandescent	100	2,800
Light blue incandescent	100	4,000
Daylight incandescent	100	5,000
Tungsten-halogen	100	3,100
Tungsten-halogen with light blue filter	100	4,000
Tungsten-halogen with blue filter	100	5,000
Fluorescent		
Cool white	62	4,100
Cool white deluxe	87	4,200
Warm white	53	2,900
Warm white deluxe	77	2,800
Natural	55	3,450
Lite white	49	4,100
Daylight	56	6,500
Cool green	70	6,450
RE-730	70–79	3,000
RE-735	70–79	3,500
RE-74l	70–79	4,100
RE-750	70–79	5,000
RE-830	80–89	3,000
RE-835	80–89	3,500
RE-84l	80–89	4,100
RE-850	80–89	5,000
Chroma 50	92	5,000
Chroma 75	95	7,500
High Intensity Discharge		
Standard mercury	15	5,700
Mercury deluxe warm white	50	3,300
Coated mercury vapor deluxe white (250 W)	50	3,900
Deluxe high pressure sodium (70 W)	65	2,200
White high pressure sodium (95 W)	80	2,500
Standard metal halide (175 W)	65	4,200
Standard clear metal halide (175 W)	65	3,100
Standard coated metal halide (175 W)	70	3,000
Standard high wattage metal halide (1000 W)	65	3,400
High CRI warm clear metal halide (150 W)	85	3,000
High CRI neutral clear metal halide (250 W)	85	4,100
High CRI daylight clear metal halide (250 W)	92	5,500
Compact metal halide (70 W)	80	3,000
Compact metal halide (150 W)	80	4,300
Combined metal halide coated/HPS	65	3,000

TABLE 2   Lamp Designations and Properties

Proposed ANSI Lamp Designation	Design Volts	Watts	Design Life (Hrs.)	Initial Candlepower	Beamspread 50%	Beamspread 10%	Filament Shield	Notes
			Aluminum Reflector (AR) Lamps					
20AR37/NSP6	12	20	3,000	7,000	6°	—	N	
20AR37/SP20	12	20	3,000	1,400	18°	—	N	
20AR37/FL30	12	20	3,000	350	32°	—	N	
20AR48/SP10	12	20	2,000	5,000	10°	—	Y	
20AR48/G/SP10	12	20	2,000	4,500	10°	—	Y	Gold reflector
20AR48/24V/SP10	24	20	2,000	4,500	10°	—	Y	
20AR48/FL15	12	20	2,000	2,000	15°	—	Y	
20AR48/G/FL15	12	20	2,000	1,500	15°	—	Y	Gold reflector
15AR56/SP15	6	15	3,000	1,400	14°	—	N	
50AR56/SP10	12	50	3,000	11,000	10°	—	N	
50AR56/NFL25	12	50	3,000	1,900	25°	—	N	
20AR70/SP10	12	20	2,000	7,000	10°	—	Y	
20AR70/FL30	12	20	2,000	1,000	30°	—	Y	
50AR70/SP10	12	50	2,000	15,000	10°	—	Y	
50AR70/G/SP10	12	50	2,000	13,500	10°	—	Y	Gold reflector
50AR70/FL30	12	50	2,000	2,000	30°	—	Y	
50AR70/G/FL30	12	50	2,000	1,800	30°	—	Y	Gold reflector
75AR70/SP10	12	75	2,000	19,000	10°	—	Y	
75AR70/FL30	12	75	2,000	4,000	30°	—	Y	
35AR111/6V/VNSP3	6	35	2,000	45,000	3°	—	Y	
35AR111/VNSP3	12	35	2,000	45,000	3°	—	Y	
35AR111/SP10	12	35	2,000	15,000	10°	—	Y	
35AR111/FL30	12	35	2,000	2,000	30°	—	Y	
50AR111/NSP5	12	50	2,000	50,000	5°	—	Y	
50AR111/SP10	12	50	2,000	20,000	10°	—	Y	
50AR111/FL30	12	50	2,000	3,000	30°	—	Y	
75AR111/SP10	12	75	2,000	25,000	10°	—	Y	
75AR111/FL30	12	75	2,000	4,500	30°	—	Y	
75AR111/WFL60	12	75	2,000	1,300	60°	—	Y	
100AR111/SP10	12	100	2,000	45,000	10°	—	Y	
100AR111/FL30	12	100	2,000	7,000	30°	—	Y	
100AR111/WFL60	12	100	2,000	2,000	60°	—	Y	

Continued on next page

Proposed ANSI Lamp Designation	Design Volts	Watts	Design Life (Hrs.)	Initial Candlepower	Beamspread 50%	10%	Filament Shield	Notes
				Mirrored Reflector (MR) Lamps				
20MR11/NSP10 (FTB)*	12	20	3,500	5,500	10°	—	N	
20MR11/SP15 (FTC)	12	20	3,500	1,760	17°	—	N	
20MR11/NFL30 (FTD)	12	20	3,500	600	30°	—	N	
35MR11/NSP8 (FTE)	12	35	3,500	9,000	8°	—	N	
35MR11/SP20 (FTF)	12	35	3,500	3,000	20°	—	N	
35MR11/NFL30 (FTH)	12	35	3,500	1,300	30°	—	N	
50MR11/NSP10	12	35	3,000	11,000	10°	—	N	
50MR11/SP20	12	35	3,000	4,400	20°	—	N	
50MR11/NFL30	12	35	3,000	2,600	30°	—	N	
20MR16/VNSP7 (EZX)	12	20	3,000	8,200	7°	12°	N	
20MR16/NSP15 (ESX)	12	20	3,000	3,600	13°	19°	N	
20MR16/FL40 (BAB)	12	20	4,000	525	40°	59°	N	
35MR16/NSP12 (FRB)	12	35	4,000	8,700	12°	—	N	
35MR16/SP20 (FRA)	12	35	4,000	3,900	20°	—	N	
35MR16/FL40 (FMW)	12	35	4,000	1,600	40°	—	N	
42MR16/VNSP9 (EZY)	12	42	3,500	13,100	9°	15°	N	
42MR16/NFL25 (EYS)	12	42	4,000	2,400	27°	47°	N	
50MR16/NSP15 (EXT)	12	50	4,000	10,200	14°	24°	N	
50MR16/NFL25 (EXZ)	12	50	4,000	3,400	27°	49°	N	
50MR16/NFL30 (EXK)	12	50	4,000	2,450	32°	52°	N	
50MR16/FL40 (EXN)	12	50	4,000	1,850	40°	64°	N	
50MR16/WFL55(FNV)	12	50	4,000	1,150	55°	—	N	
75MR16/NSP15 (EYF)	12	75	4,000	12,000	14°	24°	N	
75MR16/NFL25 (EYJ)	12	75	4,000	4,900	25°	35°	N	
75MR16/FL40 (EYC)	12	75	4,000	2,100	42°	64°	N	
				Parabolic Aluminum Reflector (PAR) Lamps				
40PAR16/H/NSP10	120, 130	40	2,000	5,000	10°	—	N	
40PAR16/H/NFL25	120, 130	40	2,000	1,300	27°	—	N	
55PARI6/H/NSP12	120, 130	55	2,000	5,000	12°	—	N	
55PARI6/H/NFL30	120, 130	55	2,000	1,300	30°	—	N	
60PAR16/H/NSP10	120, 130	60	2,000	7,500	10°	—	N	
60PARI6/H/NFL25	120, 130	60	2,000	2,000	27°	—	N	
75PAR16/H/NSP12	120, 130	75	2,000	7,500	12°	—	N	
75PAR16/H/NFL30	120, 130	75	2,000	2,000	30°	—	N	

*Codes in parentheses refer to former ANSI designations.

Continued on next page

Proposed ANSI Lamp Designation	Design Volts	Watts	Design Life (Hrs.)	Initial Candlepower	Beamspread 50%	Beamspread 10%	Filament Shield	Notes
35PAR20/H/NSP8	120	50	2,500	3,000	8°	—	N	
35PAR20/H/NFL30	120	50	2,500	900	30°	—	N	
35PAR20/H/WFL40	120	50	2,500	600	40°	—	N	
50PAR20/H/NSP10	120, 130	50	2,000	6,000	10°	—	N	
50PAR2O/H/NFL25	120, 130	50	2,000	1,850	26°	—	N	
50PAR20/CB/H/NFL25	120, 130	50	2,000	1,850	26°	—	N	Cool beam option
50PAR30/H/NSP11	120, 130	50	2,000	10,500	11°	—	N	
50PAR30/H/NFL25	120, 130	50	2,000	2,700	24°	—	N	
50PAR30/CB/H/NFL25	120, 130	50	2,000	2,700	24°	—	N	Cool beam option
50PAR30/H/FL35	120, 130	50	2,000	1,600	36°	—	N	
50PAR30/HIR/NSP7	120, 130	50	3,000	19,500	7°	—	N	IR-reflecting
50PAR30/HIR/NFL25	120, 130	50	3,000	4,000	23°	—	N	IR-reflecting
50PAR30/HIR/FL35	120, 130	50	3,000	2,400	33°	—	N	IR-reflecting
75PAR30/H/NSP11	120, 130	75	2,000	15,000	11°	—	N	
75PAR30/H/NFL25	120, 130	75	2,000	3,500	27°	—	N	
75PAR30/CB/H/NFL35	120, 130	75	2,000	3,500	27°	—	N	Cool beam option
75PAR30/H/FL35	120, 130	75	2,000	2,500	36°	—	N	
25PAR36/VNSP5	5.5	25	1,000	19,700	—	5.5° × 4.5°	Y	
25PAR36/NSP9	12	25	2,000	2,600	10° × 8°	19° × 17°	Y	
25PAR36/WFL30	12	25	2,000	360	37° × 26°	49° × 41°	Y	
25PAR36/VWFL55	12	25	2,000	160	55°	—	Y	
35PAR36/H/VNSP5	12	35	4,000	25,000	5°	—	N	
35PAR36/H/NSP8	12	35	4,000	8,000	8°	—	N	
35PAR36/H/WFL30	12	35	4,000	900	25° × 35°	—	N	
50PAR36/H/VNSP5	12	50	4,000	40,000	5°	—	N	
50PAR36/H/NSP8	12	50	4,000	11,000	8°	—	N	
50PAR36/H/WFL30	12	50	4,000	1,300	25° × 35°	—	N	
50PAR36/VNSP6	12	50	2,000	19,000	6°	—	Y	
50PAR36/NSP10	12	50	2,000	1,100	10°	20° × 17°	Y	
50PAR36/WFL35	12	50	2,000	1,300	39° × 27°	48° × 41°	Y	
50PAR36/VWFL55	12	50	2,000	600	55°	80° × 80°	Y	
45PAR/H/NSP9	120, 130	45	2,000	11,500	9°	—	N	
45PAR/H/SP11	120, 130	45	2,000	8,800	11°	—	N	
45PAR/H/FL30	120, 130	45	2,000	1,700	32°	—	N	
60PAR/HIR/SP10	120, 130	60	3,000	18,500	10°	—	N	IR-reflecting
60PAR/HIR/FL30	120, 130	60	3,000	3,650	29°	—	N	IR-reflecting
60PAR/HIR/WFL55	120, 130	60	3,000	1,250	53°	—	N	IR-reflecting

Continued on next page

Proposed ANSI Lamp Designation	Design Volts	Watts	Design Life (Hrs.)	Initial Candlepower	Beamspread 50%	Beamspread 10%	Filament Shield	Notes
75PAR/H/NSP8	120, 130	75	2,500	18,400	8°	—	N	
75PAR/H/NFL25	120, 130	75	2,500	4,000	26°	—	N	
90PAR/H/NSP8	120, 130.	90	2,000	23,000	8°	—	N	
90PAR/H/SP10	120, 130	90	2,000	18,500	12°	—	N	
90PAR/CB/H/SP10	120, 130	90	2,000	18,500	12°	—	N	Cool beam option
90PAR/H/FL30	120, 130	90	2,000	4,000	30°	—	N	
90PAR/CB/H/FL30	120, 130	90	2,000	4,000	30°	—	N	Cool beam option
100PAR/HIR/SP10	120, 130	100	3,000	30,000	10°	—	N	IR-reflecting
100PAR/HIR/FL35	120, 130	100	3,000	3,600	33°	—	N	IR-reflecting
150PAR/H/NSP9	120, 130	150	3,000	37,500	9°	—	N	
150PAR/H/SP10	120, 130	150	3,000	25,000	10°	—	N	
150PAR/H/FL30	120, 130	150	3,000	7,500	30°	—	N	
150PAR/H/VWFL55	120	150	3,000	2,500	55°	—	N	
Q150PAR/SP10	120	150	4,000	29,000	10°	—	N	
Q150PAR/FL20	120	150	4,000	7,200	22°	—	N	
Q250PAR/SP10	120	150	6,000	52,000	10°	—	N	
Q250PAR/FL20	120	150	6,000	12,000	22°	—	N	
25PAR46/VNSP5	5.5	25	1,000	55,000	—	5.5° × 4.5°	Y	
150PAR46/MFL20	125	150	2,000	8,000	26° × 13°	39° × 25°	N	Med side prong
200PAR46/NSP10	120, 130	200	2,000	31,000	12° × 8°	23° × 19°	N	Med side prong
200PAR46/MFL20	120, 130	200	2,000	11,500	27° × 13°	40° × 24°	N	Med side prong
120PAR56/VNSP7	12	120	2,000	60,000	8° × 6°	15° × 10°	N	Cool beam option
120PAR56/MFL15	12	120	2,000	19,000	18° × 9°	29° × 15°	N	
120PAR56/WFL25	12	120	2,000	5,625	35° × 18°	50° × 25°	N	
200PAR56/MFL15	120	200	2,000	15,000	22° × 13°	34° × 22°	N	
240PAR56/VNSP8	12	240	2,000	140,000	9° × 6°	17° × 10°	N	
240PAR56/MFL15	12	240	2,000	46,000	19° × 8°	28° × 15°	N	
240PAR56/WFL25	12	240	2,000	13,000	35° × 18°	50° × 27°	N	
300PAR56/NSP9	120	300	2,000	68,000	10° × 8°	20° × 14°	N	Cool beam option
300PAR56/MFL15	120, 130	300	2,000	24,000	23° × 11°	34° × 19°	N	
300PAR56/MFL15	120	300	2,000	32,000	21° × 10°	30° × 17°	N	Cool beam
300PAR56/WFL25	120, 130	300	2,000	11,000	37° × 18°	57° × 27°	N	
300PAR56/WFL25	120	300	2,000	11,400	37° × 19°	53° × 28°	N	Cool beam

Continued on next page

Proposed ANSI Lamp Designation	Design Volts	Watts	Design Life (Hrs.)	Initial Candlepower	Beamspread 50%	Beamspread 10%	Filament Shield	Notes
Q500PAR56/NSP11	120	500	4,000	96,000	13° × 8°	32° × 15°	N	
Q500PAR56/MFL20	120	500	4,000	43,000	26° × 10°	42° × 20°	N	
Q500PAR56/WFL30	120	500	4,000	19,000	44° × 20°	66° × 34°	N	
120PAR64/NSP7	6	120	3,000	180,000	—	9° × 5°	Y	
500PAR64/NSP10	120	500	2,000	110,000	12° × 7°	19° × 14°	N	
500PAR64/MFL17	120, 130	500	2,000	37,000	23° × 11°	35° × 19°	N	
500PAR64/WFL36	120, 130	500	2,000	13,000	42° × 20°	55° × 32°	N	
Q1000PAR64/NSP12	120	1,000	4,000	200,000	15° × 8°	31° × 14°	N	
Q1000PAR64/MFL15	120	1,000	4,000	80,000	28° × 12°	45° × 22°	N	
Q1000PAR64/WFL35	120	1,000	4,000	33,000	48° × 24°	72° × 45°	N	
Reflector (R) Lamps								
15R14SC/SP15	12	15	2,000	800	15°	31°	N	Single contact base
15R14SC/FL35	12	15	2,000	120	36°	102°	N	Single contact base
25R14SC/SP15	12	25	2,000	1,200	16°	32°	N	Single contact base
25R14SC/FL35	12	25	2,000	200	36°	102°	N	Single contact base
25R14/WFL60	120	25	1,500	150	60°	120°	N	
30R20/FL40	120, 130	30	2,000	300	38°	—	N	
50R20/FL40	120, 130	50	2,000	550	38°	—	N	
100R25/25°	120	100	2,000	60	—	70°	N	
75R/FL120	120	75	2,000	460	—	120°	N	
300R/SP40	120	300	2,000	14,000	40°	—	N	
300R/FL120	120	300	2,000	2,900	120°	—	N	
Elliptical Reflector (ER) Lamps								
50ER30/FL30	120, 130	50	2,000	1,300	28°	70°	N	
75ER30/FL30	120, 130	75	2,000	1,800	28°	70°	N	
120ER30/FL30	120, 130	120	2,000	2,900	28°	70°	N	

TABLE 3 Lamp Specifications

Lamp Description	Designation	Atmosphere	Light Output (%)	Kelvin Color Temperature (K)	Color Rendering Index (CRI)	Life Hours	Initial Lumens	Mean Lumens
Cool white	CW	Cool	100	4,100	62	20,000+	3,050	2,650
Cool white deluxe	CWX	Cool	70	4,200	87	20,000+	2,200	1,800
Warm white	WW	Warm	102	2,900	53	20,000+	3,100	2,700
Warm white deluxe	WWX	Warm	68	2,800	77	20,000+	2,200	1,805
Soft white	SW	Warm	68	3,000	79	20,000+	2,150	1,800
Natural	N	Warm	66	3,450	55	20,000+	2,100	1,870
Lite white	W	Neutral	102	4,100	49	20,000+	3,050	2,650
Daylight	D	Cool	83	6,500	56	20,000+	2,600	2,250
Cool Green	CG	Cool	83	6,450	70	20,000+	2,850	2,350
RE–730	Spec 30	Warm	103	3,000	70	20,000+	3,200	2,880
RE–735	Spec 35	Neutral	103	3,500	73	20,000+	3,200	2,880
RE–741	Spec 41	Cool	103	4,100	70	20,000+	3,200	2,880
RE–830	30U	Warm	105	3,000	85	20,000+	3,300	2,970
RE–835	35U	Neutral	105	3,500	85	20,000+	3,300	2,970
RE–841	41U	Cool	105	4,100	85	20,000+	3,300	2,970
RE–850	50U	Cool	105	5,000	85	20,000+	3,280	2,950
Chroma 50	C50	Cool	70	5,000	92	20,000+	2,200	1,915
Chroma 75	C75	Cool	64	7,500	95	20,000+	2,000	1,720
Red	R	—	6	—	—	20,000+	195	60
Pink	PK	—	35	—	—	20,000+	1,160	695
Gold	GO	—	60	—	—	20,000+	2,400	1,765
Green	G	—	140	—	—	20,000+	4,400	2,200
Blue	B	—	35	—	—	20,000+	1,200	720

TABLE 4 Efficacy of Electric Light Sources

Lamp Type	Lamp Wattage Range	Initial Efficacy (Lumens per Watt)	Kelvin Color Temperature (K)	Color Rendering Index (CRI)	Design Life (Hours)
Incandescent	6–1,500	4–20	2,700–2,800	100	750–4,000
Tungsten halogen	50–1,500	18–22	2,900–3,100	100	1,000–4,000
Fluorescent	4–215	10–65	2,700–7,500	53–95	6,000–24,000+
Compact fluorescent	5–39	28–48	2,700–4,100	81–82	1,250–10,000
Mercury vapor	40–1,000	19–59	3,300–5,900	15–52	12,000–24,000+
High-pressure sodium	33–1,000	31–127	1,800–2,800	22–80	7,500–24,000+
Low-pressure sodium	18–180	58–185	1,740–1,750	–44	14,000–18,000
Metal halide	32–1,500	35–95	3,000–4,400	65–70	3,000–20,000

TABLE 5 **Brightness Table** (Approximate Candelas per Square Inch)

Lamp Description			Brightness
Incandescent			150.0
Fluorescent			
Preheat			
8 W	T5	(12″)	8.1
15 W	T8	(18″)	6.7
15 W	T12	(18″)	4.1
20 W	T12	(24″)	4.6
Rapid Start			
30 W	T12	(36″)	5.3
32 W	T8	(48″)	7.4
40 W	T8	(60″)	7.4
40 W	T10	(48″)	6.6
40 W	T12	(48″)	5.4
40 W	T12	(48″ ES)	4.7
40 W	T12	6″ ($22\frac{7}{16}$″ U-bent)	5.0
High Output			
24″	T12	(35 W)	6.1
48″	T12	(60 W)	7.3
72″	T12	(85 W)	7.3
96″	T12	(110 W)	7.3
96″	T12	(95 W ES)	6.6
Very-Hi Output			
48″	T12	(116 W)	12.0
72″	T12	(162 W)	12.0
96″	T12	(212 W)	12.0
96″	T12	(185 W ES)	11.2
Instant Start			
40 W	T12	(48″)	5.3
40 W	T12	(60″)	2.3
Slimline			
42″	T8	(23 W)	5.3
64″	T8	(35 W)	5.3
72″	T8	(37.5 W)	5.0
96″	T8	(50 W)	5.0
48″	T12	(38.5 W)	5.0
72″	T12	(56 W)	5.0
96″	T12	(75 W)	5.0
96″	T12	(6 W ES)	4.5
Circline			
20 W	T9	($6\frac{1}{2}$″ Diam.)	5.9
22 W	T9	($8\frac{1}{4}$″ Diam.)	5.2
32 W	T9	(12″ Diam.)	4.8
40 W	T9	(16″ Diam.)	4.8

TABLE 6 Relative Output of Colored Lamps

Lamp Color Description	Light Output (%)
Incandescent—Tinted Lamps	
Clear	100
Pink	75
Yellow-white	85
Green-white	55
Blue-white	40
White (silica coat)	100
Incandescent—Sign Lamps	
Clear	100
White	85
Ivory	73
Flame tint	58
Rose	35
Red	5
Orange	35
Yellow	65
Green	5
Blue	3
Lumiline Lamps	
Clear	100
White	85
Fluorescent	
Cool white	100
Cool white deluxe	72
Warm white	102
Warm white deluxe	72
Natural	69
Lite white	104
Daylight	85
Cool green	93
RE–730	105
RE–735	105
RE–741	105
RE–830	108
RE–835	108
RE–841	108
RE–850	108
Chroma 50	72
Chroma 75	66
Blue	39
Gold	79
Red	6
Pink	45
Green	160
Deep blue	17

TABLE 7   Relative Lamp Watts

Filament (Clear Color)		
	30 W	Clear
	60 W	Pink
	90 W	Blue-white
	200 W	Red
	90 W	Amber
	36 W	Yellow or gold
	300 W	Green
	300 W	Blue
Filament (Diffuse Color)		
	30 W	Silica coat
	39 W	Pink tint
	36 W	Gold tint
	60 W	Green tint
	75 W	Blue tint
Fluorescent		
	10 W	Cool white
	22 W	Pink
	165 W	Red
	13 W	Yellow or gold
	11 W	Yellow-green
	6 W	Green
	22 W	Blue
	65 W	Deep blue

TABLE 8   Relative Brightness for Equal Attraction

White light	10
Yellow light	12
Red light	3
Green light	4
Blue light	6

TABLE 9   Voltage Drop Guidelines: Chart for Selecting Secondary Voltage Tap to Be Used with Various Wire Sizes for Given Distances Between Transformer and Lamps

Distance (Ft) from Transformer to Lamps for 100 Watt Load

Wire Size (Gauge)	Less Than 30 Ft	30	60	90	120	150	180	210	240	270	300
14	12 V	13 V	14 V	——————————— Use Larger Wire Size. ———————————							
12	12 V	13 V	13 V	14 V	——————————— Use Larger Wire Size. ———————————						
10	12 V	13 V	13 V	14 V	14 V	——————— Use Larger Wire Size. ———————					
8	12 V	12 V	12 V	13 V	13 V	13 V	14 V	14 V	14 V	Use Larger Wire Size.	

Distance (Ft) from Transformer to Lamps for 300 Watt Load

Wire Size (Gauge)	Less Than 10 Ft	10	20	30	40	50	60	70	80	90	100	110	120
12	12 V	13 V	13 V	14 V	——————————— Use Larger Wire Size. ———————————								
10	12 V	12 V	13 V	13 V	14 V	14 V	——————— Use Larger Wire Size. ———————						
S	12 V	12 V	12 V	13 V	13 V	13 V	14 V	14 V	14 V	—— Use Larger wire Size. ——			
6	12 V	12 V	12 V	12 V	13 V	13 V	13 V	13 V	14 V	14 V	14 V	14 V	14 V

Distance (Ft) from Transformer to Lamps for 500 Watt Load

Wire Size (Gauge)	Less Than 10 Ft	10	20	30	40	50	60	70	80	90	100	110	120
10	12 V	13 V	14 V	14 V	——————————— Use Larger Wire Size. ———————————								
8	12 V	12 V	13 V	13 V	14 V	——————— Use Larger Wire Size. ———————							
6	12 V	12 V	13 V	13 V	13 V	14 V	14 V	14 V	—— Use Larger Wire Size. ——				
4	12 V	12 V	12 V	12 V	13 V	13 V	13 V	13 V	14 V	14 V	14 V	14 V	14 V

NOTE: Confirm tap selection by measurement of voltage at lamp terminals when all of the lamps are operating.

TABLE 10   Trigonometric Functions: Sines and Cosines of Angles

$\theta°$	$\sin \theta$	$\cos \theta$	$\theta°$	$\sin \theta$	$\cos \theta$	$\theta°$	$\sin \theta$	$\cos \theta$	$\theta°$	$\sin \theta$	$\cos \theta$
0	0.0000	1.000	26	0.438	0.899	52	0.788	0.616	72	0.951	0.309
1	.0175	1.000	27	.454	.891	53	.799	.602	73	.956	.292
2	.0349	0.999	28	.470	.833	54	.809	.588	74	.961	.276
3	.0523	.999	29	.485	.875	55	.819	.574	75	.966	.259
4	.0698	.998	30	.500	.866	56	.829	.559	76	.970	.242
5	.0872	.996	31	.515	.857						
6	.105	.995	32	.530	.848						
7	.122	.993	33	.545	.839	57	.839	.545	77	.974	.225
8	.139	.990	34	.559	.829	58	.848	.530	78	.978	.208
9	.156	.988	35	.574	.819	59	.857	.515	79	.982	.191
10	.174	.985	36	.588	.809	60	.866	.500	80	.985	.174
11	.191	.982	37	.602	.799	61	.875	.485	81	.988	.156
12	.208	.978	38	.616	.788						
13	.225	.974	39	.629	.777						
14	.242	.970	40	.643	.766	62	.883	.470	82	.990	.139
15	.259	.966	41	.656	.755	63	.891	.454	83	.993	.122
16	.276	.961	42	.669	.743	64	.899	.438	84	.995	.105
17	.292	.956	43	.682	.731	65	.906	.423	85	.996	.0872
18	.309	.951	44	.695	.719	66	.914	.407	86	.9976	.0698
19	.326	.946	45	.707	.707						
20	.342	.940	46	.719	.695						
21	.358	.934	47	.731	.682	67	.921	.391	87	.9986	.0523
22	.375	.927	48	.743	.669	68	.927	.375	88	.9994	.0349
23	.391	.921	49	.755	.656	69	.934	.358	89	.9998	.0175
24	.407	.914	50	.766	.643	70	.940	.342	90	1.0000	0.0000
25	.423	.906	51	.777	.629	71	.946	.326			

TABLE 11   Lamp Lumen Depreciation Factors

Lamp Description	Shape	Nominal Wattage	Lamp Lumen Depreciation (LLD) Factors
Incandescent			
Extended Service	A,PS	15–70	0.85
General Service	A,PS,S	to–40	0.85
		50–1,500	0.89
Projector	PAR 38-64	75–1,000	0.84
Reflector	R 40	150–500	0.86
	R 52-57	500–1,000	0.81
Rough Service	A,PS	50–200	0.79
Showcase	T-10	25–40	0.78
Silver Bowl	A,PS	200–500	0.75
Three Light	A,T	30–150	0.85
	PS	100–300	0.72
Tungsten-Halogen	T	200–1,500	0.96
Vibration	A-19	50	0.72
Fluorescent			
Cool white	T12	40	0.87
Cool white deluxe	T12	40	0.82
Warm white	T12	40	0.87
Warm white deluxe	T12	40	0.82
Natural	T12	40	0.89
Lite white	T12	40	0.87
Daylight	T12	40	0.87
Cool green	T12	40	0.82
RE–700 Series	T8	40	0.90-
RE–800 Series	T12	40	0.90-
	T12	30	0.90
	T8	40	0.93
	T8	32	0.93
	T8	25	0.93
Chroma 50	T12	40	0.87
Chroma 75	T12	40	0.86
High-Intensity Discharge			
Standard mercury clear	E28	250	0.88
Mercury warm deluxe white	E28	250	0.81
Mercury deluxe white	E28	250	0.81
Deluxe high-pressure sodium	B17	70	0.80
White high-pressure sodium	B17	95	0.80
Low-pressure sodium	T16	55	0.87
Standard clear metal halide	E28	175	0.74V*
			0.69H**
	BT56	1,000	0.76
Standard coated metal halide	E28	175	0.71V
			0.65H
	BT56	1,000	0.76
High CRI metal halide	T7	150	0.89
High CRI metal halide	T8	250	0.80
Compact metal halide	T6½	70	0.82
Compact metal halide	T7	150	0.89

*Vertical lamp orientation
**Horizontal lamp orientation

TABLE 12   Lamp Lumen Depreciation

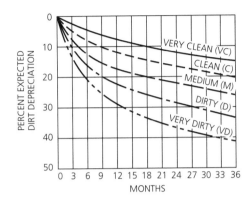

Months	Luminaire Distribution Type																			
	Direct				Semi–direct				Direct-Indirect				Semi-Indirect				Indirect			
Percent Expected Dirt Depreciation	10	20	30	40	10	20	30	40	10	20	30	40	10	20	30	40	10	20	30	40
Room Cavity Ratio																				
1	.98	.96	.94	.92	.97	.92	.89	.84	.94	.87	.80	.76	.94	.87	.80	.73	.90	.80	.70	.60
2	.98	.96	.94	.92	.96	.92	.88	.83	.94	.87	.80	.75	.94	.87	.79	.72	.90	.80	.69	.59
3	.98	.95	.93	.90	.96	.91	.87	.82	.94	.86	.79	.74	.94	.86	.78	.71	.90	.79	.68	.58
4	.97	.95	.92	.90	.95	.90	.85	.80	.94	.86	.79	.73	.94	.86	.78	.70	.89	.78	.67	.56
5	.97	.94	.91	.89	.94	.90	.84	.79	.93	.86	.78	.72	.93	.86	.77	.69	.89	.78	.66	.55
6	.97	.94	.91	.88	.94	.89	.83	.78	.93	.85	.78	.71	.93	.85	.76	.68	.89	.77	.66	.54
7	.97	.94	.90	.87	.93	.88	.82	.77	.93	.84	.77	.70	.93	.84	.76	.68	.89	.76	.65	.53
8	.96	.93	.89	.86	.93	.87	.81	.75	.93	.84	.76	.69	.93	.84	.76	.68	.88	.76	.64	.52
9	.96	.92	.88	.85	.93	.87	.80	.74	.93	.84	.76	.68	.93	.84	.75	.67	.88	.75	.63	.51
10	.96	.92	.87	.83	.93	.86	.79	.72	.93	.84	.75	.67	.92	.83	.75	.67	.88	.75	.62	.50

TABLE 13   Luminance Maintenance Categories

Procedure for Determining Luminaire Maintenance Categories

To assist in determining Luminaire Dirt Depreciation (LDD) factors, luminaires are separated into six categories (I through VI). To arrive at categories, luminaires are arbitrarily divided into sections, a Top Enclosure and a Bottom Enclosure, by drawing a horizontal line through the light center of the lamp or lamps. The characteristics listed for the enclosures are then selected as best describing the luminaire. Only one characteristic for the top enclosure and one for the bottom enclosure should be used in determining the category of a luminaire. Percentage of uplight is based on 100% for the luminaire. The maintenance category is determined when there are characteristics in both enclosure columns. If a luminaire falls into more than one category, the lower numbered category is used.

Maintenance Category	Top Enclosure	Bottom Enclosure
I	1. None.	1. None
II	1. None 2. Transparent with 15% or more uplight through apertures. 3. Translucent with 15% or more uplight through apertures. 4. Opaque with 1% or more uplight through apertures.	1. None 2. Louvers or baffles
III	1. Transparent with less than 15% upward light through apertures. 2. Translucent with less than 15% upward light through apertures. 3. Opaque with less than 15% uplight through apertures.	1. None 2. Louvers or baffles
IV	1. Transparent unapertured. 2. Translucent unapertured. 3. Opaque unapertured.	1. None 2. Louvers
V	1. Transparent unapertured. 2. Translucent unapertured. 3. Opaque unapertured.	1. Transparent unapertured 2. Translucent unapertured
VI	1. None 2. Transparent unapertured. 3. Translucent unapertured. 4. Opaque unapertured.	1. Transparent unapertured 2. Translucent unapertured 3. Opaque unapertured

Reprinted from the *IES Lighting Handbook*. Used with permission from the Illuminating Engineering Society of North America.

TABLE 14 Luminaire Dirt Depreciation (LDD) Factors for Six Luminaire Categories (I through VI) and for Five Degrees of Dirtiness

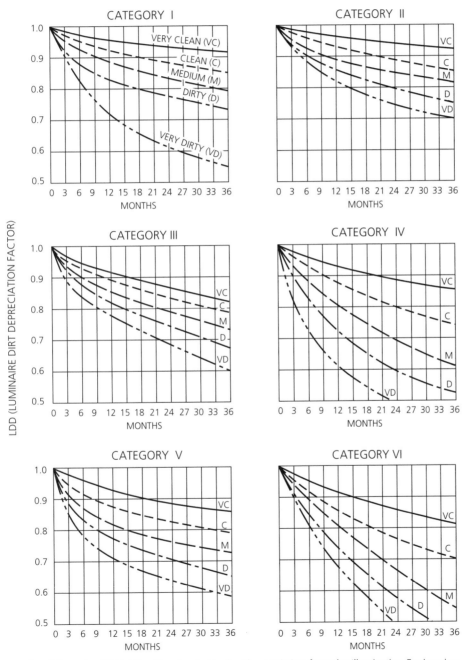

Reprinted from the IES Lighting Handbook. Used with permission from the Illuminating Engineering Society of North America.

TABLE 15   Sample Coefficient of Utilization Table

Coefficients of Utilization—Zonal Cavity Method
Effective Floor Cavity Reflectance 0.20

| RC | 80 | | | | 70 | | | | 50 | | | 30 | | | 10 | | | 0 |
RW	70	50	30	10	70	50	30	10	50	30	10	50	30	10	50	30	10	0
0	86	86	86	86	84	84	84	84	80	80	80	77	77	77	74	74	74	72
1	82	80	78	76	80	78	76	75	75	74	72	72	71	70	70	69	68	67
2	77	74	71	68	76	72	70	67	70	68	66	68	66	64	66	64	63	62
3	73	68	64	61	71	67	63	60	65	62	59	63	61	58	61	59	58	56
4	69	63	58	55	67	62	58	55	60	57	54	59	56	53	57	55	53	51
5	64	58	53	49	63	57	52	49	55	52	49	54	51	48	53	50	48	47
6	60	53	48	44	59	52	48	44	51	47	44	50	46	44	49	46	43	42
7	56	48	43	39	55	48	43	39	47	42	39	46	42	39	45	41	39	38
8	52	44	39	35	51	43	38	35	42	38	35	42	38	35	41	37	34	33
9	48	39	34	31	47	39	34	31	38	34	31	38	33	31	37	33	30	29
10	44	36	30	27	43	35	30	27	35	30	27	34	30	27	33	29	27	26

Note: All candela, lumens, luminance, coefficient of utilization and VCP values in this report are based on relative photometry which assumes a ballast factor of 1.000. Any calculations prepared from these data should include an appropriate ballast factor.

TABLE 16   Recommended Illuminance Values

	General Lighting			Task Lighting		
	Public Spaces	*Simple Orientation*	*Occasional Visual Tasks*	*Large Visual Tasks*	*Small Visual Tasks*	*Very Small Visual Tasks*
	2–5 fc	*5–10 fc*	*10–20 fc*	*20–50 fc*	*50–100 fc*	*100–200 fc*
Activity						
GENERAL						
Circulation						
Corridors				■		
Elevators				■		
Lobbies				■		
Stairs				■		
Service						
Toilets and washrooms				■		
Storage						
Active			■			
Inactive		■				
HOME/HOSPITALITY FACILITIES						
Bathrooms, for grooming				■		
Bedrooms, for reading				■		
Cleaning			■			
Conversation areas		■				
Dining		■				
Kitchen, critical seeing					■	
Laundry				■		
Sewing						■
INDUSTRY						
Assembly						
Simple				■		
Moderately difficult					■	
Difficult						■
Inspection						
Simple				■		
Moderately difficult					■	
Difficult						■
Locker Rooms			■			

Continued on next page

	General Lighting			Task Lighting		
	Public Spaces	*Simple Orientation*	*Occasional Visual Tasks*	*Large Visual Tasks*	*Small Visual Tasks*	*Very Small Visual Tasks*
	2–5 fc	*5–10 fc*	*10–20 fc*	*20–50 fc*	*50–100 fc*	*100–200 fc*
Activity						
OFFICES						
Accounting					■	*
Conference rooms				■		
Drafting, high contrast					■	
Drafting, low contrast						■
General/private offices				■	**	
Lounges and reception			■			
SCHOOLS						
Assembly						
Auditoriums			■			
Social activity		■				
Classrooms						
General				■		
Lecture demonstration						■
Science laboratories					■	
STORES						
Circulation			■			
Feature Displays						■
Merchandise					■	
Sales transactions				■	***	
Wrapping and packaging				■		

*If #4 pencil and harder leads are used for handwritten tasks.
**If tasks involve poor copies, photographs, maps, 6 point type.
***If handwritten carbon copies.
Based upon the recommended illumination levels, *IES Handbook,* 1987

TABLE 17 **Consolidated Listing of Illuminance Categories:**
Illuminance Categories and Illuminance Values for Generic
Types of Activities in Interiors

Type of Activity	Illuminance Category	Ranges of Illuminances		Reference Workplane
		Lux	Footcandles	
Public spaces with dark surroundings	A	20–30–50	2–3–5	
Simple orientation for short temporary visits	B	50–75–100	5–7.5–10	General lighting throughout spaces
Working spaces where visual tasks are only occasionally performed	C	100–150–200	10–15–20	
Performance of visual tasks of high contrast or large size	D	200–300–500	20–30–50	
Performance of visual tasks of medium contrast or small size	E	500–750–1000	50–75–100	Illuminance on task
Performance of visual tasks of low contrast or very small size	F	1000–1500–2000	100–150–200	
Performance of visual tasks of low contrast and very small size over a prolonged period	G	2000–3000–5000	200–300–500	Illuminance on task obtained by a combination of general and local (supplemental lighting)
Performance of very prolonged and exacting visual task	H	5000–7500–10,000	500–750–1000	
Performance of very special visual tasks of extremely low contrast and small size	I	10,000–15,000–20,000	1000–1500–2000	

Reprinted from the IES Lighting Handbook. Used with permission from the Illuminating Engineering Society of North America.

TABLE 18 Weighting Factors to be Considered in Selecting Specific Illuminance Within Ranges of Values for Each Category

A. For Illuminance Categories A through C

Room and Occupant Characteristics	Weighting Factor		
	−1	0	+1
Occupant ages	Under 40	40–55	Over 55
Room surface reflectances*	Greater than 70 percent	30 to 70 percent	Less than 30 percent

B. For Illuminance Categories D through I

Task and Worker Characteristics	Weighting Factor		
	−1	0	+1
Workers' ages	Under 40	40–55	Over 55
Speed and/or accuracy[1]	Not important	Important	Critical
Reflectance of task background[2]	Greater than 70 percent	30 to 70 percent	Less than 30 percent

*Average weighted surface reflectances, including wall, floor, and ceiling reflectances, if they encompass a large portion of the task area or visual surround. For instance, in an elevator lobby, where the ceiling height is 7.6 meters [25 feet], neither the task nor the visual surround encompasses the ceiling, so only the floor and wall reflectances would be considered.

[1] In determining whether speed and/or accuracy is not important, important, or critical the following questions need to be answered: What are the time limitations? How important is it to perform the task rapidly? Will errors produce an unsafe condition or product? Will errors reduce productivity and be costly? For example, in reading for leisure there are no time limitations and it is not important to read rapidly. Errors will not be costly and will not be related to safety. Thus, speed and/or accuracy is not important. If, however, a worker is involved in exacting work, accuracy is critical because of the close tolerances, and time is important because of production demands.

[2] The task background is that portion of the task upon which the meaningful visual display is exhibited. For example, on this page the meaningful visual display includes each letter which combines with other letters to form words and phrases. The display medium, or task background, is the paper, which has a reflectance of approximately 85 percent.

Reprinted from the IES Lighting Handbook. Used with permission from the Illuminating Engineering Society of North America.

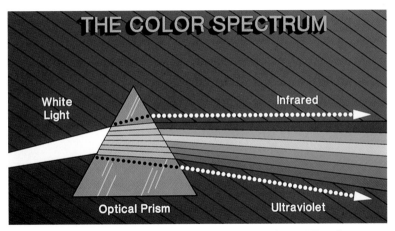

Plate 1. Optical prism. Image used courtesy of General Electric.

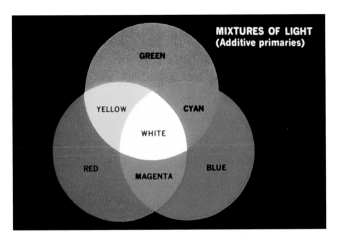

Plate 2. Mixtures of primary and secondary colors of light. Image used courtesy of General Electric.

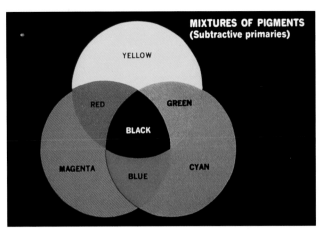

Plate 3. Mixtures of primary and secondary colors of pigment. Image used courtesy of General Electric.

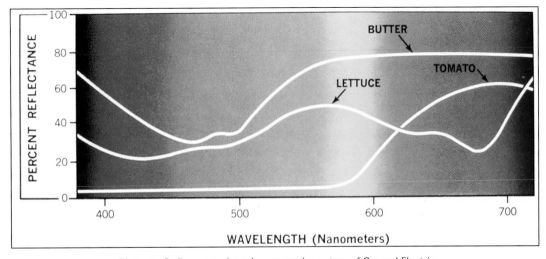

Plate 4. Reflectance chart. Image used courtesy of General Electric.

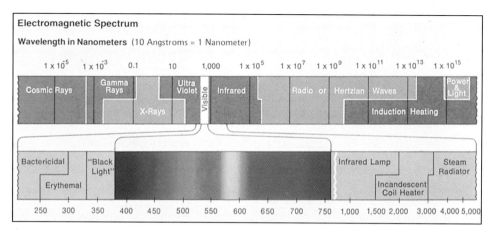

Plate 5. The color spectrum. Image used courtesy of Philips Lighting.

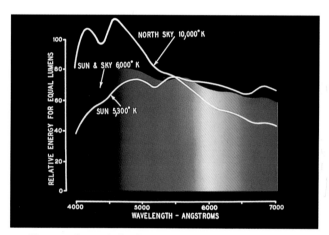

Plate 6. Spectral distribution chart for natural daylight.

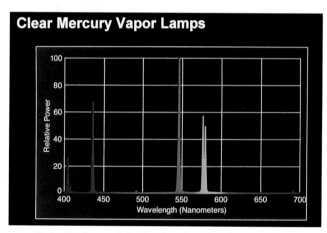

Plate 7. Spectral distribution chart for clear mercury vapor. Image used courtesy of Philips Lighting.

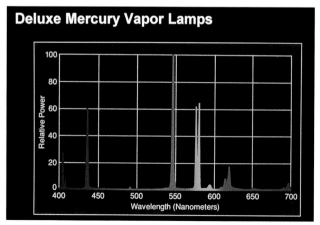

Plate 8. Spectral distribution chart for phosphor-coated mercury vapor lamps. Image used courtesy of Philips Lighting.

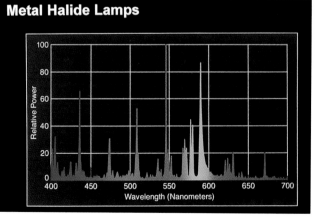

Plate 9. Spectral distribution chart for metal halide lamps. Image used courtesy of Philips Lighting.

Ceramalux Lamps

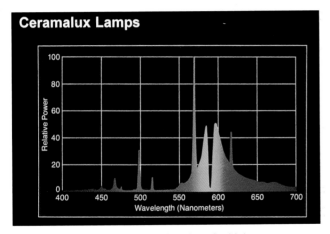

Plate 10. Spectral distribution chart for high pressure sodium lamps. Image used courtesy of Philips Lighting.

White SON Lamps

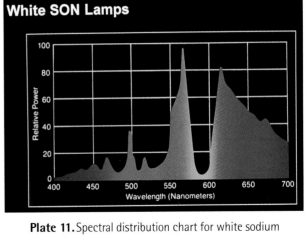

Plate 11. Spectral distribution chart for white sodium lamps. Image used courtesy of Philips Lighting.

Plate 12. Spectral distribution chart for low pressure sodium lamps.

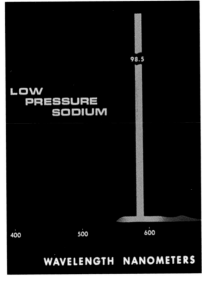

Spectral Distribution of Cool White Lamps

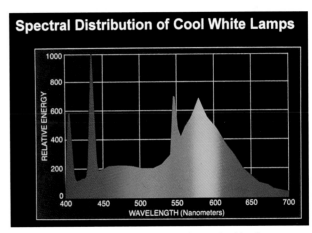

Plate 13. Spectral distribution chart for cool white fluorescent lamps. Image used courtesy of Philips Lighting.

Spectral Distribution of Warm White Lamps

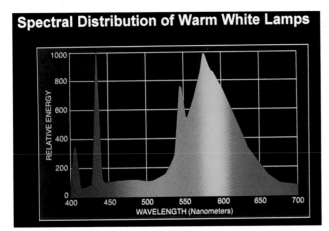

Plate 14. Spectral distribution chart for warm white fluorescent lamps. Image used courtesy of Philips Lighting.

Spectral Distribution of Cool White Deluxe Lamps

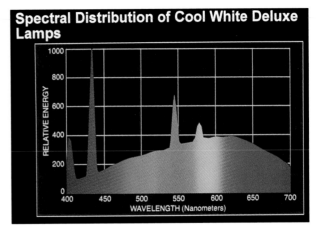

Plate 15. Spectral distribution chart for cool white deluxe fluorescent lamps. Image used courtesy of Philips Lighting.

Spectral Distribution of Warm White Deluxe Lamps

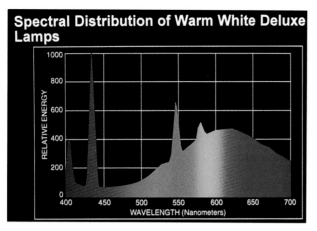

Plate 16. Spectral distribution chart for warm white deluxe fluorescent lamps. Image used courtesy of Philips Lighting.

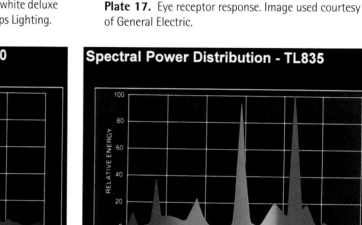

Plate 17. Eye receptor response. Image used courtesy of General Electric.

Spectral Power Distribution - TL830

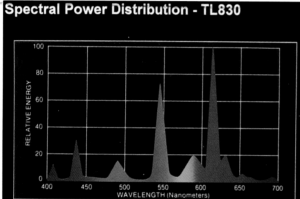

Plate 18. Rare earth 8-3000K lamp. Image used courtesy of Philips Lighting.

Spectral Power Distribution - TL835

Plate 19. Rare earth 8-3500K lamp. Image used courtesy of Philips Lighting.

Spectral Power Distribution - TL841

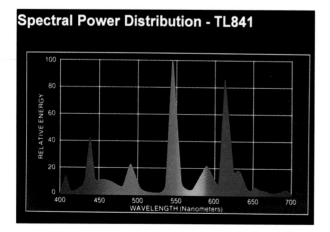

Plate 20. Rare earth 8-4100K lamp. Image used courtesy of Philips Lighting.

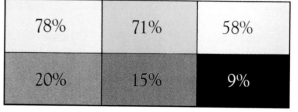

78%	71%	58%
20%	15%	9%

Plate 21. Surface finish reflectances.

REFERENCES

Anderson, Bruce, with Michael Riordan. The Solar Home Book. Andover: Brick House Publishing Co., 1976.

Arnheim, Rudolf. The Dynamics of Architectural Form. Berkeley: University of California Press, 1977.

Evans, Benjamin H., AIA. Daylight in Architecture. New York: McGraw-Hill Book Company, 1981.

Flynn, John E. "A Study of Subjective Responses to Low Energy and Nonuniform Lighting Systems." Lighting Design & Application February 1977: 6–14.

—— "The Psychology of Light." Series of 8 Articles. Electrical Consultant December 1972–August 1973.

Flynn, John E., and Samuel M. Mills. Architectural Lighting Graphics. New York: Reinhold Publishing Corporation, 1962.

Flynn, John E., and Arthur W. Segil. Architectural Interior Systems. New York: Van Nostrand Reinhold Co., 1970.

Flynn, John E. and Terry J. Spencer. "The Effects of Light Source Color on User Impression and Satisfaction." Journal of the Illuminating Engineering Society April 1977: 167–179.

Flynn, John E., Terry J. Spencer, Osyp Martyniuk, and Clyde Hendrik. "Interim Study of Procedures for Investigating the Effect of Light on Impression and Behavior. Journal of the Illuminating Engineering Society October 1993: 87–94.

Gordon, Gary. "The Design Department." Series of 6 Articles. Architectural Lighting November 1986–May 1987.

Gordon, Gary, with Mark Loeffler. "Specialty Lighting." Encyclopedia of Architecture: Design, Engineering, and Construction. New York: John Wiley & Sons, 1989.

Graham, Frank D. Audels Handy Book of Practical Electricity. New York: Theo. Audel & Co., 1941.

Gregory, Richard L. Eye and Brain, 4th ed. Princeton: Princeton University Press, 1990.

Guide to Dimming Low Voltage Lighting. Coopersburg: Lutron Electronics Co., 1989.

Guide to Fluorescent Lamps. Somerset: Philips Lighting Company, 1988.

Guide to High Intensity Discharge Lamps. Somerset: Philips Lighting Company, 1991.

Guide to Incandescent Lamps. Somerset: Philips Lighting Company, 1986.

Hall, Edward T. The Hidden Dimension. Garden City: Doubleday, 1966.

High Intensity Discharge Lamps. Cleveland: General Electric Company, 1975.

Incandescent Lamps. Cleveland: General Electric Company, 1984.

Kahn, Louis I. Light is the Theme. Fort Worth: Kimbell Art Foundation, 1975.

Lamp Specification and Application Guide. Somerset: Philips Lighting Company, 1993.

Light and Color. Cleveland: General Electric Company, 1978.

Marsteller, John. "A Philosophy of Light: Recalling Richard Kelly's Three Functional Elements." Interior Design February 1987: 78–80.

Mehrabian, Albert. Public Spaces and Private Spaces. New York: Basic Books Inc., 1976.

Moore, Fuller. Concepts and Practice of Architectural Daylighting. New York: Van Nostrand Reinhold Company, 1985.

Parker, Bertha Morris. Electricity. Evanston: Row, Peterson and Company, 1944.

Product Catalog. Danvers: Osram Sylvania, 1993.

Rea, Mark S., ed. Lighting Handbook. 8th ed. New York: Illuminating Engineering Society of North America, 1993.

Robb, Christina. "Light: An Illumination." The Boston Globe Magazine 1 September 1985: 12+.

Smith, Robert L. "Lessons in Luminance." Lighting Design & Application August 1992: 10–12.

Spectrum: 9200 Lamp Catalog. 21st ed. Cleveland: General Electric Company, 1993.

Tanizaki, Jun'ichiro. In Praise of Shadows. New Haven: Leete's Island Books, 1977.

The ABC's of Electronic Ballasts Rosemont: Advance Transformer Co., 1989.

Thomson, Garry. The Museum Environment. London: Butterworths, 1978.

CREDITS

Luminaire drawings

Many of the drawings in Chapter 12 are based on luminaires manufactured by Edison Price Incorporated. The following illustrations are based on luminaires first designed by Edison Price:

Figure 12.6   for the First Unitarian Church, Rochester, 1963.

Figure 12.7   for the Hartford Fire Insurance Building, 1961.

Figure 12.8   the first parabolic, low-brightness, fluorescent downlight was designed for the Upjohn Executive Headquarters Building, 1961.

Figure 12.10   for the CIT Building Headquarters Lobby, 1958.

Figure 12.12   for the Philadelphia Academy of Music, 1957.

Figure 12.14   for the Knoll Chicago Showroom, 1954.

Figure 12.28   for the Chicago Civic Center, 1965.

Figure 12.29   for the Munson-Williams-Proctor Museum, 1960.

Figure 12.30   for the Museum of Modern Art, 1958.

Figure 12.32   for the Munson-Williams-Proctor Museum, 1960.

Figure 12.33   for the Lyndon Baines Johnson Library, 1971.

Figure 12.34   for the Lyndon Baines Johnson Library, 1971.

Figure 12.37   for the Seagram Building Lobby, 1957.

Figure 12.38   for 9 West 58 Street, New York City, 1971.

Figure 12.45   for the Yale Art Gallery Building, 1953.

Figure 12.47   for St. John's College, 1965.

Photographs

All projects were designed by Gary Gordon Architectural Lighting, Inc.

Figure 2.1	Prudential Insurance Company of America, Grad Associates PA. Photo by Peter L. Goodman.
Figure 2.2	Armenian Evangelical Church, Lee H. Skolnick Architect. Photo by Stan Reiss.
Figure 2.3	Australia Broadcasting Corporation, Zivkovic Associates Architects. Photo by Ashley Ranson.
Figure 2.4	Prudential Insurance Company of America, Grad Associates PA. Photo by Peter L. Goodman.
Figure 2.5	Armenian Evangelical Church, Lee H. Skolnick Architect. Photo by Stan Reiss.
Figure 2.6	Armenian Evangelical Church, Lee H. Skolnick Architect. Photo by Stan Reiss.
Figure 2.7	One Fifth Avenue, Pentagram Architectural Services PC. Photo by Peter Mauss/Esto.
Figure 2.8	Prudential Insurance Company of America, Grad Associates PA. Photo by Peter L. Goodman.
Figure 2.15	St. Mark's Bookshop, Zivkovic Associates Architects. Photo by Ashley Ranson.
Figure 2.16	City Bakery, Turett Collaborative Architects. Photo by Paul Warchol.
Figure 2.17	One Fifth Avenue, Pentagram Architectural Services PC. Photo by Peter Mauss/Esto.
Figure 2.18	Tommy Boy Records, Turett Collaborative Architects. Photo by Paul Warchol.
Figure 3.2	Private Residence, New York City, Sidnam/Petrone Architects. Photo by Peter L. Goodman.
Figure 3.4	Canteen Showroom, Andaloro Associates. Photo by Peter Paige.
Figure 3.6	Lillian Vernon Residence, Hardy Holzman Pfeiffer Associates.
Figure 3.7	Sedona Store, Andaloro Associates. Photo by George Mott.
Figure 3.9	Morton Productions, BumpZoid. Photo by Langdon Clay.
Figure 3.11	Omon Ltd., Zivkovic Associates Architects. Photo by Ashley Ranson.
Figure 3.12	Offices for Sultra Corporation, Andaloro Associates. Photo by Richard Lee.
Figure 3.14	Omon Ltd., Zivkovic Associates Architects. Photo by Ashley Ranson.
Figure 3.15	Lillian Vernon Residence, Hardy Holzman Pfeiffer Associates.
Figure 3.16	Tommy Boy Records, Turett Collaborative Architects. Photo by Paul Warchol.

Figure 3.17   City Bakery, Turett Collaborative Architects. Photo by Paul Warchol.

Figure 3.18   Offices for Sultra Corporation, Andaloro Associates. Photo by Richard Lee.

Figure 3.19   Offices for Sultra Corporation, Andaloro Associates. Photo by Richard Lee.

Figure 3.21   Photo by Photosphere.

Figure 3.23   Photo by Photosphere.

Figure 3.24   Photo by Photosphere.

Figure 3.25   Photo by Photosphere.

Figure 3.26   Photo courtesy of GE Lighting.

Figure 3.27   Photo courtesy of GE Lighting.

Figure 3.34   Private Residence, New York City, Sidnam/Petrone Architects. Photo by Peter L. Goodman.

Figure 3.35   Prudential Insurance Company of America, Grad Associates PA. Photo by Peter L. Goodman.

Figure 3.36   Private Residence, New Jersey, Frank and Marcotullio Design Associates. Photo by Michael Gordon.

Figure 13.1   Offices for Sultra Corporation, Andaloro Associates. Photo by Richard Lee.

Figure 13.2   Photo courtesy of Philips Lighting.

Figure 13.3   Residence for Adam Rose and Peter McQuillan, Stuart Mager Incorporated. Photo by David Mager.

Figure 13.5   Offices for Gary Gordon Architectural Lighting, Donna Selene Seftel Architect.

Figure 13.23   Prudential Insurance Company of America, Grad Associates PA. Photo by Peter L. Goodman.

INDEX